IMAGES
of America

SOUTHBURY

IMAGES
of America

SOUTHBURY

Virginia Palmer-Skok

ARCADIA
PUBLISHING

ISBN 978-0-7385-1316-4

Published by Arcadia Publishing
Charleston, South Carolina

Printed in the United States of America

Library of Congress Catalog Card Number: 2003107570

For all general information, contact Arcadia Publishing:
Telephone 843-853-2070
Fax 843-853-0044
E-mail sales@arcadiapublishing.com
For customer service and orders:
Toll-free 1-888-313-2665

Visit us on the Internet at www.arcadiapublishing.com

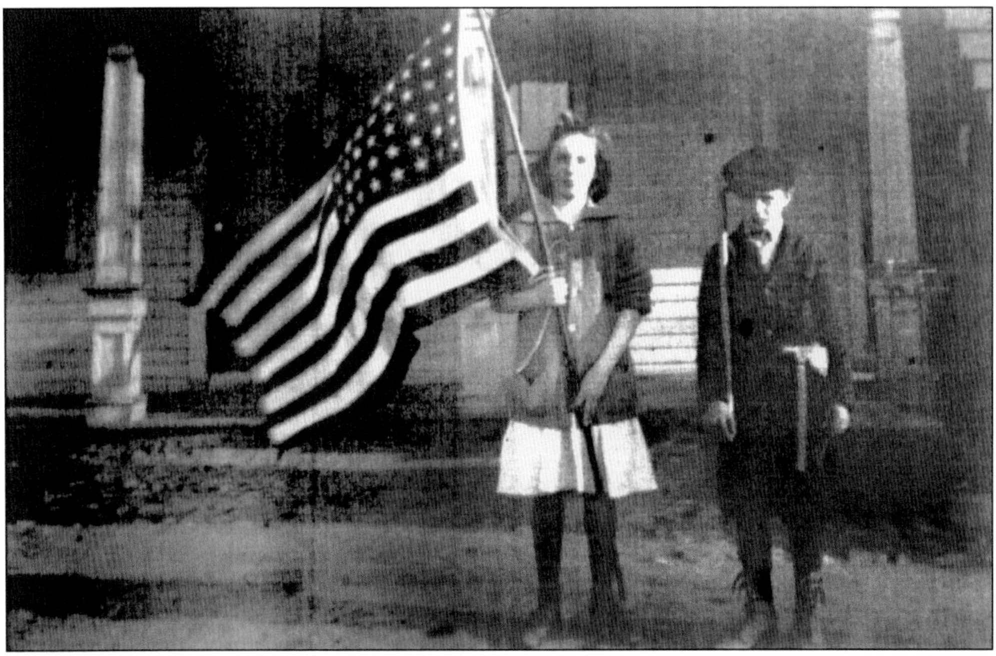

Patriotic Celebration. Young children display patriotic fervor with a 48-star flag. (SHS.)

Contents

Acknowledgments

I would like to take the opportunity to thank those individuals and organizations, such as the Southbury Historical Society, that have donated photographs to be used in this book. This publication would not have been possible without the generosity and foresight of those benefactors.

I would also like to thank Catherine Palmer, Dorothy Manville, and Andrew Skok for dedicating many hours and important insights that have greatly contributed to this piece and made it possible.

The photographic contributors are the Southbury Historical Society (SHS), Dorothy Green Manville (DM), Andrew Skok (AS), Betsey Stiles (BS), Beverly Iorio (BI), Melvin and Charlotte Wheeler (MCW), Tom Lautenschlager (TL), Richard Cromwell (RC), Esther Townsend (ET), Althea McGahie (AM), Richard Swanson (RS), Mary and James Weaver (MJW), Alan Brinley (ALB), Paul Hotchkiss (PH), George Stone Sr. (GS), Howard Hornbecker (HH), Samuel Green III (SG), Arza Bennett (AB), Marty Ludorf (MC), Cathy and Paul Palmer (CCP), the Historical Society of Glastonbury (GHS), and the Connecticut Historical Society (CHS).

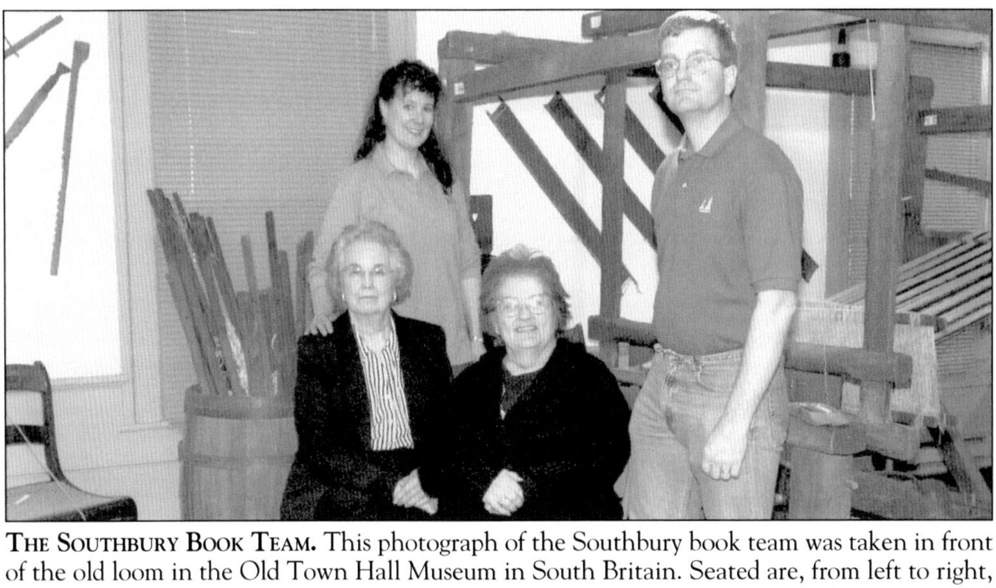

The Southbury Book Team. This photograph of the Southbury book team was taken in front of the old loom in the Old Town Hall Museum in South Britain. Seated are, from left to right, Catherine Palmer (chairman of the historic buildings commission) and Dorothy G. Manville (president of the Southbury Historical Society). Standing are, from left to right, Virginia Palmer-Skok (author) and Andrew Skok.

INTRODUCTION

Southbury has seen many changes over its 300-plus years of history. In 1673, 15 families left Stratford because of religious differences and settled in Ancient Woodbury, also known as Pomperaug Plantation. This land was purchased from the Pootatuck Indians. Many ancestors of the original families have not left the area, including the Hinmans, Stiles, Curtisses, and Mitchells, to name a few. As Colonial settlements were primarily along the coast, Pomperaug Plantation was considered very remote because it was one of the farthest inland settlements. Later in 1674, the small community was renamed Woodbury, meaning a dwelling in the woods.

Additional purchases of land grew the new colony. In 1679, the Kettletown area was purchased. It is thought that it was originally purchased in 1659 for a kettle from the Pagassett tribe, who were not the rightful owners. The area was called "kitle town." Soon to follow came other purchases of land, which included parts of what was to become the future Southbury. These included the Shepaug Purchase in 1686 and the Quassapaug Purchase in 1687. In 1706, the Kettletown area was purchased for a third time.

The second ecclesiastical society of Ancient Woodbury was incorporated in 1731 and called Southbury. In 1787, the General Assembly granted Southbury incorporation as a separate town from Woodbury.

Education was important in Colonial times, and by law, the ecclesiastical societies were responsible for it. In 1770, the White Oak section of town held school in the Congregational church. In the 1760s, Bullet Hill School was built. Additional school districts were added and numbered for each ecclesiastical society. They included White Oak, Bullet Hill, Southford, Kettletown, Hulls Hill, Translyvania, South Britain School, Pierce Hollow, Purchase, Pootatuck, and Wapping.

For more than 100 years, the community was primarily agrarian. Waterpower had a profound effect, starting in the 1800s, when manufacturing plants and mills sprung up along brooks and streams. Waterpower contributed to the growth of industries, especially in South Britain. Businesses included tanneries, clothiers, mills (cider, textile, sasso, and grist), brick kilns, and distilleries. Local products were hats, tacks, buttons, brads, wagon wheels, shears, knives, silver spoons, thimbles, hoop skirts, and bustles. It is thought that in the mid-1800s, Southbury had as many as 60 small factories and shops. Many of the small businesses left when more efficient methods of industry developed in cities such as Waterbury.

Transportation advances brought even more changes to town. When railroads started running through town, people began traveling back and forth to larger communities for work and trading.

The town has attracted many people over its history, whether it be for religious dissension, escaping revolutions in foreign countries, employment, play, retirement, or even to just enjoy its rural charm, including stonewalls and farms. Location and major roadways made commuting distance to larger cities palatable. In the 20th century, Southbury became a haven for city dwellers looking for recreation as well as a country retreat for vacation or retirement. Many who came for vacation made summer homes permanent dwellings. A surge of people, including notables, came to buy property to be able to enjoy the resplendent beauty of the area. A few who have lived here include Victor Borge, Ed Sullivan, Barbara Hershey, and Tony Marvin. In the late 1960s, a retirement community was built in Heritage Village.

The many settlers and their associated history have brought a unique flavor to the community, making it live up to its name as identified on the seal of the town, Unica Unique, the one and only.

One

Around Town

A Town Meeting gives everyone a chance to speak out, but it is not, I think, too democratic, for there are always two or three people who talk all the time, louder and louder. By eleven thirty, it is a question of who can shout the loudest. In the end, everyone votes on all issues, just as they had made their minds up to vote before ever coming to the meeting.

—Gladys Taber, *Stillmeadow Sampler*, 1959.

A mere 50-some years after the Pilgrims landed in Plymouth, Southbury was settled as a part of Ancient Woodbury. The town has a fascinating history from its earliest settlers, at the time of the Laurentian glaciers to the present day. As one of the fastest growing communities in Connecticut, it has a rich and enthralling past that has changed with the times.

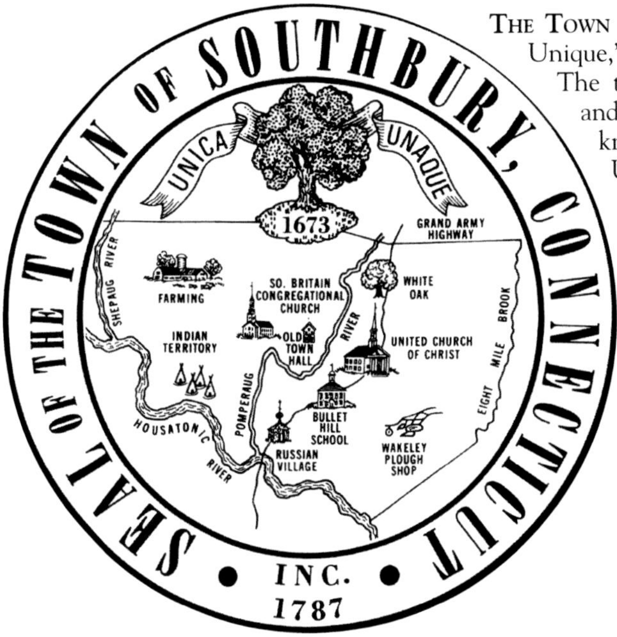

THE TOWN SEAL. The town seal reads, "Unica Unique," meaning "the one and only." The town is unique in both its beauty and magnificent history. It is the only known town of that name in the United States. (CPP.)

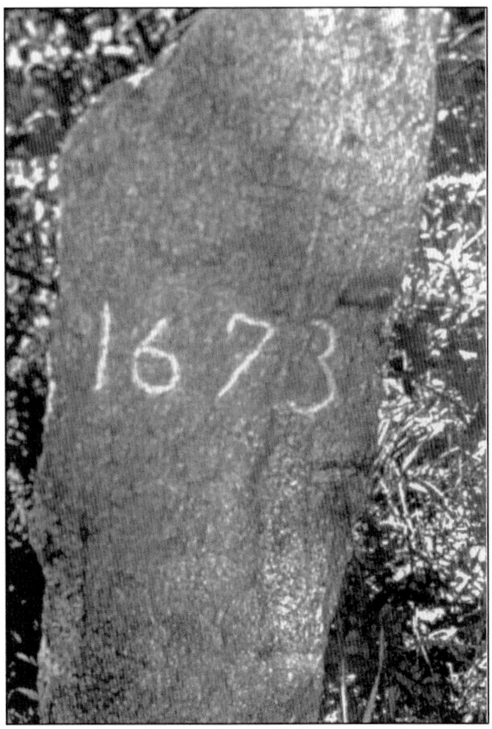

THE WHITE OAK MARKER. This marker denotes the site where original settlers camped in the area that is known as Ancient Woodbury. It is located along Crook Horn Road near Old Field Road and Route 67. A white oak tree stood on the site and gave its name to this section of town. A piece of the original tree, which fell down, was saved by Shadrich Osborn in 1908 and is on display at the Old Town Hall Museum. (SHS.)

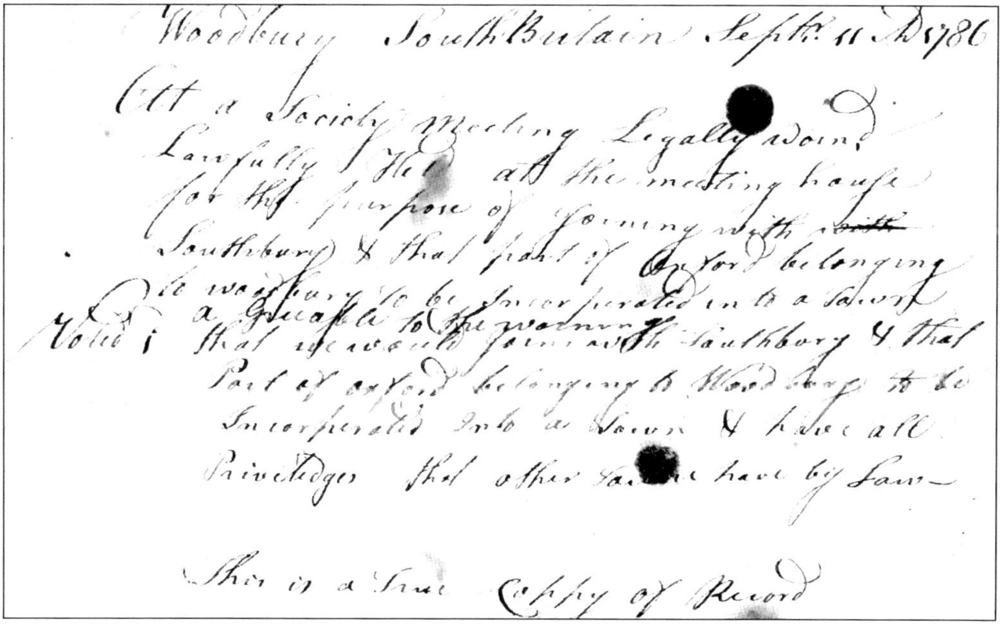

Woodbury South Britain Septr 11 AD 1786

At a Society Meeting Legally warned & Lawfully Held at the meeting house for the purpose of Joining with Southbury & that part of Oxford belonging to Woodbury to be Incorporated into a Town

Voted ; that we would Join with Southbury & that Part of Oxford belonging to Woodbury to be Incorporated Into a Town & have all Priviledges that other Towns have by Law

This is a True Coppy of Record

SOUTHBURY TOWNSHIP PAPERS. These documents were found recently in near-perfect condition in the Stile family attic. The papers show a request for incorporation of South Britain, a part of Oxford, and Southbury as a township. In 1787, the General Assembly gave Southbury the right of incorporation separate from Ancient Woodbury. The town area included Southbury proper, South Britain, and part of Oxford. The same year, the town of Bethlehem (Bethlem) was incorporated. When Southbury incorporated, there were 1,738 residents. The grand list was £15,000. The population dropped in the 1850 census to about 1,484. In 1900, there were 1,238 residents. A short time after incorporation, county lines changed, and Southbury became part of New Haven County. Until then, Southbury had been part of Litchfield County. (SHS.)

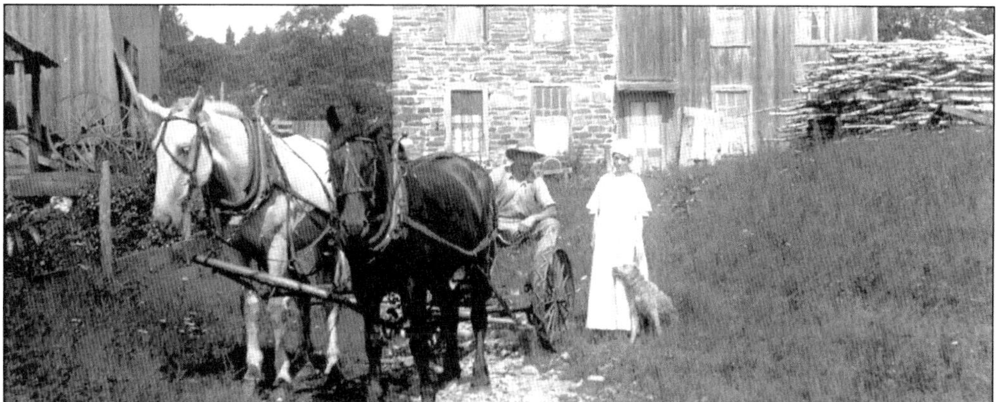

THE OLD STONE HOUSE. William and Lottie Lautenschlager stand in front of their house in August 1914 with their dog. The house, on Route 172, is thought to be oldest house in town. Inhabitants of Ancient Woodbury were given seven pounds to build a well-fortified house to protect their families. In 1704–1705, the house was built from stone quarried in Roxbury and transported by oxen-drawn wagons by the Bronson brothers. It was built with a lookout on the roof near the chimney. Prior to the building of the fort, settlers left the settlement temporarily for Stratford in 1675, when King Philip's War broke out. (TL.)

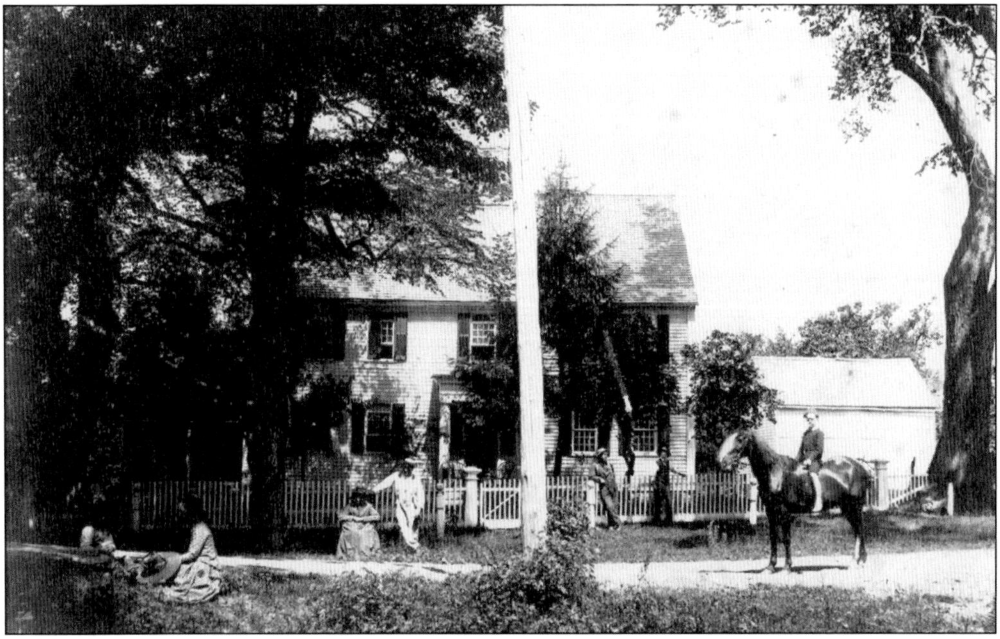

A Family at Home. Lt. Francis Stiles and his wife sit in chairs in front of their home with their son Gidney leaning against the fence in the late 1800s. The Stiles family are among the town's earliest inhabitants. They lived in the White Oak section. (RC.)

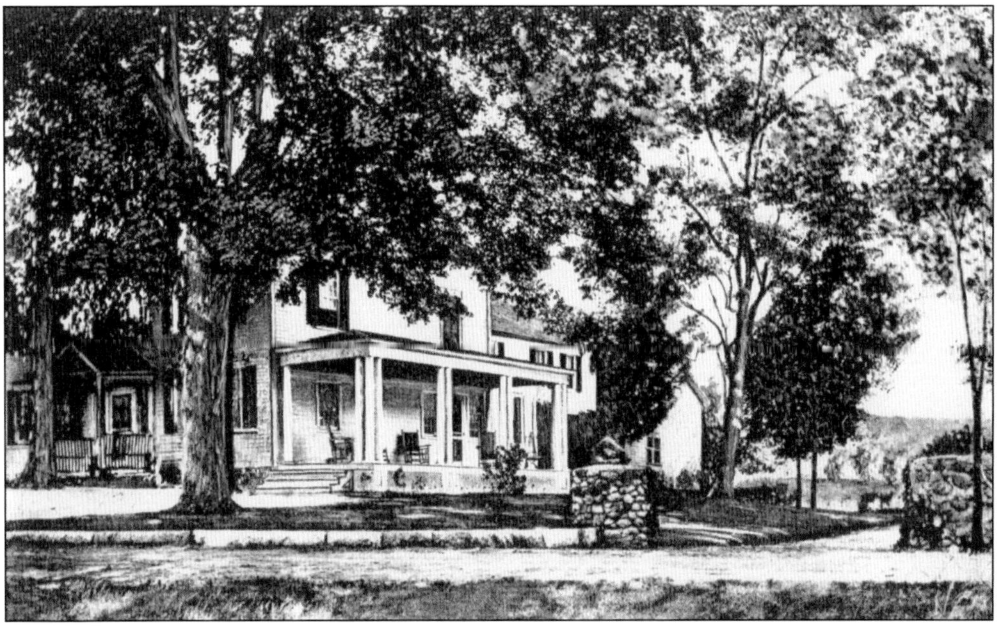

The Oldfield House. This house was used frequently in photographer Wallace Nutting's pictures. Erected between 1818 and 1820, it is the former home of John Mosley. In later years, it was owned by Albert Aston and his wife, Ruth, who donated the land for the green of the United Church of Christ. It is on the corner of the present intersection of Bucks Hill, Route 6, and Route 67. (TL.)

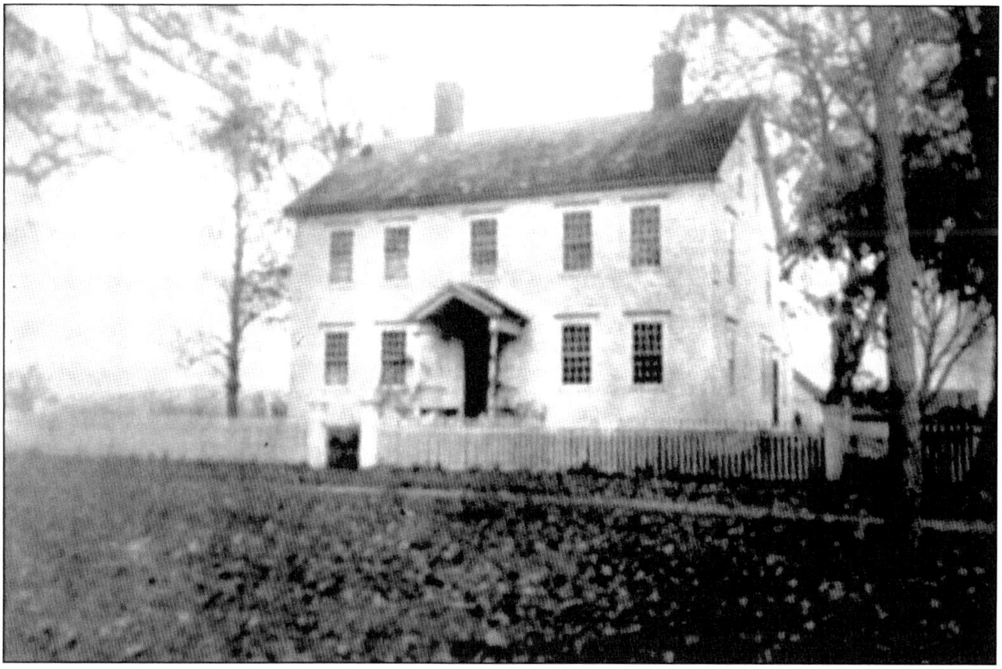

The Timothy Hinman House. The owner, Timothy Hinman, was a Yale graduate of 1784. He owned the burial ground that was deeded to the ecclesiastical society for Old Back (Middleground Graveyard). (SHS.)

The Old Mansion House on Mansion House Road. The house shown was built by Mitchel S. Mitchell and included a ballroom. The 1991 survey of historic properties says the house was built in 1827 as a "house of public entertainment." Other references claim a date of 1828. A paper was found in the stair post listing the six workmen who completed the house in 1829. Among them was James English, who later became governor of Connecticut. Previous owners include famous furniture maker Duncan Phyfe. He later deeded the house to his daughter Sarah Whitlock in 1854. She had 13 children and some adopted children. (TL.)

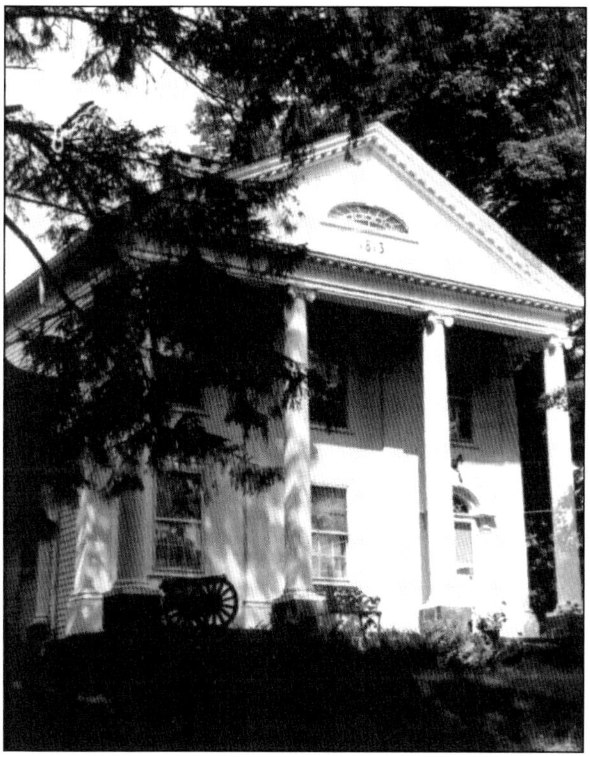

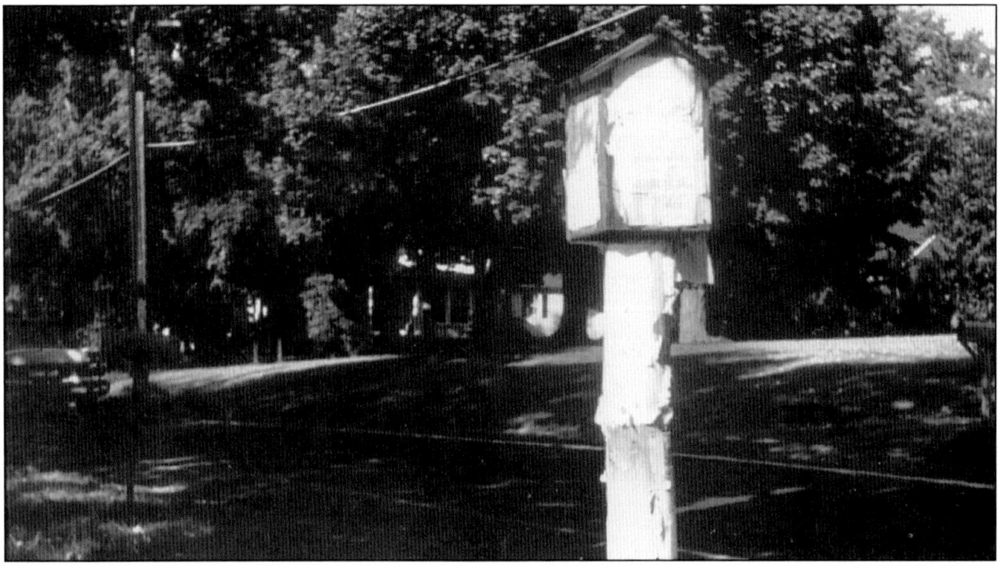

New England Signpost. Shown is one of the three town signposts that used to exist. The signpost, an important part of every New England town, was where notices were posted for all to read. In the past, things went by word of mouth or were posted on message posts. There were three in town in prominent locations: the land near United Church of Christ in front of the green, South Britain near the church area, and Southford on the backside of the intersection of Routes 188 and 67, near Southford Chapel. Another form of early communication was the tolling of church bells to signify an important event. When Lincoln died, the tolling of the bells from one community to another signaled his death and a time of mourning. People draped their houses and church alters in black in recognition of this tragedy. (SHS.)

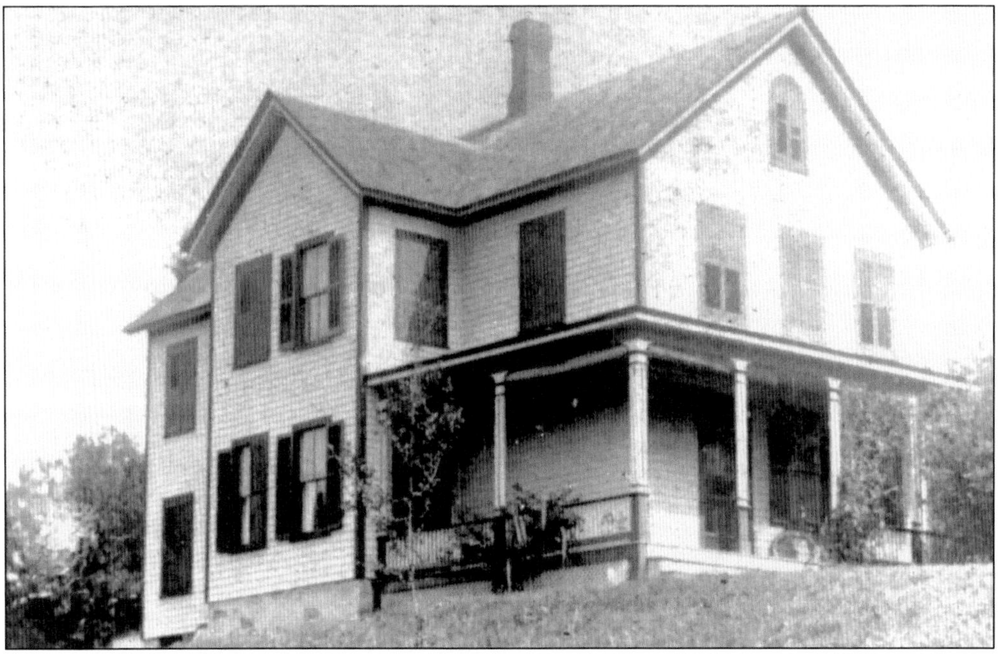

The Charles Stone House. This house was located on the road to the railroad depot. Charles was the son of Alonzo Stone. (MCW.)

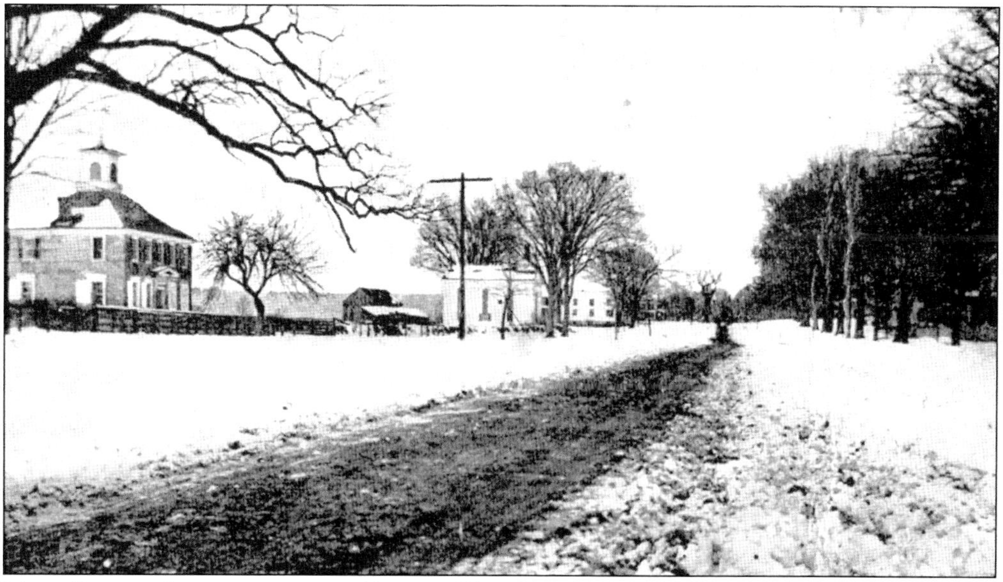

Main Street Approaching the Bullet Hill School. In this view, which looks north on Main Street, is the Bullet Hill School, which was used in the early days as a place to hold town meetings, a site for church gatherings, and a schoolhouse. As seen here, lawns were very large. Roads were laid out either north and south or east and west between set intervals. (TL.)

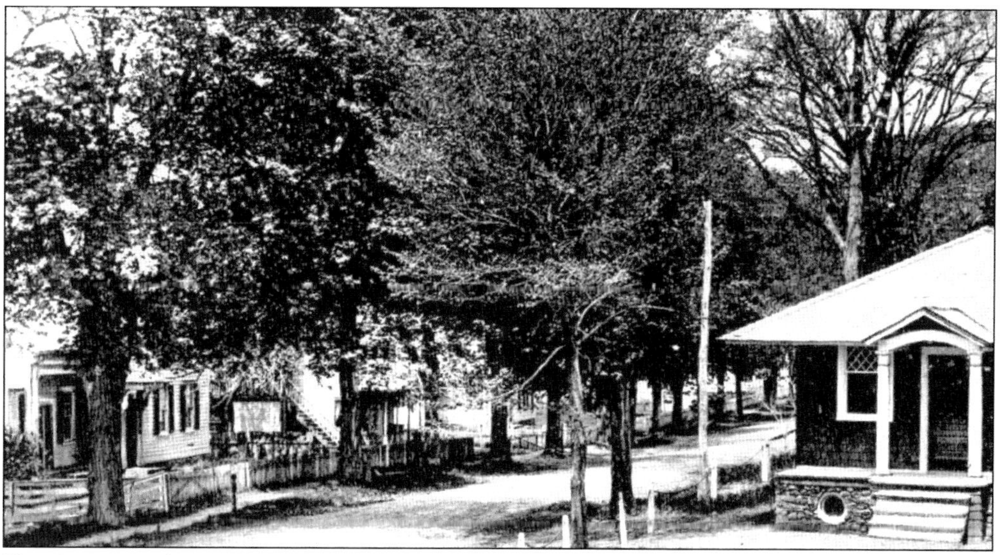

The Library, South Britain. Prior to the construction of this building, libraries existed in people's homes and in Munson Hall. In 1791, the area's first public library was established in South Britain. The South Britain Library building was built in 1904 by contractor A.H. Wilson at a cost of $746. It served as the town's only public source of reading material until 1969, when the Southbury Library was built on Main Street South. Over 1,000 books were transferred in 1969 from the South Britain Library to the new public library. The little library remained open for many years, staffed by volunteers, and eventually closed. In 1983, The town of Southbury accepted the library as one of its three historic buildings. Today, the building holds genealogical and local-history information for the historical society. (DM.)

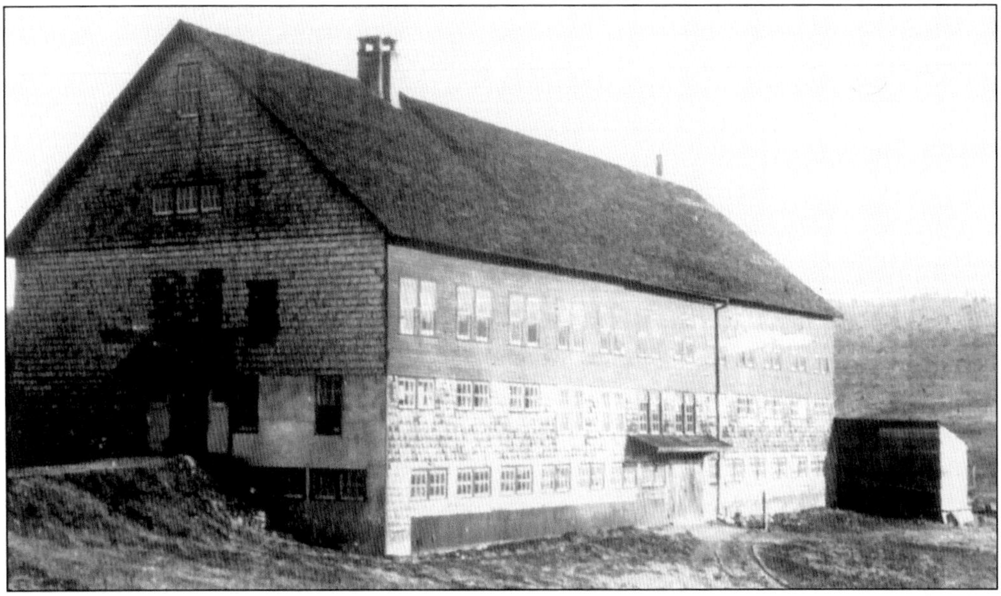

THE NUTTING BARN. Here, Wallace Nutting had the colorists of his photographs work. This location was near his estate in the area of Heritage Village. Nutting named his house and studio Nuttinghame and resided there from 1906 until 1912. Now, it is the meetinghouse in Heritage Village. Many locals were employed in his business. The ladies painted photographs with water colors. Nutting's cow barn was converted to a dormitory, studio, and workshop. Nutting also installed a swinging bridge over the Pomperaug River as a shortcut for his colorists. The Nutting barn burned. (SHS.)

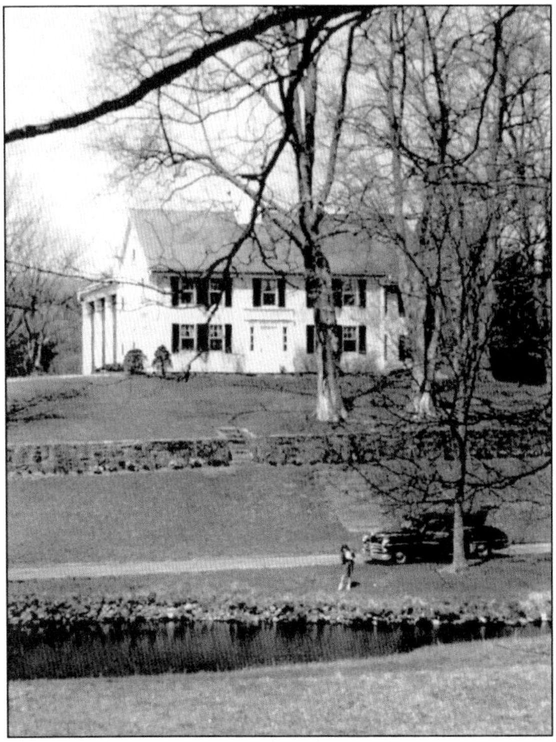

VICTOR BORGE'S HOME. Shown are the pond and house that belonged to Victor Borge in the Heritage Village area. The house is now the village's meetinghouse. It was previously owned by Wallace Nutting. It was built in the 1740s. Borge was a famous comedic pianist. Heritage Village is the consolidation of two major land holdings formerly belonging to Borge and his neighbor, Alfred P. Kreuger. Borge used his property as a place to escape from the rigors of television and theater and to raise his famous Cornish game hens. Ballantine Field is named after another former owner's son, Lt. John H. Ballantine Jr., who was killed in World War II. Another Southbury resident that was killed in a World War was Lt. C. Edward Hine, and an American Legion post was named after him in its organization in 1945. Heritage Village was opened in 1968 and is an adult community for people more than 55 years of age. (SHS.)

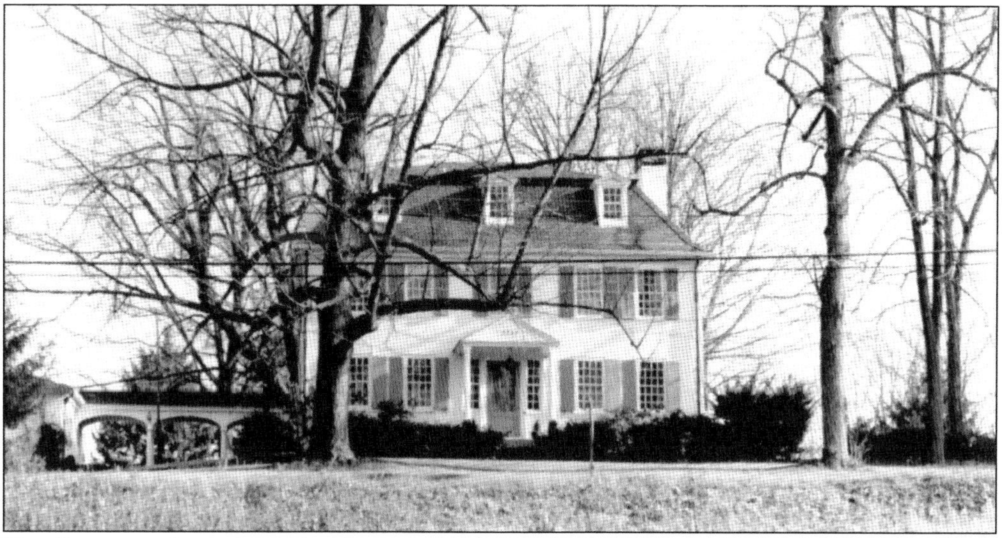

THE BENJAMIN STILES METRIC HOUSE. This house, built *c*. 1787, had a mansard roof covered with slate. Bricks were made from local clay and were said to be fired in a kiln on the side of the Pomperaug River. Legend also states that the house plans were designed by Stiles's French friend, who was an engineer working with metric measurements in Rochambeau's army. Stiles graduated from Yale in 1776 and earned a Master of Arts degree in 1778. He was one of the first attorneys in town. The family occupied the house until 1920. This residence is the subject of many Wallace Nutting photographs. The use of brick for home architecture was introduced in the 1780s. Two Yale classmates of 1776 erected mansions on Town Street. They broke the Colonial tradition in Western Connecticut of using wood. Two other brick houses of this period are in South Britain. (SHS.)

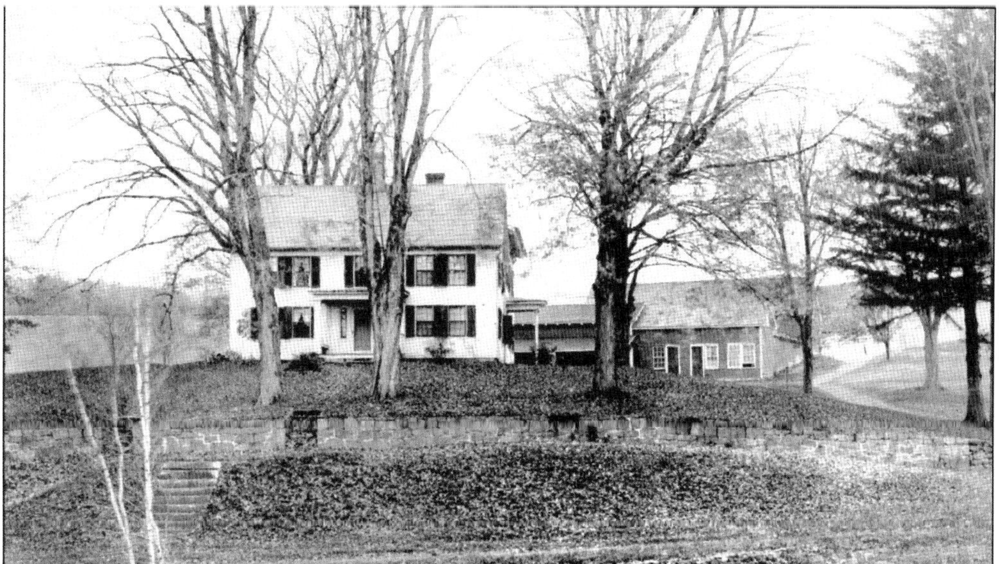

NUTTINGHAME BLOSSOMS. This is a photograph by Wallace Nutting, who, from 1906 to 1912, lived in what is now the meetinghouse in Heritage Village. He established a studio in his home. He employed many locals who painted watercolors on the platinum prints that he took. He also donated money to the United Church of Christ to install a furnace. (SHS.)

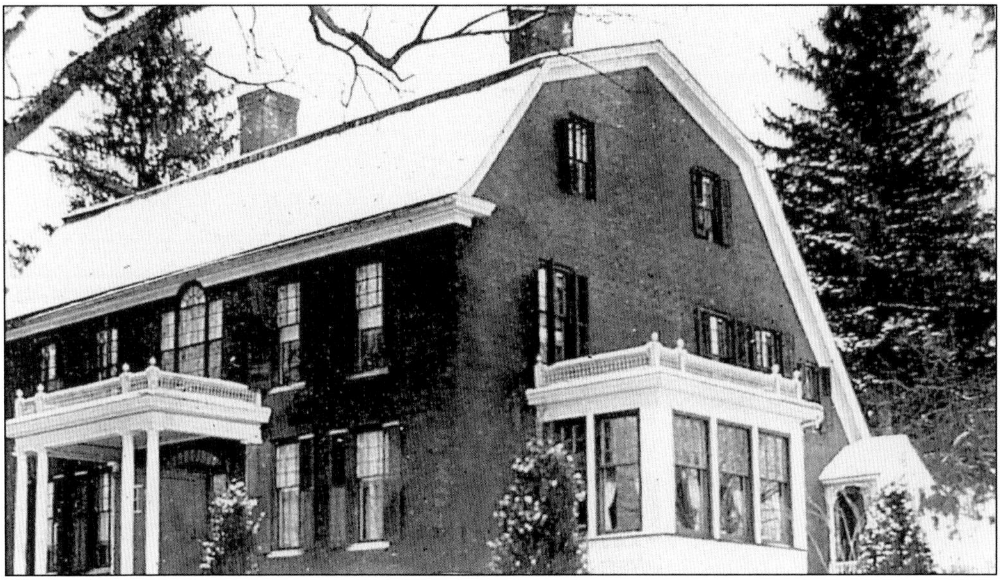

The Peter Parley House, Built c. 1777. The famous children's book author Samuel Goodrich lived in this house. It became the Lutheran Home, which was the first licensed home for the aged, in 1918. Although he only lived in Southbury for a short part of his life, Parley elected to be buried in "God's Acre where the sun shines and where rain falls upon the grassy mound." (SHS.)

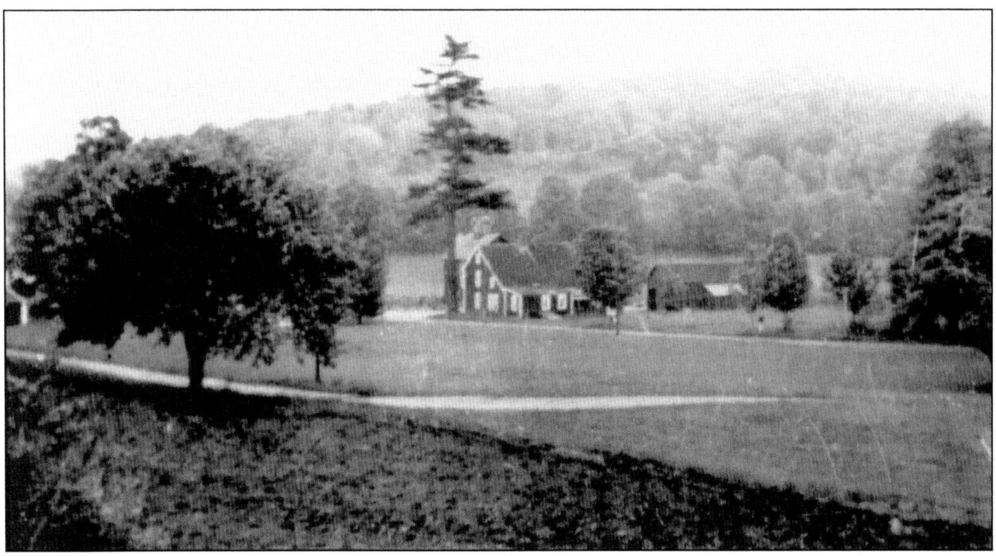

The House at Pine Tree Corners. This photograph shows a house with the tree that it was named after at Pine Tree Corners. The tree blew down in the 1938 Hurricane. The house is located at the intersection of Transylvania Road and Routes 172 and 67. (RS.)

AN EARLY HOUSE DEED. An early land document from 1784 shows the transfer of land from Nathaniel Tuttle to Capt. Ames Hicock. Local attorneys David and Benjamin Hinman officiated. (AM.)

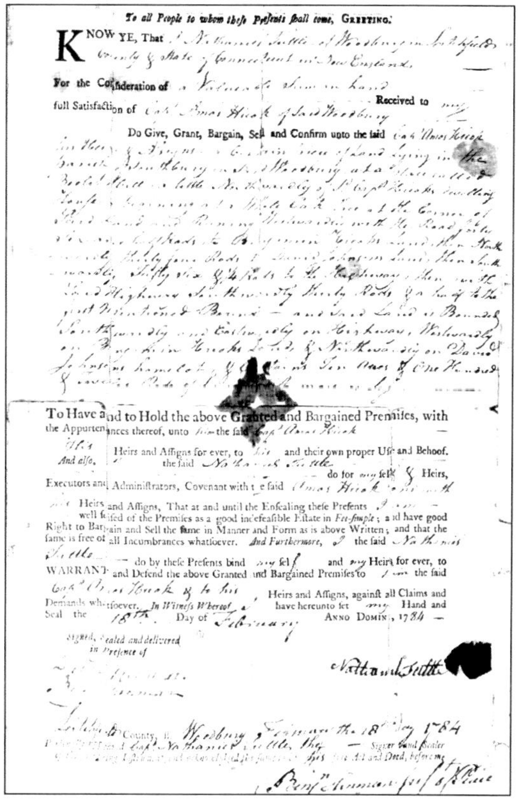

To all People to whom these Presents shall come, GREETING.

KNOW YE, That I Nathaniel Tuttle of Woodbury in Litchfield County & State of Connecticut in New England.

For the Consideration of a Valuable Sum in Land

full Satisfaction of Capt. Amos Hicock of said Woodbury Received to my

Do Give, Grant, Bargain, Sell and Confirm unto the said Capt. Amos Hicock

To Have and to Hold the above Granted and Bargained Premises, with the Appurtenances thereof, unto him the said Capt. Amos Hicock his Heirs and Assigns for ever, to his and their own proper Use and Behoof. And also, the said Nathaniel Tuttle do for my self & Heirs, Executors and Administrators, Covenant with the said Amos Hicock his Heirs and Assigns, That at and until the Ensealing these Presents I am well seised of the Premises as a good indefeasible Estate in Fee-simple; and have good Right to Bargain and Sell the same in Manner and Form as is above Written; and that the same is free of all Incumbrances whatsoever. And Furthermore, I the said Nathaniel Tuttle do by these Presents bind my self and my Heirs for ever, to WARRANT and Defend the above Granted and Bargained Premises to him the said Capt. Amos Hicock & to his Heirs and Assigns, against all Claims and Demands whatsoever. In Witness Whereof I have hereunto set my Hand and Seal the 18th Day of February ANNO DOMINI, 1784

Signed, Sealed and delivered in Presence of

Nathaniel Tuttle

Litchfield County, ss. Woodbury February the 18th Day 1784

Benj. Hinman Just. of Peace

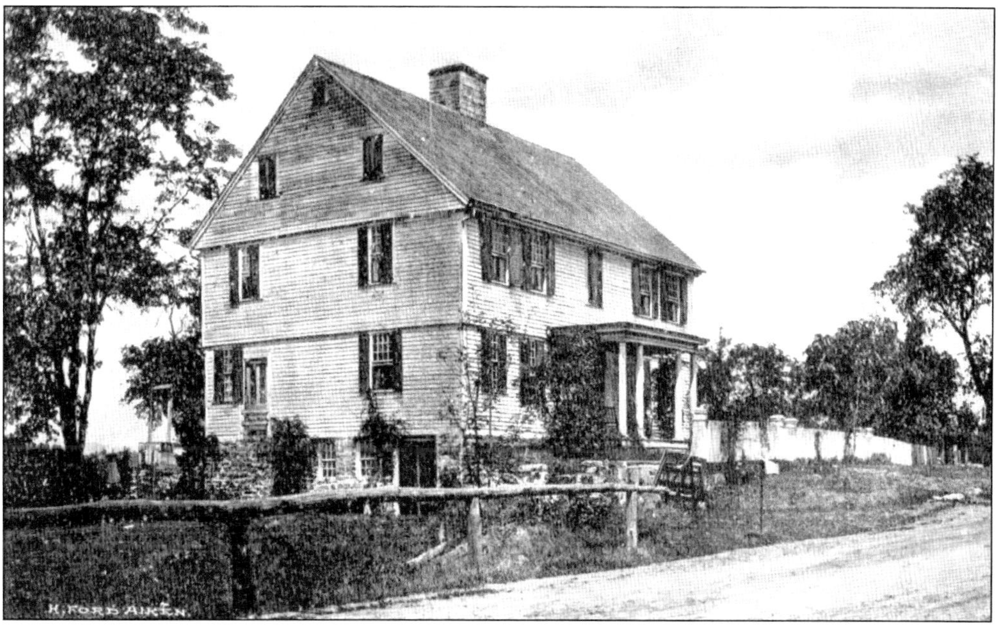

THE BENJAMIN HINMAN HOMESTEAD. This house was built in 1764 and is situated on the left side of Route 6 going north. It was built by David Hinman, the father of Benjamin. Benjamin Hinman was one of the richest men in town. He was a veteran of both the French and Indian War and the American Revolution. He commanded two regiments in the Revolution. (SHS.)

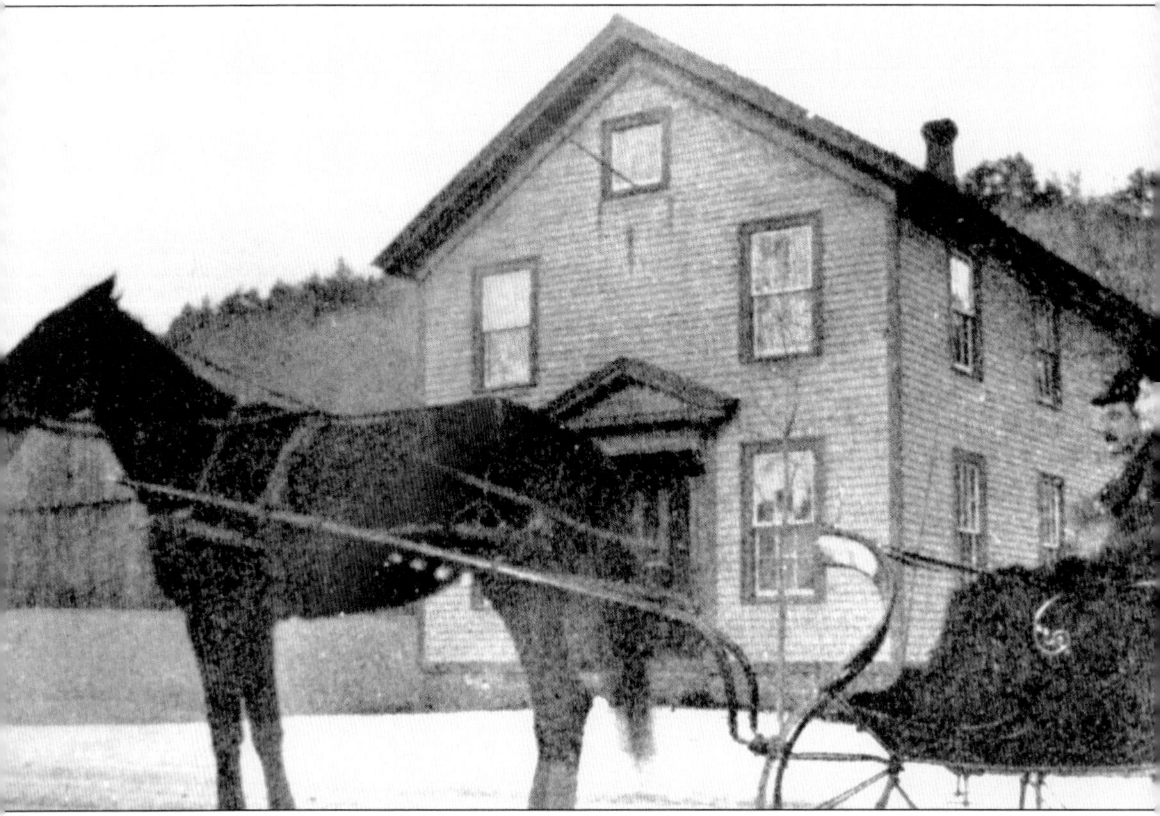

THE OLD TOWN HALL. George Mitchell is seen sleighing past a building that dates back to 1873 and is now the Old Town Hall Museum. Prior to 1868, the Ecclesiastical Society was the town's governing body. Town meetings were held in both the Congregational church on Main Street North in Southbury and the South Britain Congregational Church. In 1868, a decision was made to build a separate town hall in the business center, South Britain. The meetings would alternate between the two ecclesiastical districts. When Southbury separated from Ancient Woodbury and was incorporated in May 1787, town meetings were held alternately in the Congregational church on Main Street in Southbury and the South Britain Congregational Church on Main Street in South Britain. The construction of the town hall began in 1879. The land cost $125, and the projected building costs were not to exceed $1,375. The ladies of the South Britain Congregational Church offered to pay $1,600 for a second floor to be added. (SHS.)

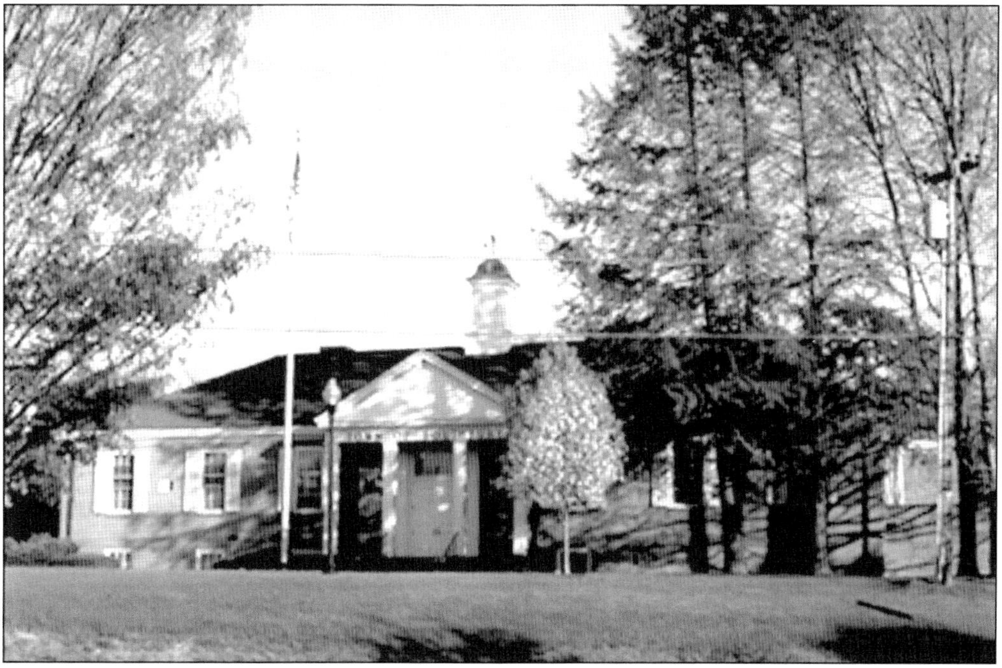

THE SECOND TOWN HALL. The town hall was built on the corner of Main Street and Peter Road. The second town hall was built in 1964. Today, it is called the town hall annex and houses the police department, parks and recreation department, and probate court. (AS.)

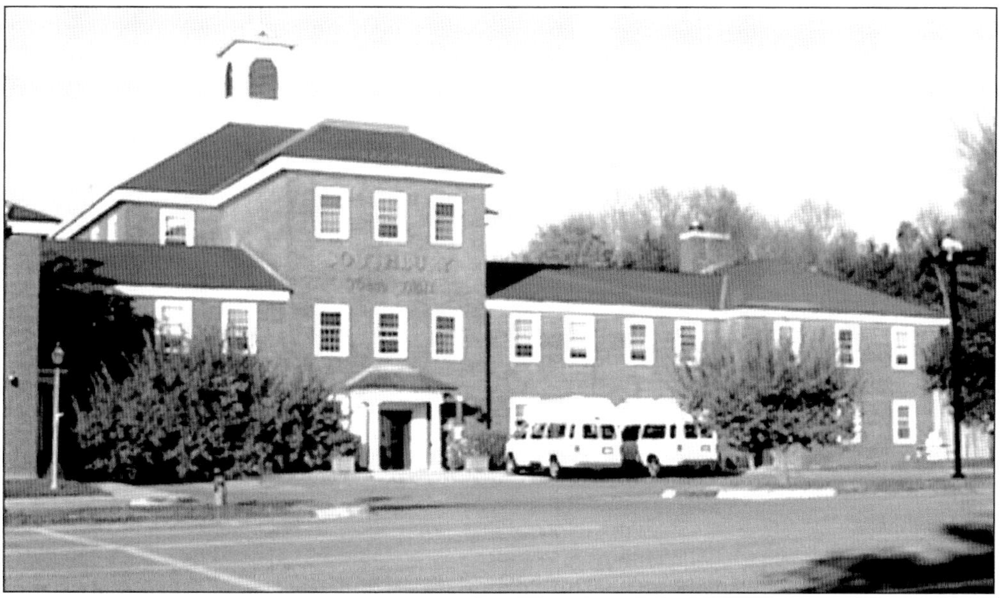

THE NEW TOWN HALL. The current and newest town hall was built in 1977. The building has an antique weather vane and cupola that were donated by Catherine McCarthy. The steeple came from the old Methodist church in South Britain and was more than 140 years old when it was given to the town. McCarthy was the only town employee that had worked in all three of the Southbury town halls. Many buildings, including this one, emulate the Georgian architectural style.(AS.)

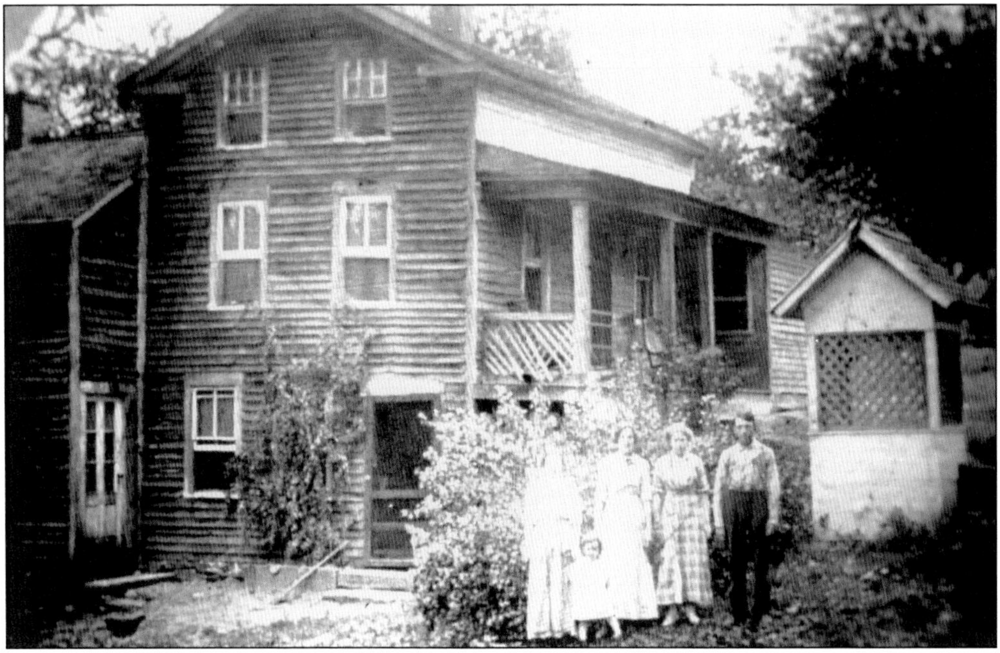

Early South Britain Home. The Georgian style evolved to the Federal style, which was characterized by sidelights and fanlights. Examples of the Renaissance Revival became fashionable, and Federal fanlights were replaced with curvilinear and triangular pediments over front doors. The most prevalent style of Greek Revival architecture attained popularity in South Britain homes in the second quarter of the 19th century. (SHS.)

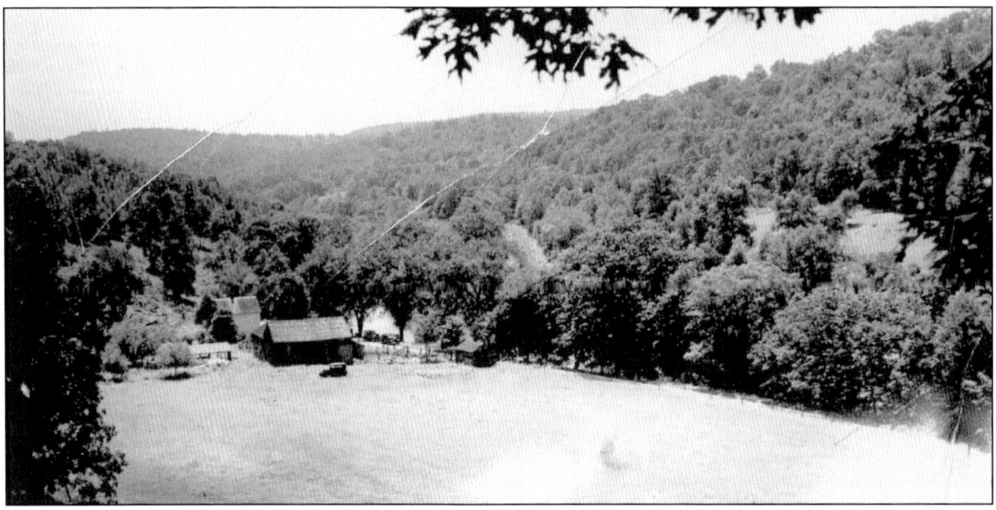

A Farm before the Construction of the Shepaug Dam. This photograph shows a homestead prior to its demise. Topography changed around town when the Shepaug Dam was built and Lake Lillinonah was flooded. The western part of Southbury was inaccessible, and land had to be annexed to Bridgewater. When the dam was completed in 1955, it filled up almost overnight. Lillinonah is named after an Indian legend that tells of a maiden who jumped into the current off Lover's Leap, below New Milford, due to her love for a white man. Her elders had selected an Indian brave for her. (MJW.)

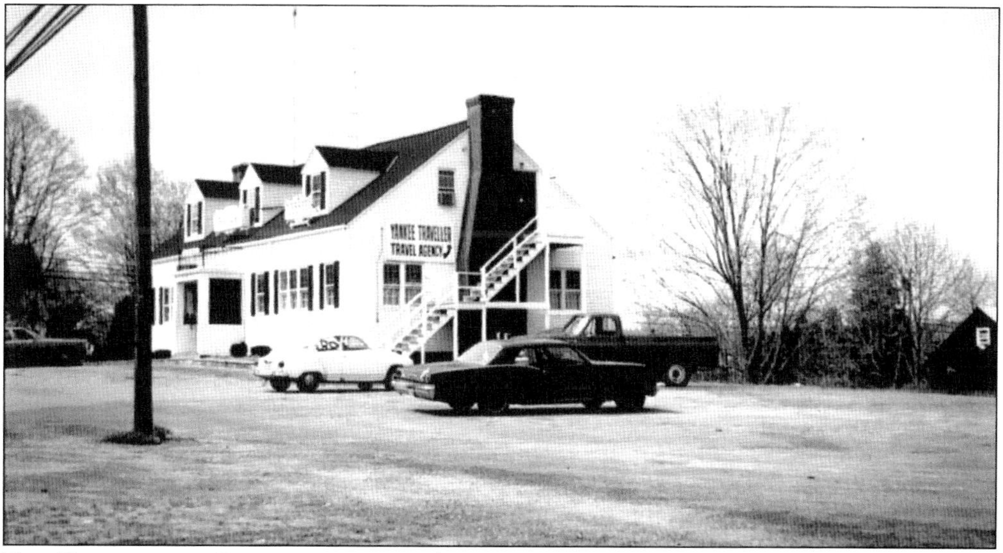

The Rathskellar Restaurant. Seen here is a local restaurant, originally the site of the Briarwood, an ice-cream parlor and restaurant. Sometimes, students from the consolidated school (now Gainfield School) went there on their lunch hours. It had a cup-of-coffee sign—just like the Maxwell House coffee logo of today—which "dripped" the coffee in lights. It was originally run by Joe and Helen Cunningham, who owned the other Briarwood on Ben Sherman Hill in Woodbury. Gordon and Julia Schielke were in business here later on. Today, the location is incorporated into 88 Main Street South. (SHS.)

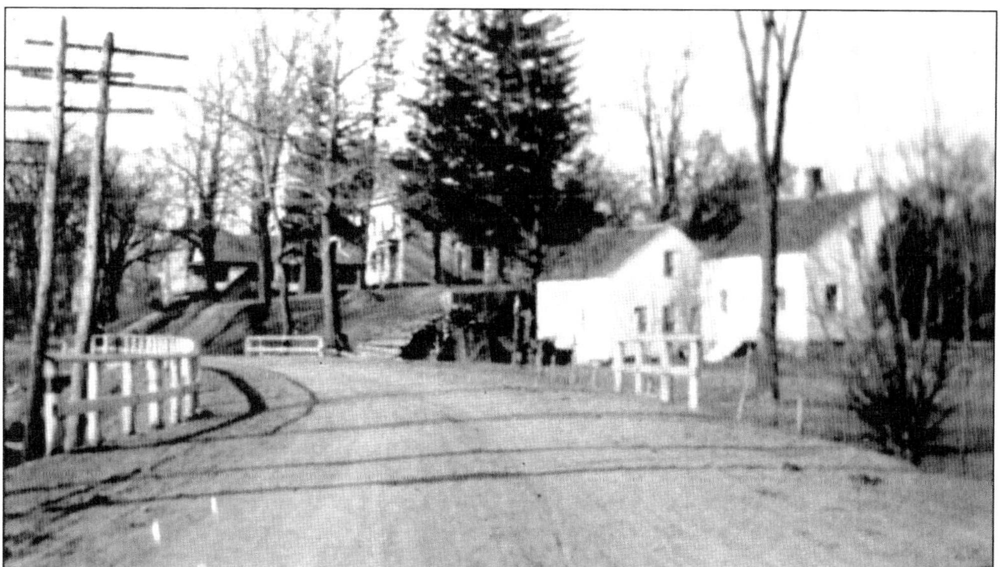

A View Looking North c. 1910–1920. The two white buildings in the foreground were the Lewis Mill. To the left, on the hill, was Nate Hicock's house (which was later demolished), and the short building in the distance was Tyler's Store. (ML.)

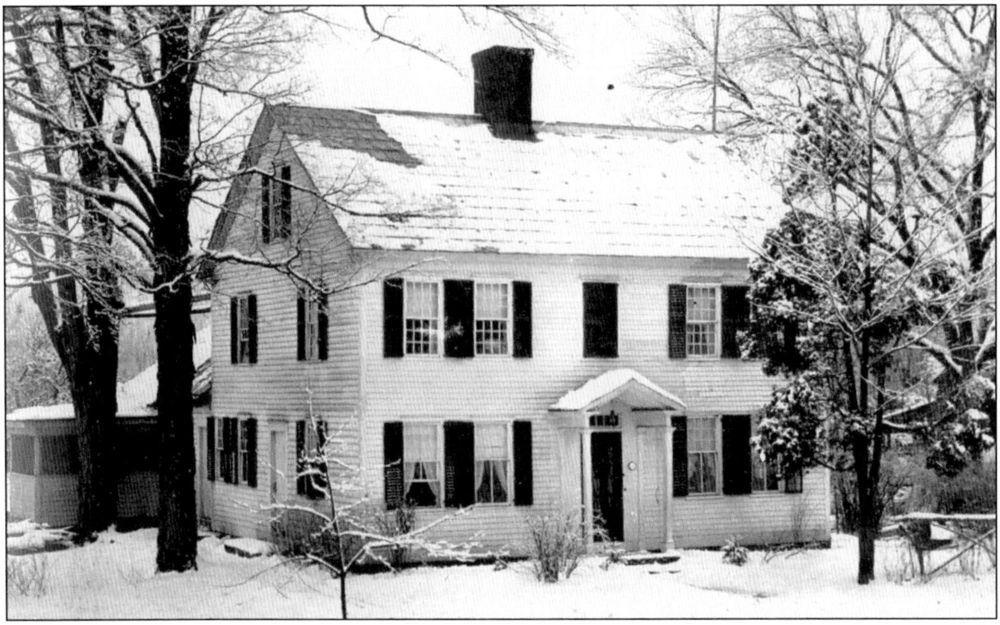

The Raymond Stiles House. Built in 1824, this house is located at 1127 Main Street North. One door was called the funeral door and was designed to transport coffins through for wakes. This area is known as Ragland and was once a common pasture for sheep. At one time, Ethan Allen, of the Green Mountain Boys fame, owned land on Saw Tooth Hill in Ragland. He sold the land in 1781. Ragland is along the present Woodbury town line. (BS.)

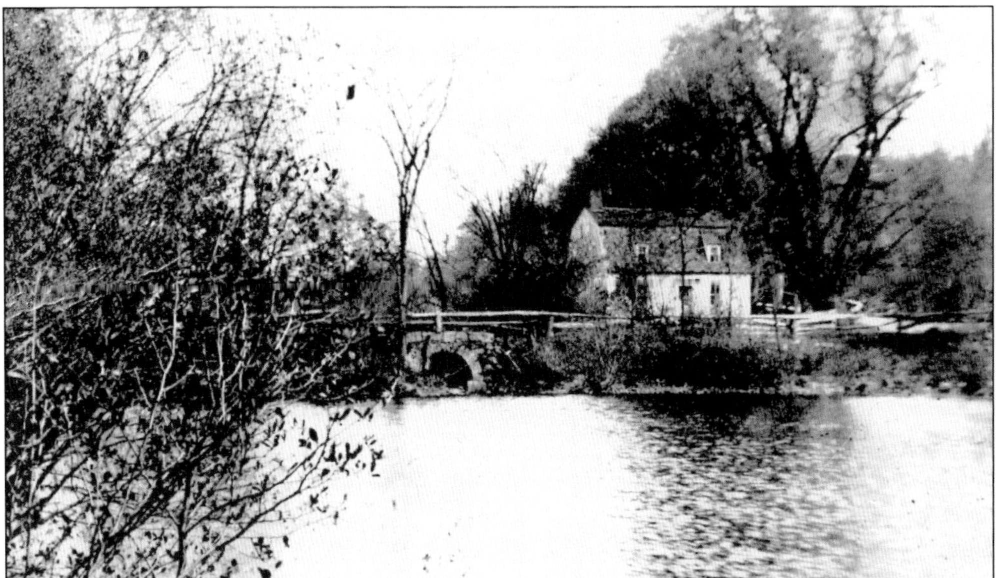

The Old Plaster House in Southford. This picture Wallace Nutting made of this home was titled *Cottage on the Floss*. The cottage was built in the mid-1800s. The nearby brook has an original keystone bridge, one of the few that exist in the state. At one time, there were also a knife shop and cider mill at this location. (GS.)

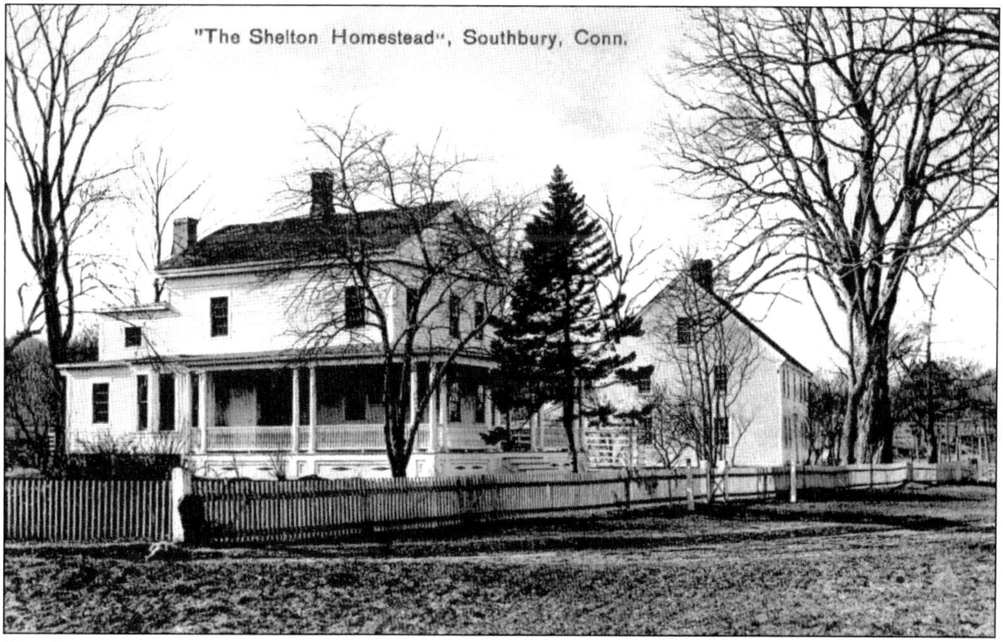

THE SHELTON HOUSE. This homestead was located at Playhouse Corners. One house was moved to the back and another was dismantled and moved to Darien in the early 1920s. The remaining structure is the current site of a real-estate office and Dr. Paterno's chiropractic practice. (TL.)

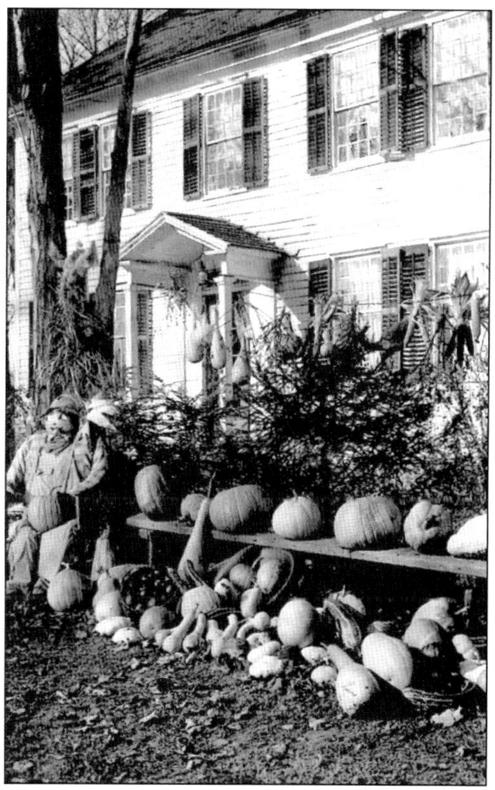

FALL DECORATIONS. The house in this photograph was decorated for the autumn season. Raymond Stiles's house was decorated this way every year. One year, a picture of one of the displays was in Life magazine. (BS and RC.)

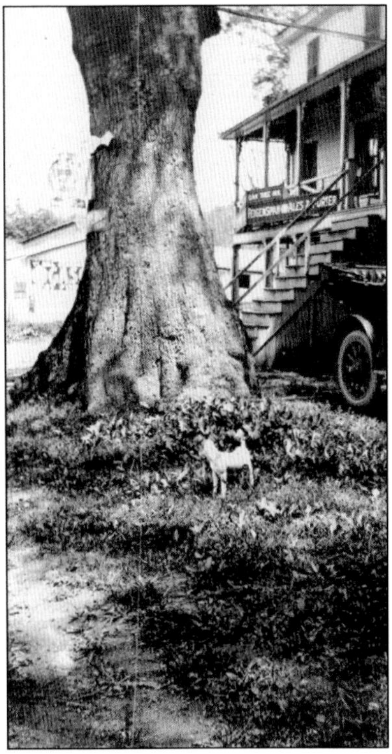

The Oak Tree Inn. This inn was named after the large tree out front. Augustus Osborne, who was at least 70 in 1912, said that there was a big hole in the tree, which she played in as a child. When the drummers arrived in town by train, they would take a room at the Oak Tree Inn and hire a livery to make their rounds. In 1912, there were kerosene lamps, slop jars (there was no running water), wash basins, and a player piano. An itinerant barber would come to the Oak Tree Inn each week. (DM.)

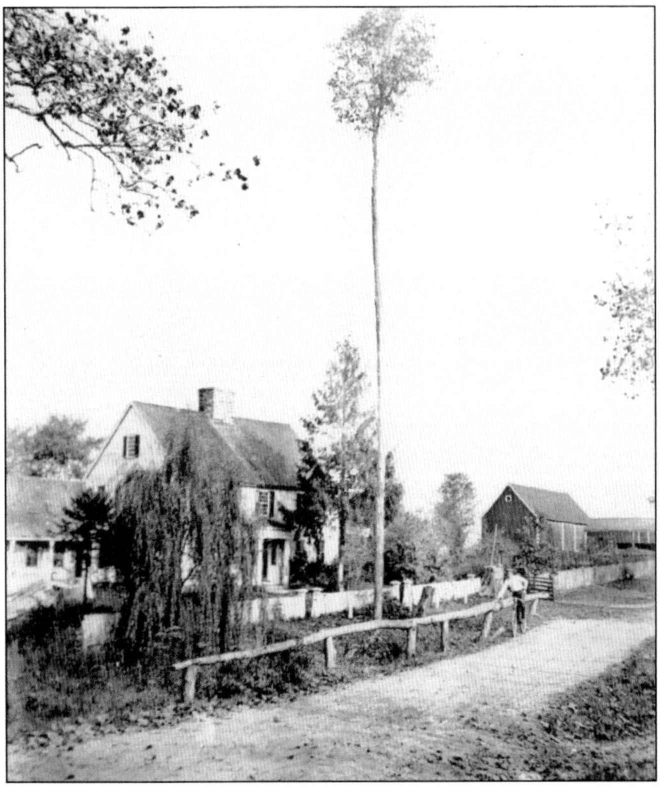

The Stiles House and Topiary Tree. Shown is the Lt. Francis Stiles house, built *c.* 1740. It was the first two-story house in Litchfield County. A secret room hid Torries and access was gained by removing attic flooring. Slave quarters were located in the basement. (RC.)

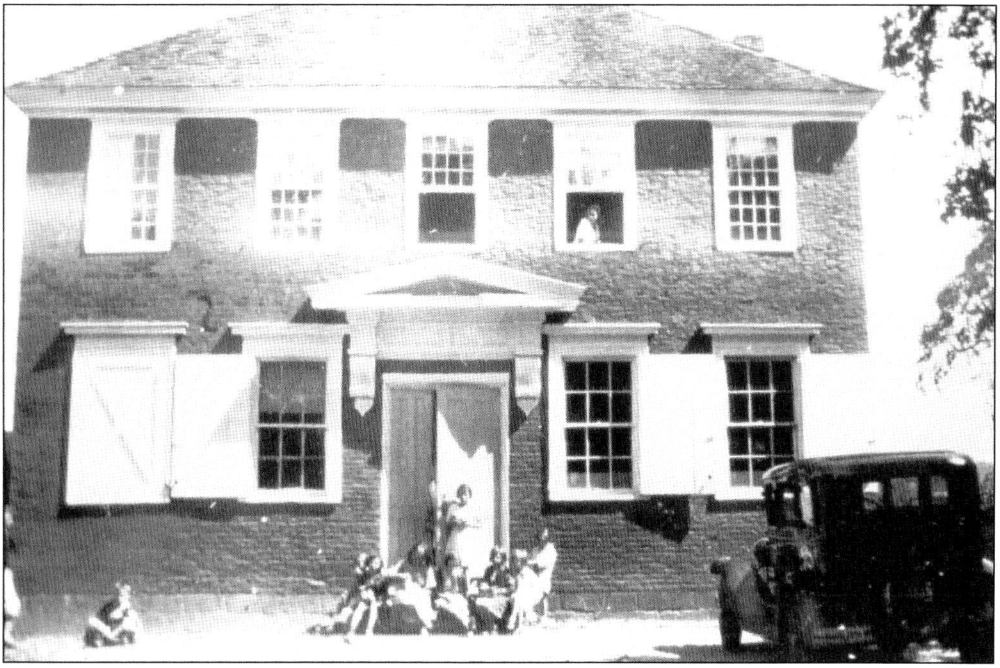

The Bullet Hill School. This is a photograph of Southbury's oldest public building. The interior has a unique architectural style. (GS.)

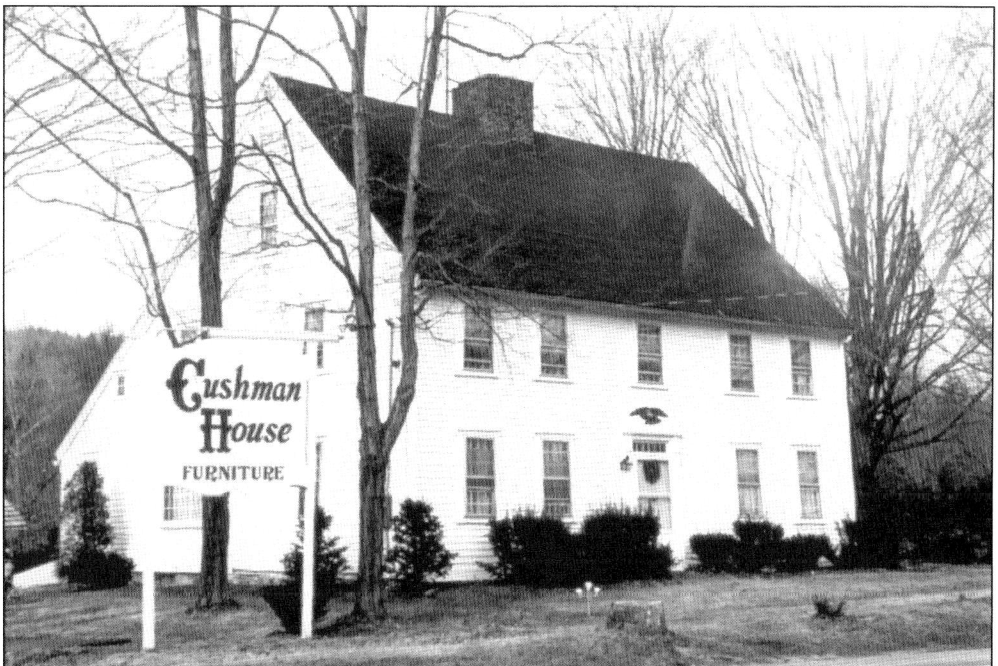

The Cushman Furniture Store. This store was located on Main Street South across from the old pumpkin patch. It burned down in the 1980s. It was once Corbin Wheeler's house. The location is the present site of 800 Main Street South. (SHS.)

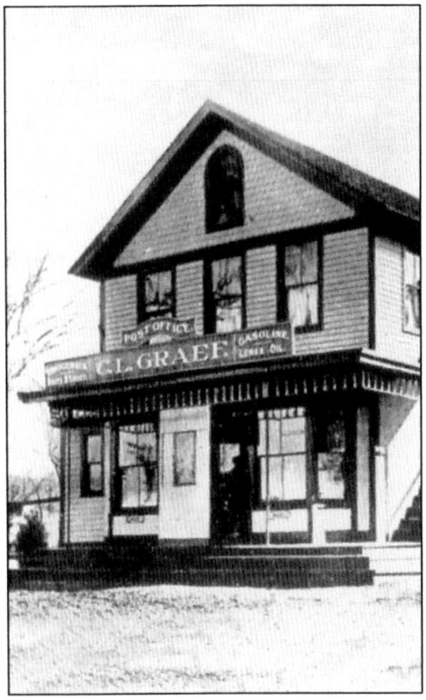

THE G.L. GRAEF STORE AND POST OFFICE IN SOUTHBURY. This store was multifunctional. It later became Green's, a general store, among others, including the Natural Merchant Health Food store that was owned by the LeFebvre family. The first South Britain post office was established in Eliot Beardsley's house on the corner of Library Road and Route 172. The South Britain post office was moved back and forth from the McCarthy store across from the Old Town Hall Museum to the Mitchell store, depending on the political party in office. At one time, the post office was located at what was John Thompson's house at the corner of Middle Road and Main Street. Southbury had two post offices burn down in town, this one and the one on Main Street that burned in 1971. (SHS.)

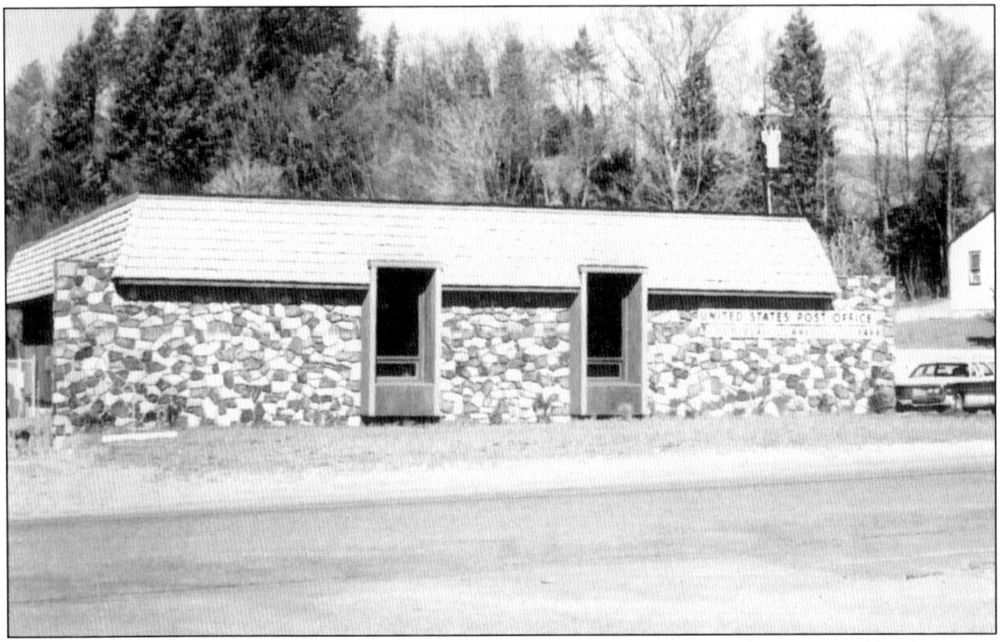

THE SOUTHBURY POST OFFICE. This photograph shows one of the sites where post office business was conducted. After the fire in the Southbury post office on Main Street, business was moved to the Grange until this building was built. Now, the building is the site of the Señor Panchos Mexican restaurant. (SHS.)

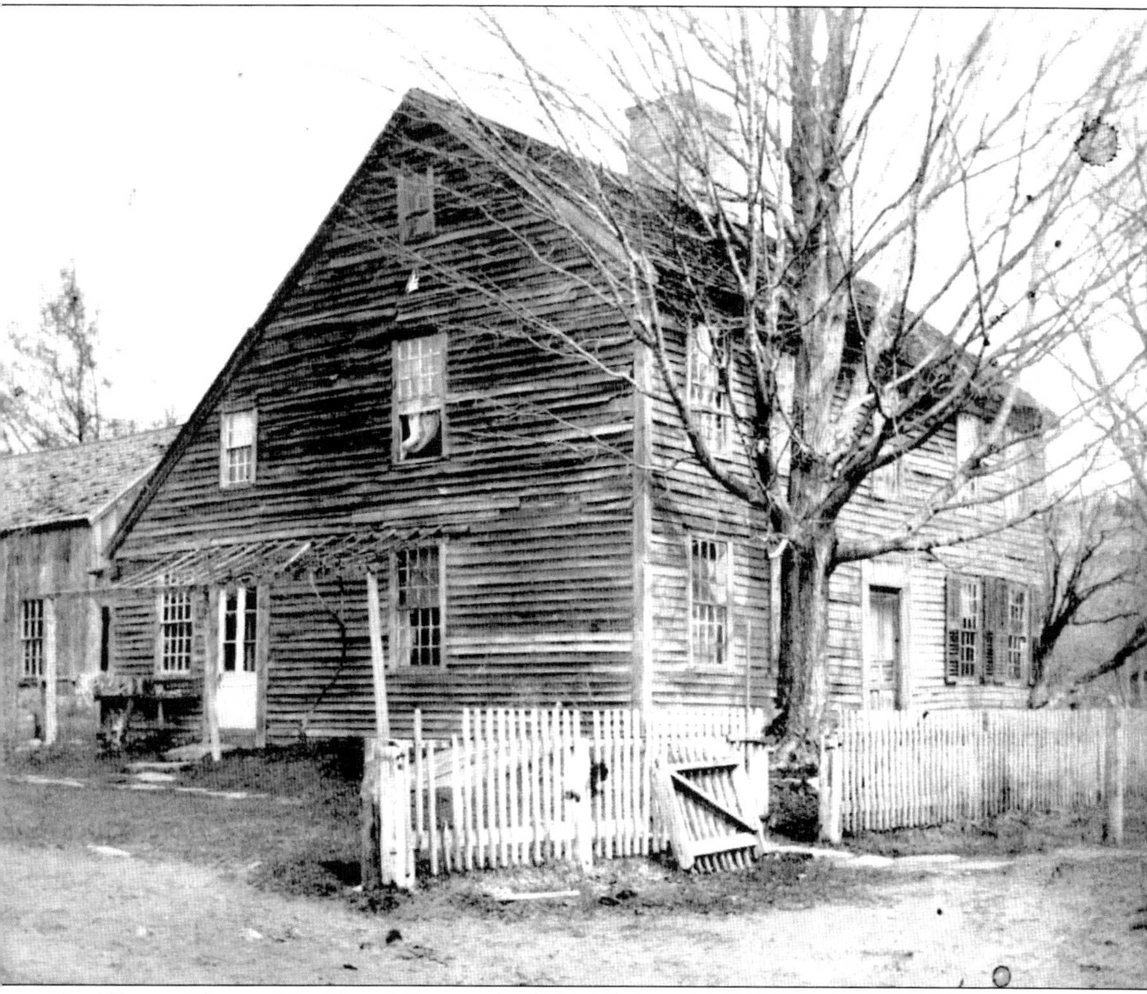

THE HICOCK HOUSE. The Hicock house, which is no longer standing, was located on Route 67 and Transylvania Road near Pine Tree Corners. The Hicock family owned many homes in the area. (TL.)

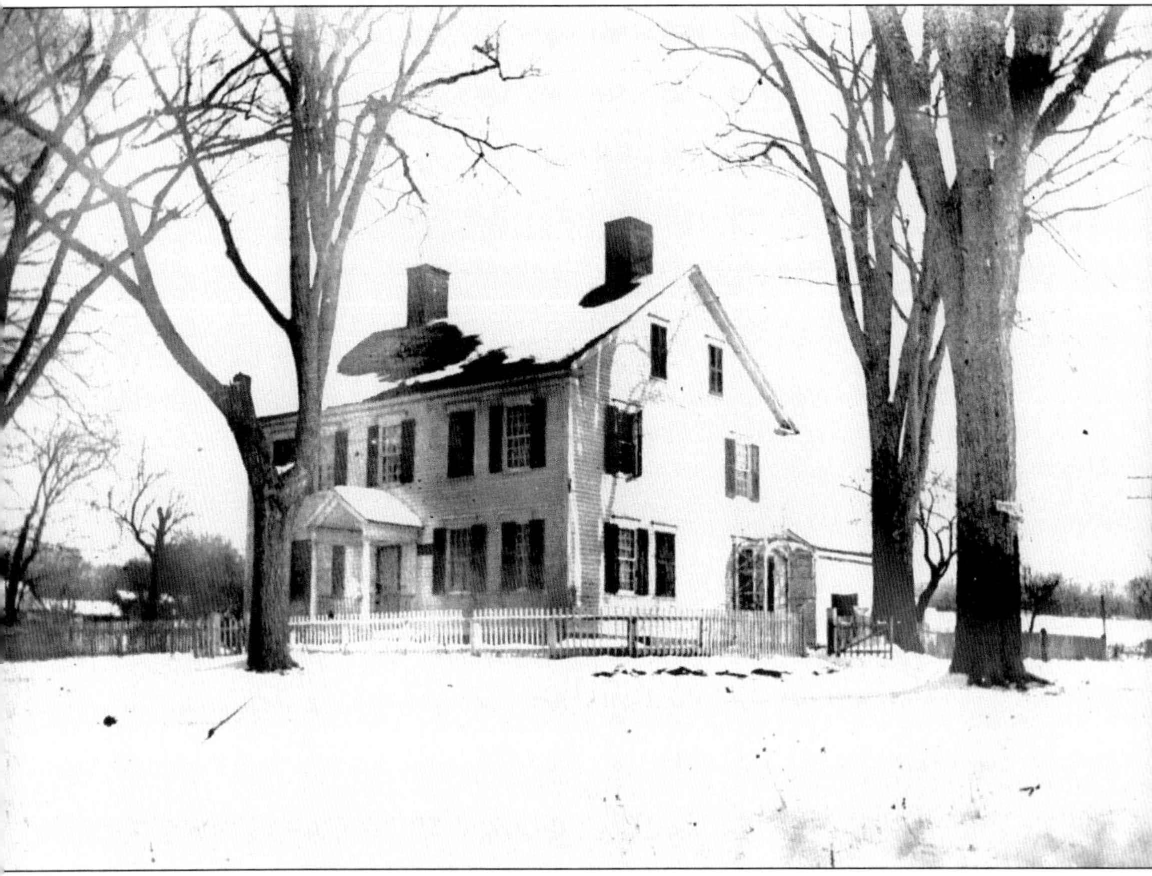

THE CONGREGATIONAL PARSONAGE. The house seen here was located on Old Waterbury Road. It is no longer serving as a parsonage. A soldier's monument can be seen on the side of the residence. The monument was moved and now is located next to the public library. The home was built by the Hine family. (SHS.)

THE RANT HOUSE. Steven Rant built the pictured windmill so that he could hear the *Grand Ole Opry* on the radio. The house was destroyed with the building of the Shepaug Dam. (MJW.)

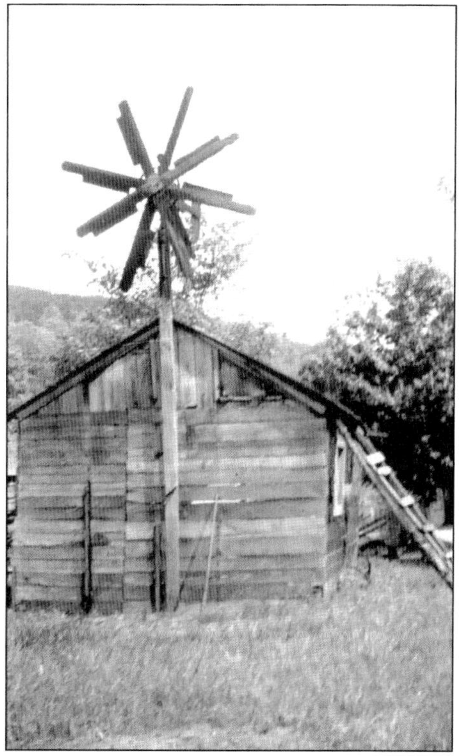

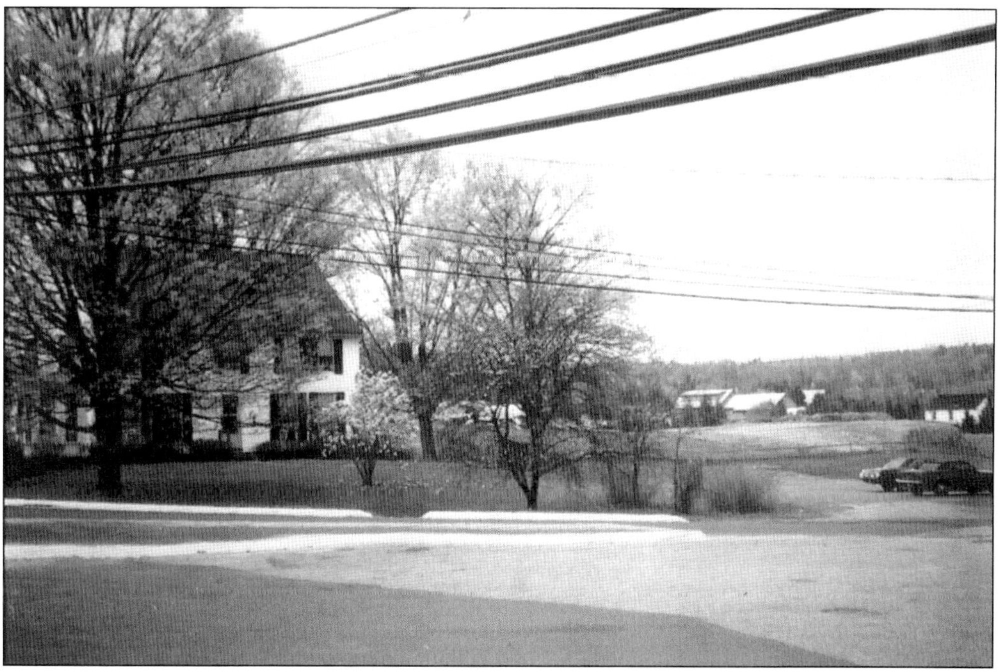

THE ELY HICOCK HOUSE. This home is the current site of Leo's restaurant. On the right is where Bennett Square is today. This view is from Poverty Road. The town treasurer of 40 years Henry Russell attended the 1902 state constitutional convention. He received a seedling of a Connecticut constitutional pine oak. It became diseased and was taken down in 2002. (SHS.)

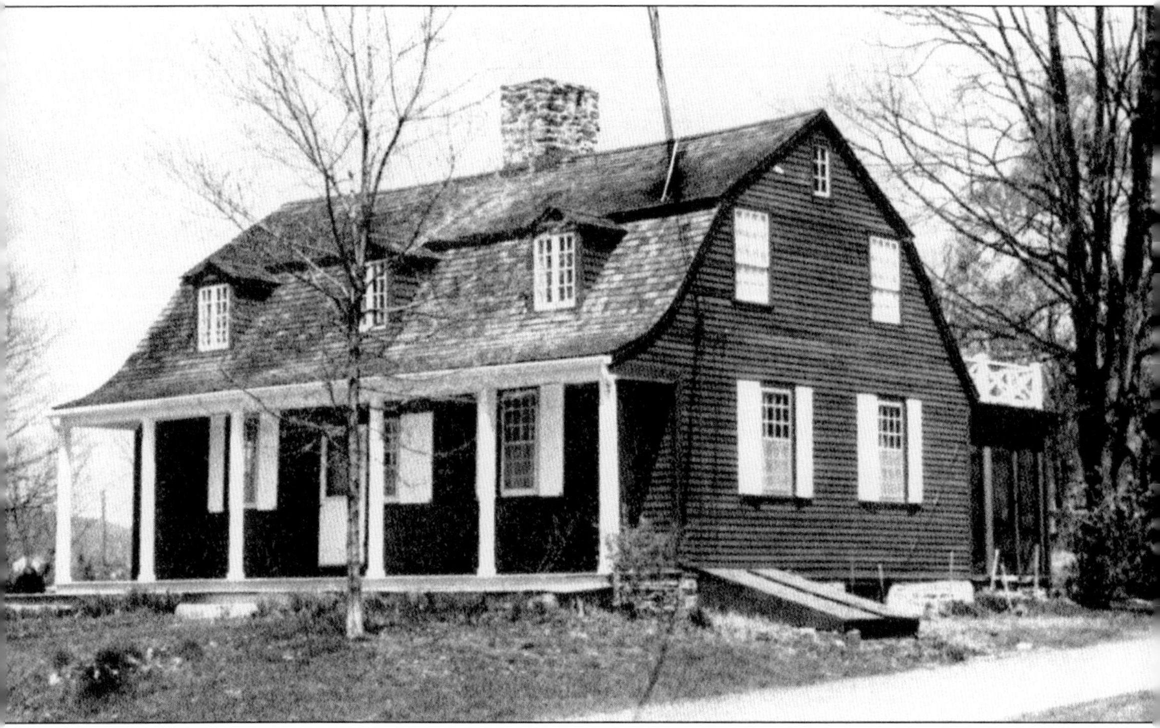

The Woodbury Savings Bank. Seen here is the Woodbury Savings Bank on Main Street in Woodbury. In 1950, a bank robbery occurred here that created excitement in Southbury. George Brewster and his brother held up the bank for $8,500. They fled to the wooded area between the Housatonic River and the Southbury Training School. A search was held by more than 200 state police officers and civilians in a five-mile area and was later called off. Five days after the heist, the robbers broke into the Wargo home and held up Catherine, her husband, Everett, and Madeline Noel by gunpoint and stole their car. After the police were notified, a running gun battle ensued along Route 67, which ended when the robbers' rear tire was shot and the Wargo car overturned. (DM.)

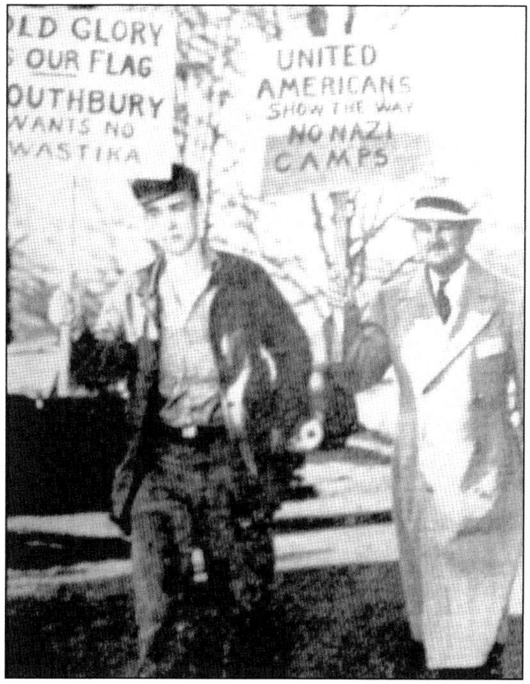

PROTESTING THE NAZI BUND. This photograph shows residents in an uproar over the Bund (the German-American Volksbund, a pro-Nazi organization in the United States during the 1930s and 1940s). In the sitzkrieg period prior to World War II, there were Nazi activities in town. In 1937, Fritz Kuhn tried to establish a camp for Bund members from New York City. A tract of 1,200 acres was purchased in Kettletown. A local storekeeper, Henry McCarthy, took notice when men stopped at his store to purchase large amounts of supplies. When the car stopped at St. Pierre's garage, a reporter recognized Hitler's number-one person on the East Coast. (SHS.)

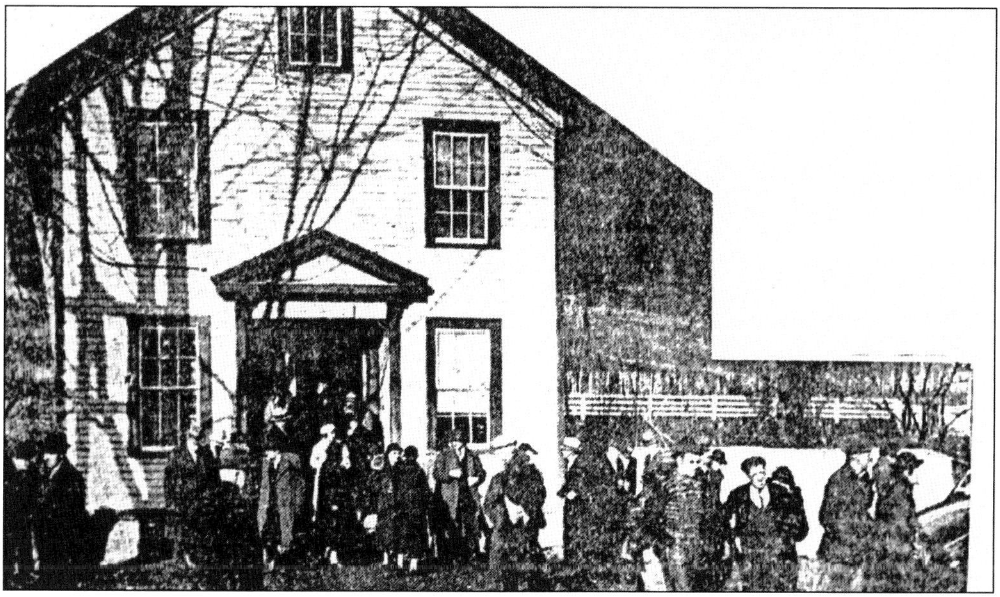

MOVING THE MEETING. A town meeting concerning the Bund was so big that it was moved from the Old Town Hall Museum to the Congregational church down the road. Selectman J. Edward Coers heard about the activity in Kettletown and jumped into action. He arrested workers under a resurrected blue law that prevented working on Sundays. He called a town meeting and helped push through both a zoning committee and ordinance to prevent the Nazi training camp. Zoning committee members included Robert C. Mitchell, Herbert Wells, Henry McCarthy, Albert Aston, and Leslie Wheeler. The Federal Bureau of Investigation collected license plate numbers from people who had visited the Bund site. When the war started, many of the owners were detained. (SHS.)

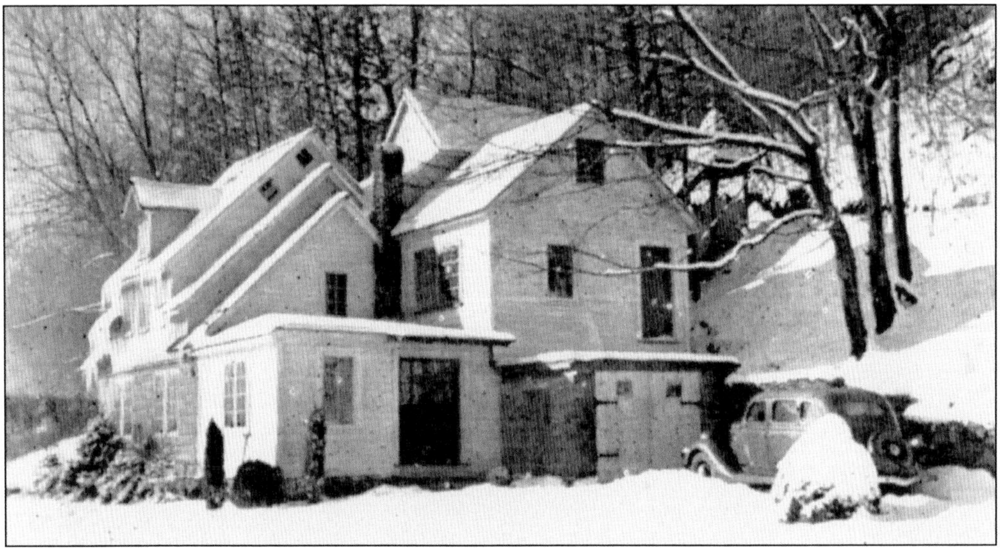

The Grebenstchikoff House. Seen here is a Russian Village house where much publishing was done. Professor George D. Grebenstchikoff was one of the founders and settlers of Russian Village, along with writer Leo Tolstoy's son Ilya. Grebenstchikoff depicted a mythical town in Siberia, his native land, in his three-volume novel called *Churaevei.* In Russian Village, he tried to recreate the vision where people of Russian descent expressed themselves artistically with music, art, poetry, and engineering to promote Russian culture outside of Russia. Grebenstchikoff wrote the epic novel *The Turbulent Giant* here. (SHS.)

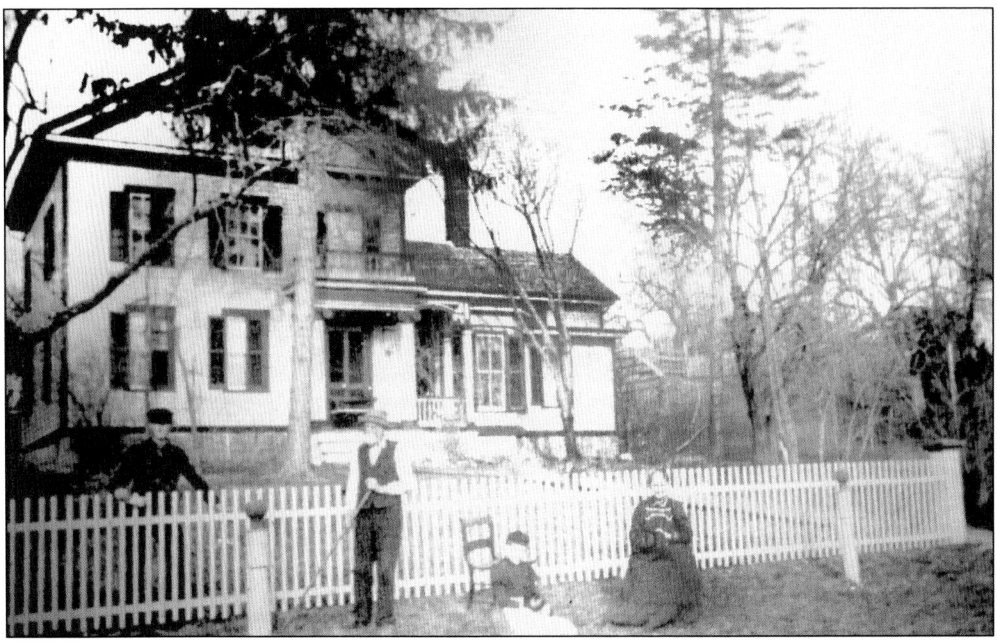

The Perry House. This house was adjacent to the Kmart plaza located on Route 67. It was burned down when the road was widened. (SHS.)

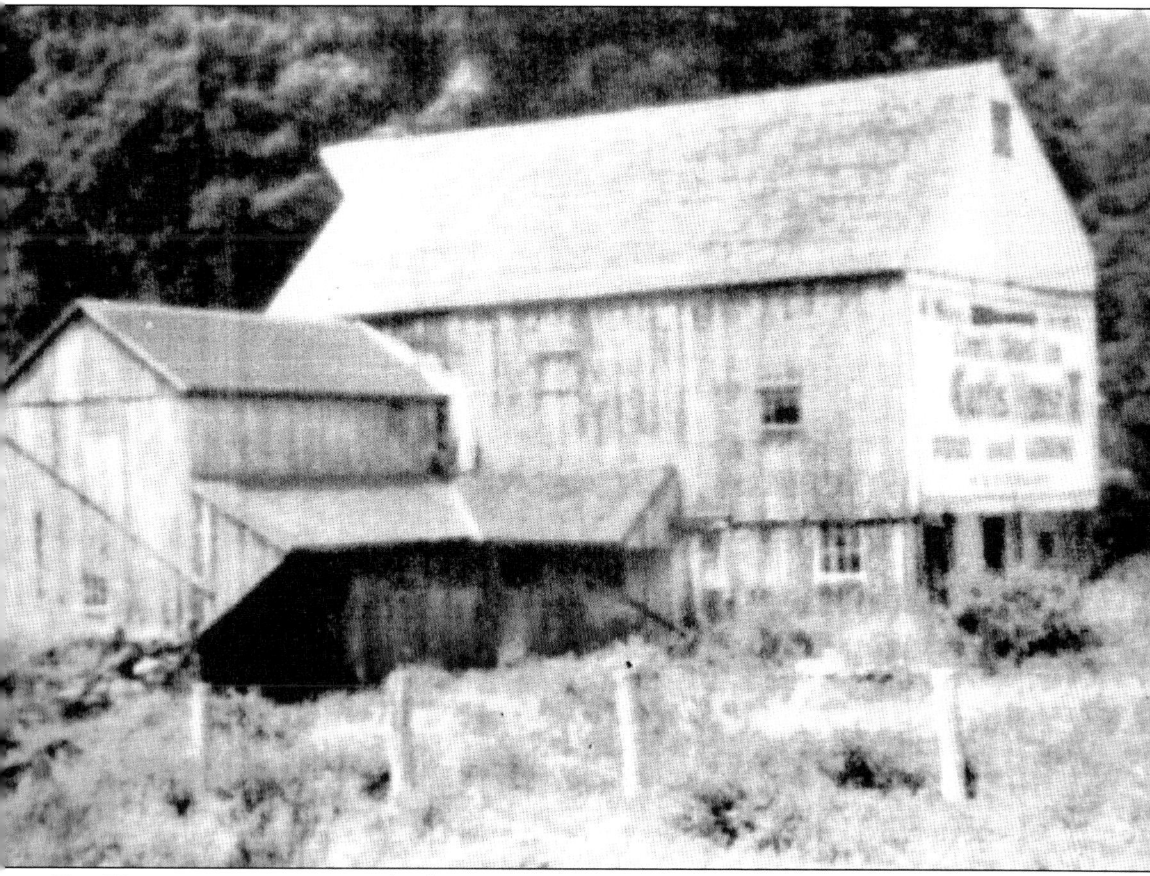

The Howard Hicock Barn. This barn, on Community House Road, is seen with a billboard advertising the Woodbury Curtis House restaurant and inn. This barn scene was painted by Alan Maver. A separate culvert was built under Route 67 because the road separated the farmer's property. Cows were moved through the culvert to pasture on the other side of the road. (ML.)

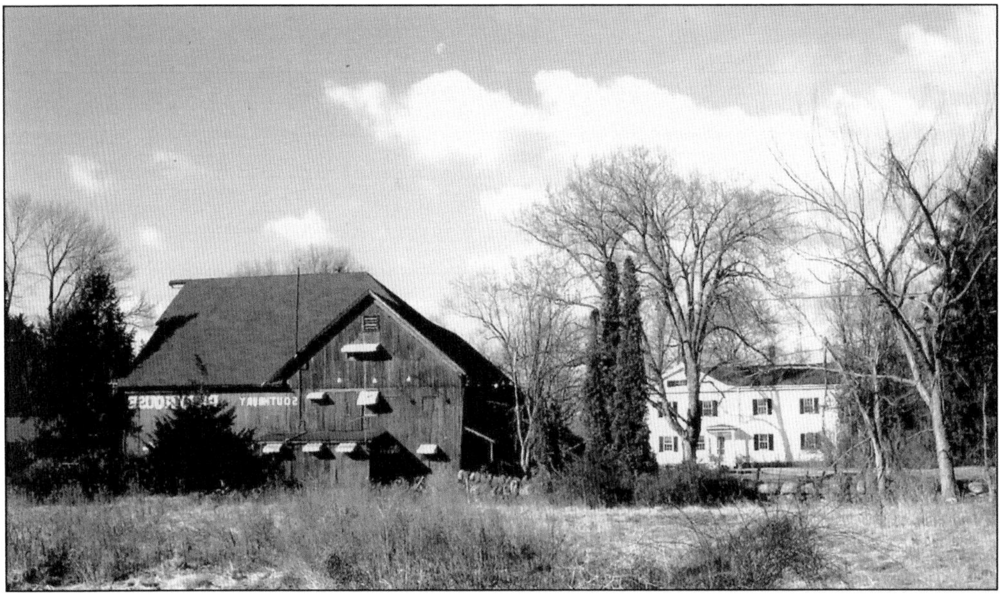

THE PLAYHOUSE AND SHELTON HOUSE. This playhouse attracted many big-name actors who wanted to perform in the country. One program featured local resident Ed Sullivan. The first performance was staged in 1946. Jack Quinn developed the playhouse out of an old barn. The barn was used to settle down cattle that came off the train en route to other destinations. It was owned by Alphonse St. Pierre. In 1968, Thomas Littleton took over the playhouse. (SHS.)

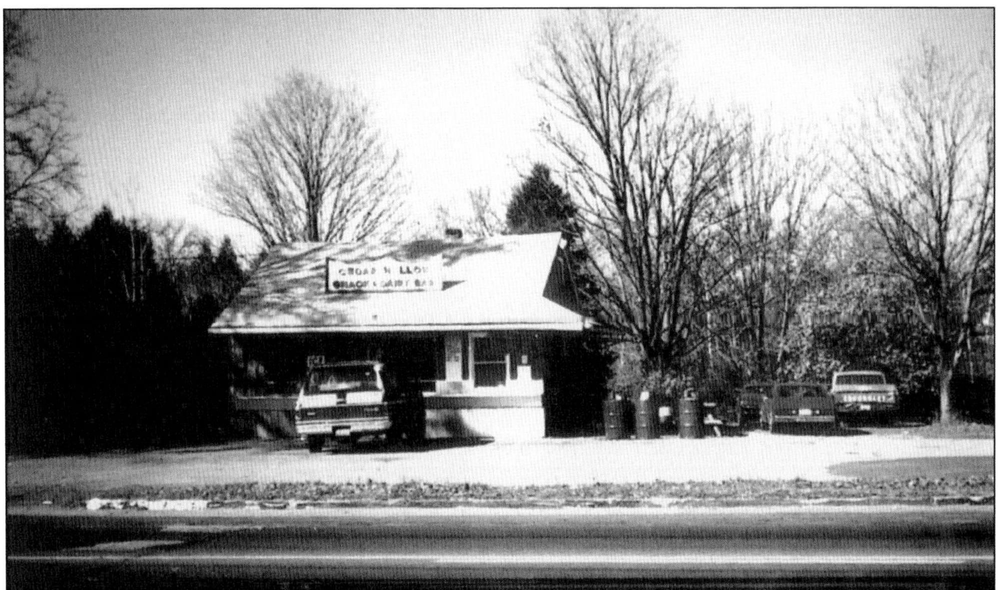

THE CEDAR HOLLOW SNACK BAR. Seen here is a famous local hamburger joint, Cedar Hollow, near Cedarland. Now it is Denmos. Another favorite hangout was Hamburg Haven on Main Street, which was where the former Antonio's was. The snack bar was formerly John Walker's service station. (SHS.)

Two

Getting There

Started this morning on the 7:45 train (to Danbury). Got my trading all done and ready for home by half past ten. Took 11:45 train home and waited in Southbury over an hour for the stage. Car fare $1.21.
—the diary of Harriet Canfield Bennett of White Oak, December 1881. (SHS.)

The type and availability of transportation has had a profound effect on the townspeople, while the building and maintenance of local roads, railroads, ferries, and bridges in Southbury and in neighboring towns had a great impact on the area.

Transportation options helped increase manufacturing, as goods and people could be moved in and out of facilities with ease. Improvements in transportation fostered growth.

Communications were limited in the early days. News traveled by word of mouth and informal and formal meetings. Methods of efficient transportation were considered critical, as they impacted everything from lifestyle to outputs from farms and industry.

People needed to travel to attend church services and schools and to conduct commerce. In the late 1600s and early 1700s, travel affected both church and education. Travel difficulties for the ever-extending settlement created the necessity to form new ecclesiastical societies with churches. The reason one- and two-room schoolhouses sprung up around the community was to ensure that students could be educated without the difficulty of commuting to a centralized school.

Residents were proud to be part of the Grand Army Highway (Route 6), which was considered a major highway at the time, connecting Maine and California.

The 19th century brought profound transformation with continued improvements to the modes of transport. As late as 1963, when Interstate 84 was opened in Southbury, the town was strongly impacted. This interstate brought quick access to jobs in New York and Hartford and attracted visitors for recreation. It also helped bring new companies to the area, including a major corporation, IBM, on Kettletown Road.

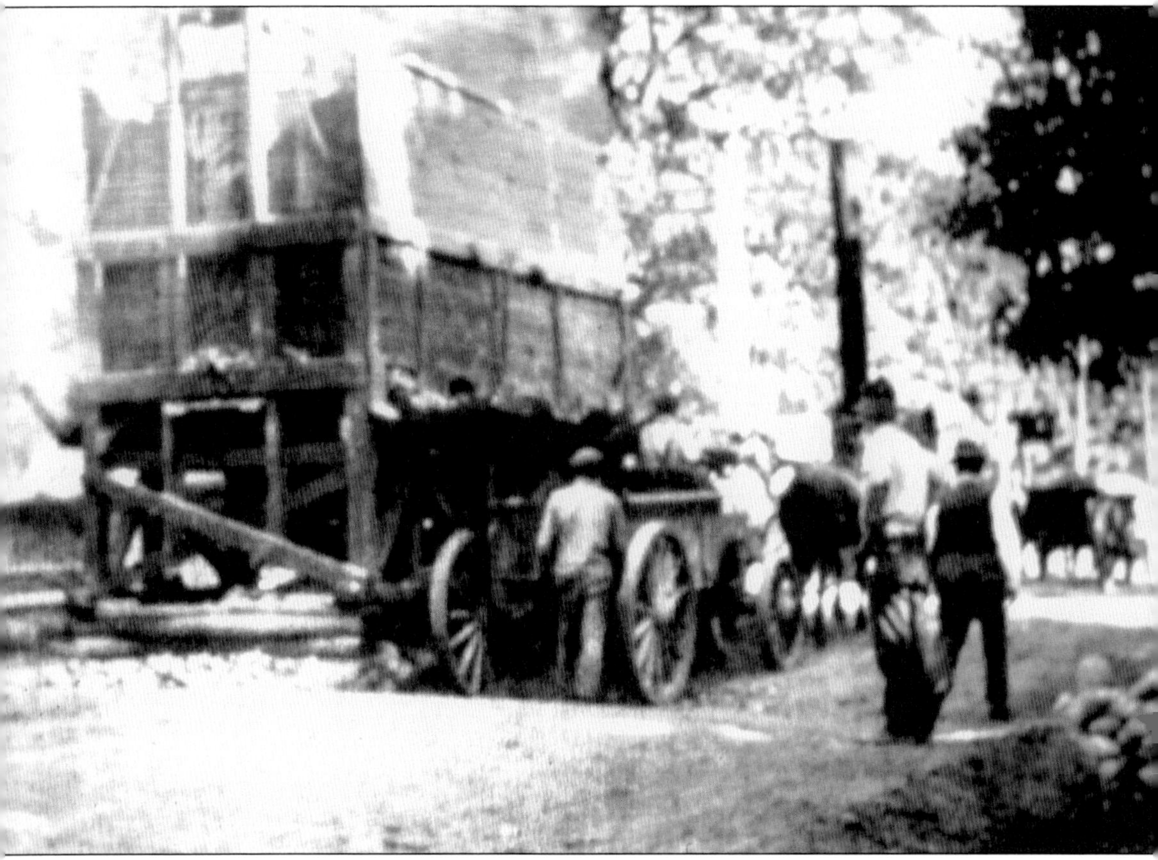

Building Main Street. Laborers used stone crushers and horse teams to pave the main thoroughfare, *c.* 1916. A few years earlier, only the state roads were paved. This included the main thoroughfare between Southbury and Woodbury, Route 6. The secondary roads were not yet graveled but remained as dirt roads. More enhancements came later on when the legislature of Connecticut passed a state aid act in 1930 to allot money for towns to improve and maintain roads. Since then, most of Southbury's roads have been paved. Some residents have made applications for and received approval to keep their dirt roads and associated rural ambiance under the Southbury Scenic Road Ordinance. (SHS.)

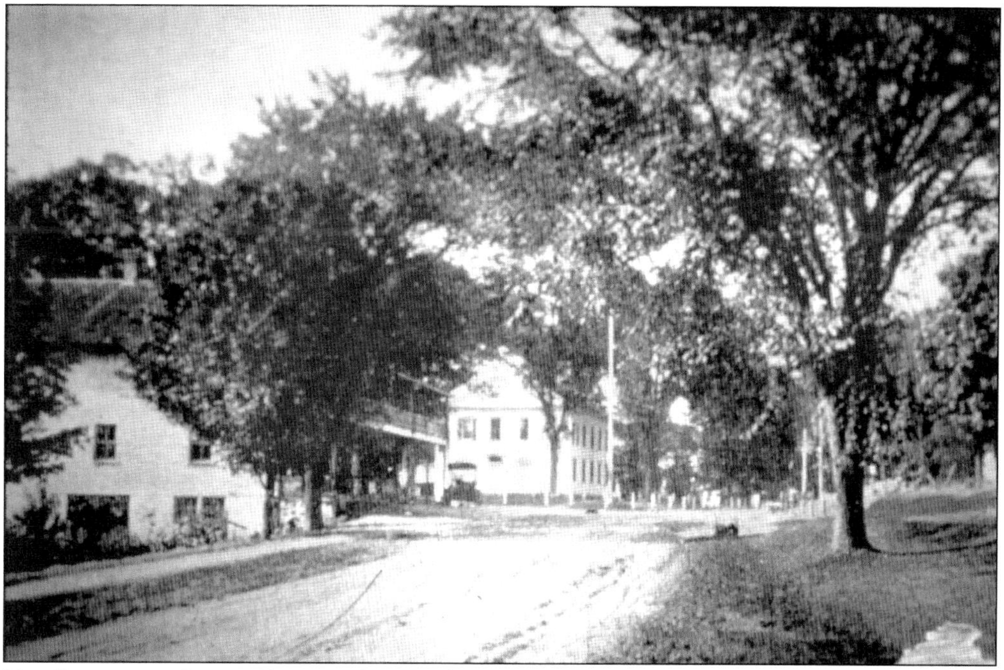

The Road into South Britain. During the first quarter of the 19th century, private investors built an elaborate system of toll roads and bridges. In the early 1800s, the state allowed people to charge tolls on turnpikes they constructed or maintained. One tollgate between the Southbury and Woodbury town lines on the Middle Turnpike was voted down in 1819. The Middle Turnpike was a toll road that crossed the Housatonic at Bennett's Bridge, connecting Southbury and Sandy Hook. (SHS.)

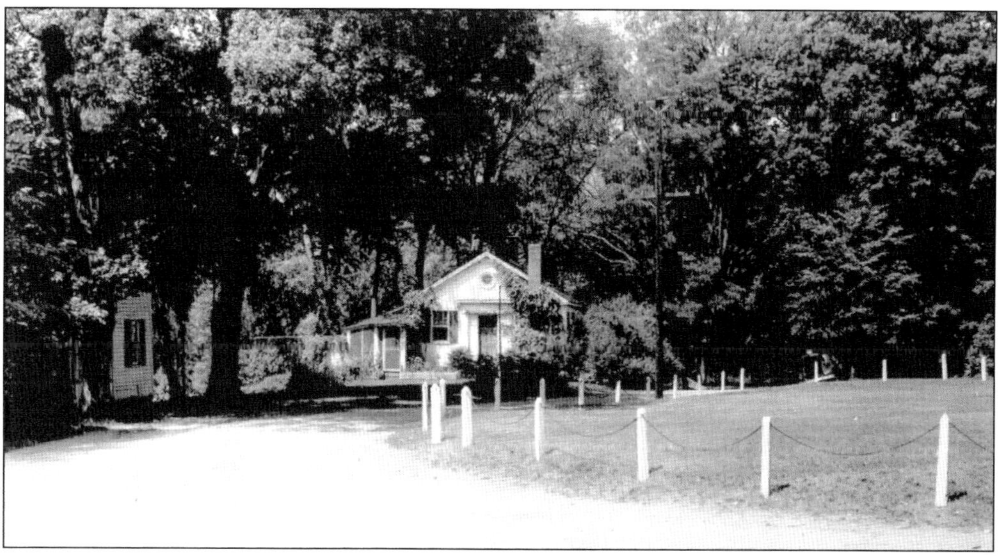

South Britain Center. The South Britain School can be seen at the edge of this scene. It was one of the town's original district schools. The dirt road leading into South Britain was commonly called the "country road." (TL.)

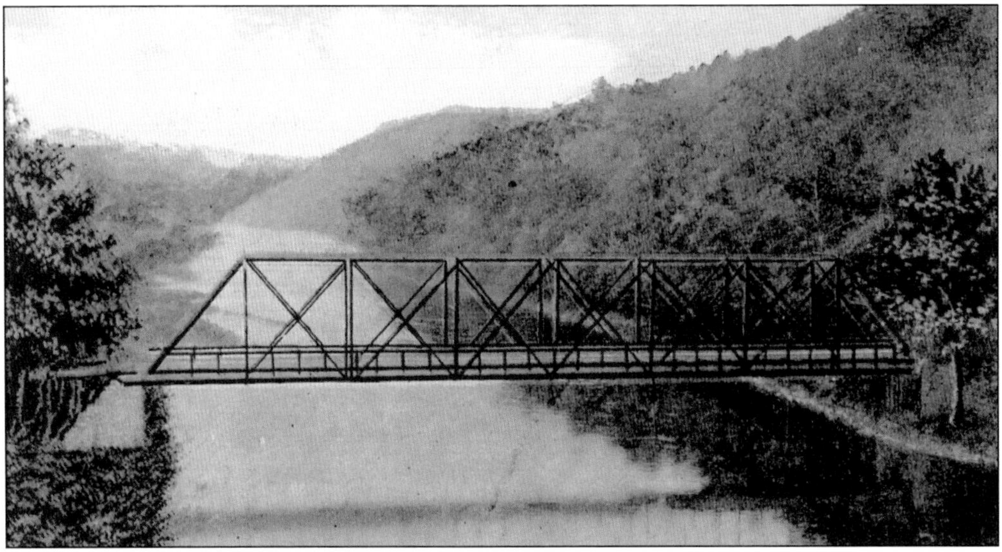

The Bridge over the Housatonic. In 1730, Peter Hubbell operated a ferry at Cockshure Island on the Housatonic River. In 1752, Wait Hinman was granted ferry rights farther down the river. Around this time, Gen. George Washington felt that the bridge was necessary for troop crossings and sent some of his men to repair it. After this time, it became known as Carlton's Bridge. (SHS.)

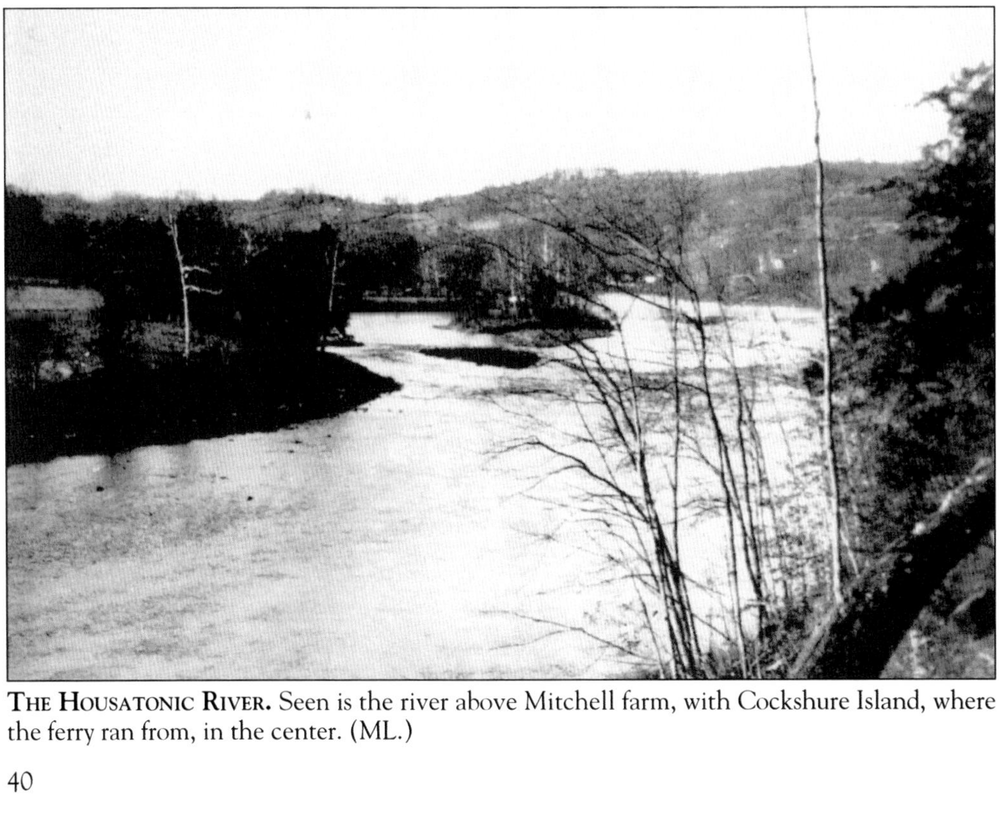

The Housatonic River. Seen is the river above Mitchell farm, with Cockshure Island, where the ferry ran from, in the center. (ML.)

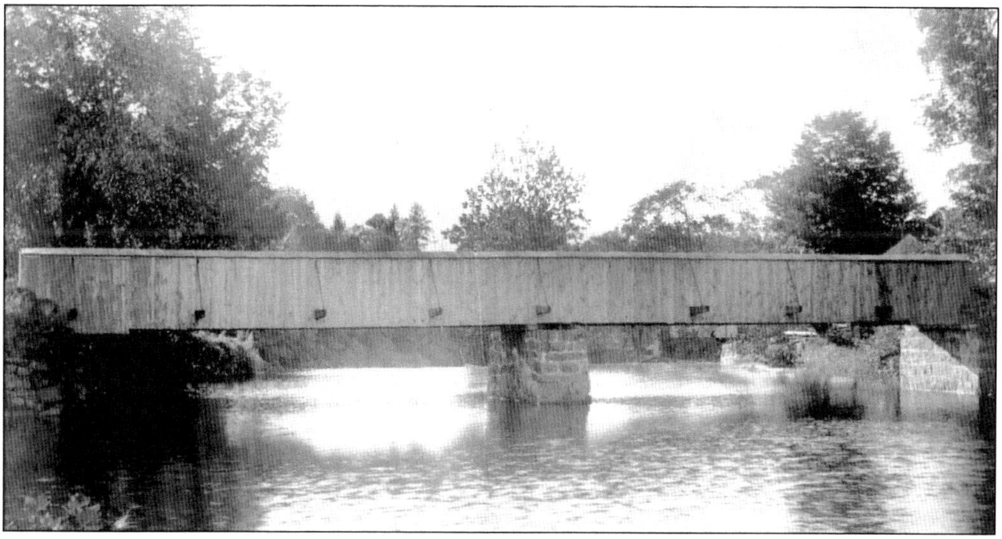

The Bridge over the Pomperaug River in South Britain. This bridge ran over Route 172 and was called Bradley's Bridge. In the old days, the normal way to cross small streams and brooks was fording, while large waterways had ferries to make the crossing. Prior to the building of bridges, low-water fords existed on the Housatonic, midway between Purchase and Hanover Brooks on the Newtown side. Traces of the fords remained after bridges were built; they were used to water horses. (SHS.)

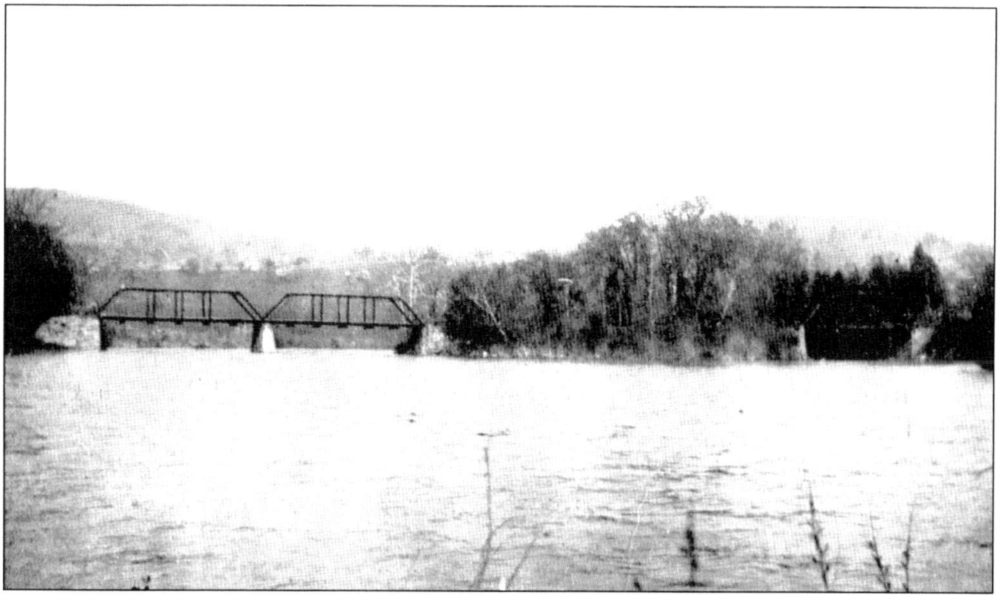

Bennett's Bridge. This bridge was blown up when Lake Zoar was flooded after the construction of the Stevenson Dam. (TL.)

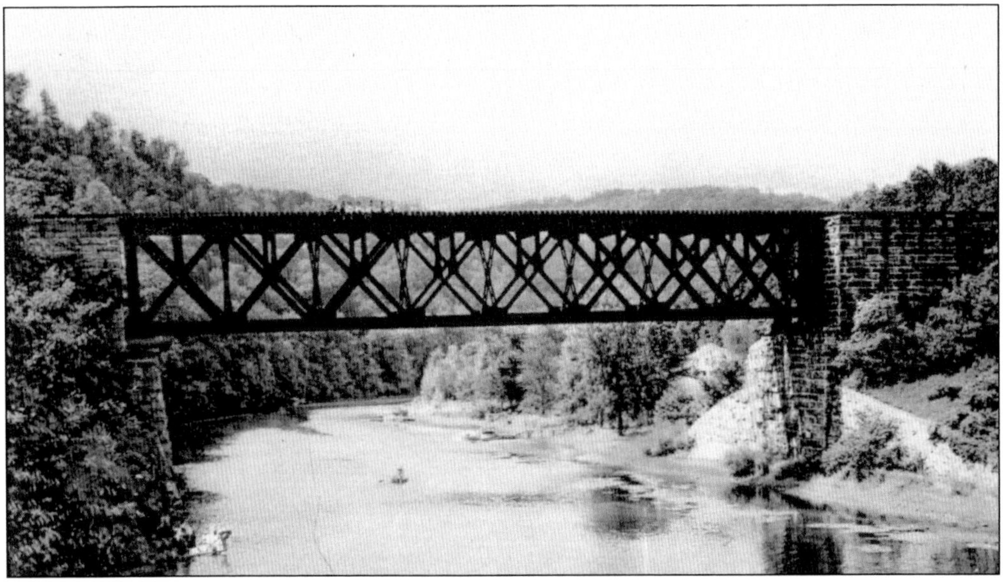

The Southbury Trestle Bridge. This bridge crosses over the Pomperaug River on Route 6. It was a train bridge in the Berkshire estates. (TL.)

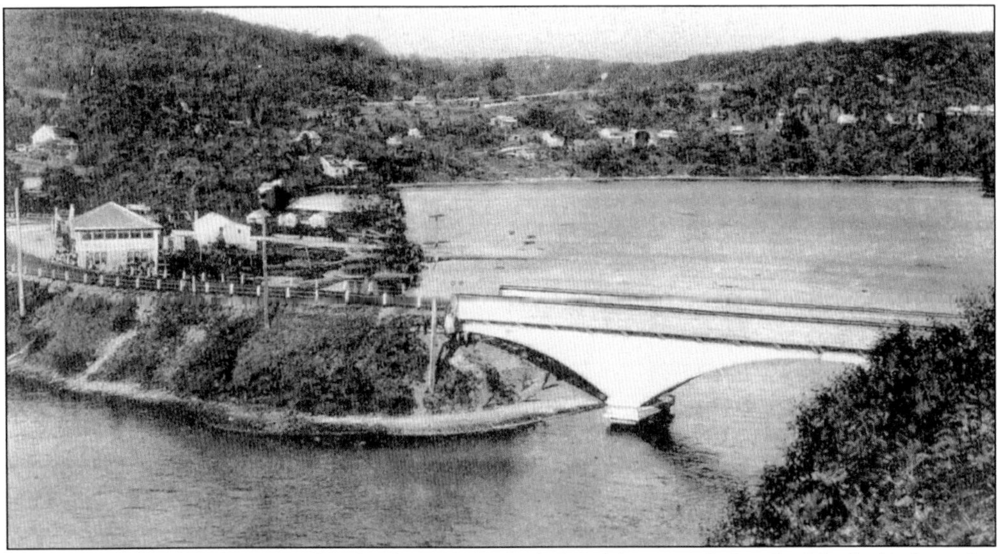

The Lake Zoar Bridge. This bridge connected Southbury and Sandy Hook. Before the flooding of Lake Zoar, Bennett's Bridge and Zoar Bridge were the principal crossings for the Housatonic. Both were run as toll bridges. This span is on the extension of River Road that crosses at the confluence of the Housatonic and Pomperaug Rivers. The distant hillside is the Fish Rock section of town. The large building on the right is Ma Hall's Toot and Come In bar. (TL.)

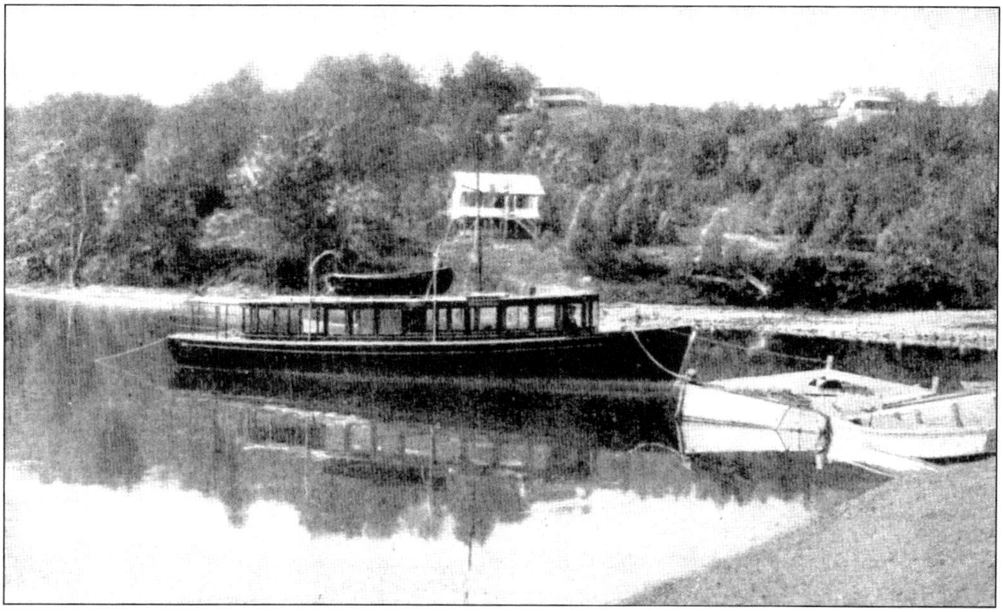

The Miss Riverside Boat at Lake Zoar. Soule-Roberts sold land in Lakeside using a boat to promote lots on Lake Zoar. The boat was piloted by Ed Scoville. (TL.)

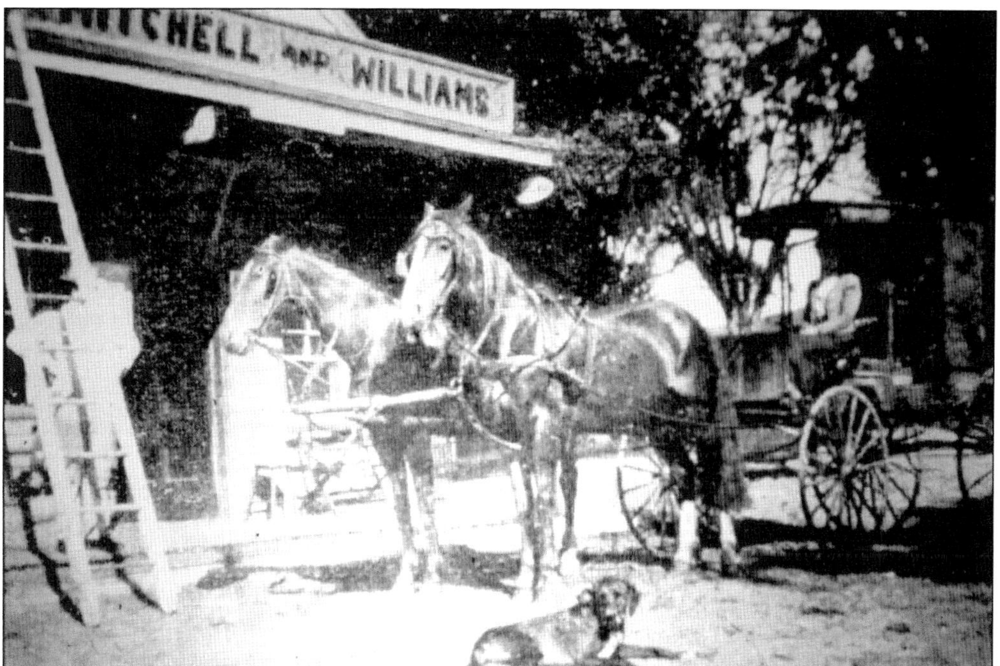

Traveling to Town. This photograph shows a family, with their horse team, headed to shop at the Mitchell and Williams store. (SHS.)

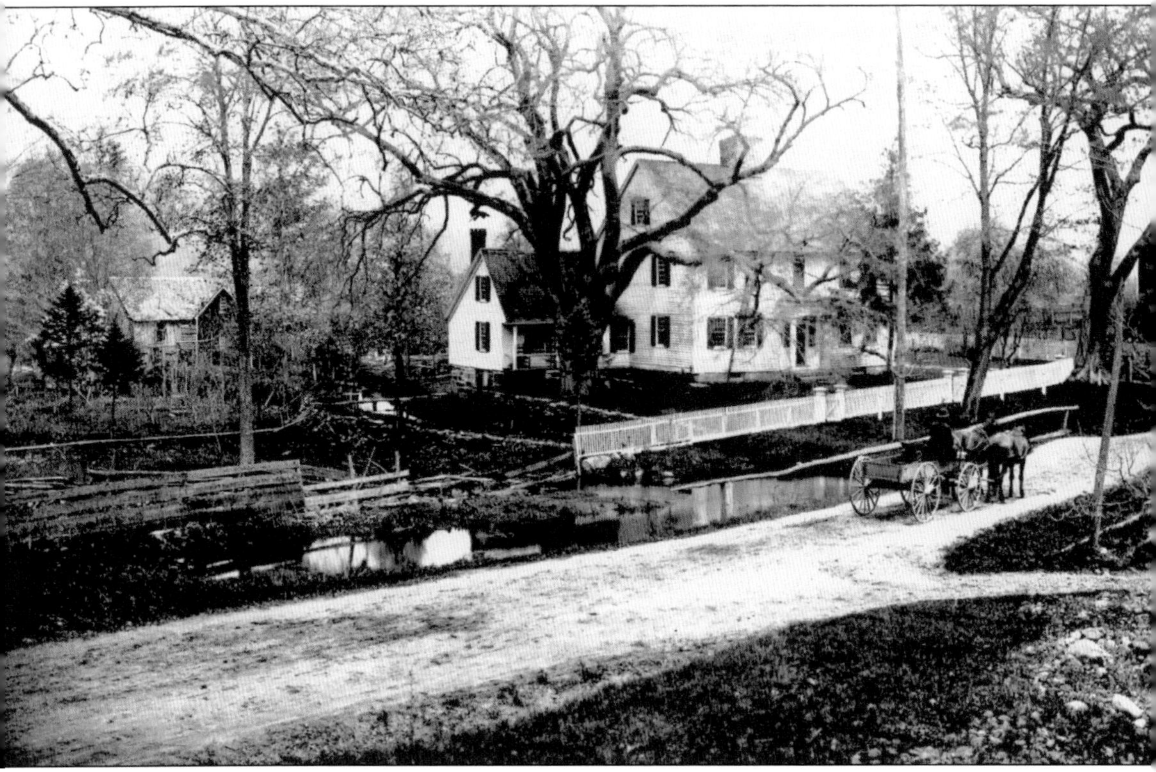

A Team Brings the Family Home. This *c.* 1900 photograph was taken in front of the Lt. Francis Stiles house in the White Oak section of town. The barn on the right was built in 1690 and won the bicentennial award for restoration. For economic reasons, when the barn was originally built, it was thatched in the back, where a passerby could not see that it was not completed. (BS.)

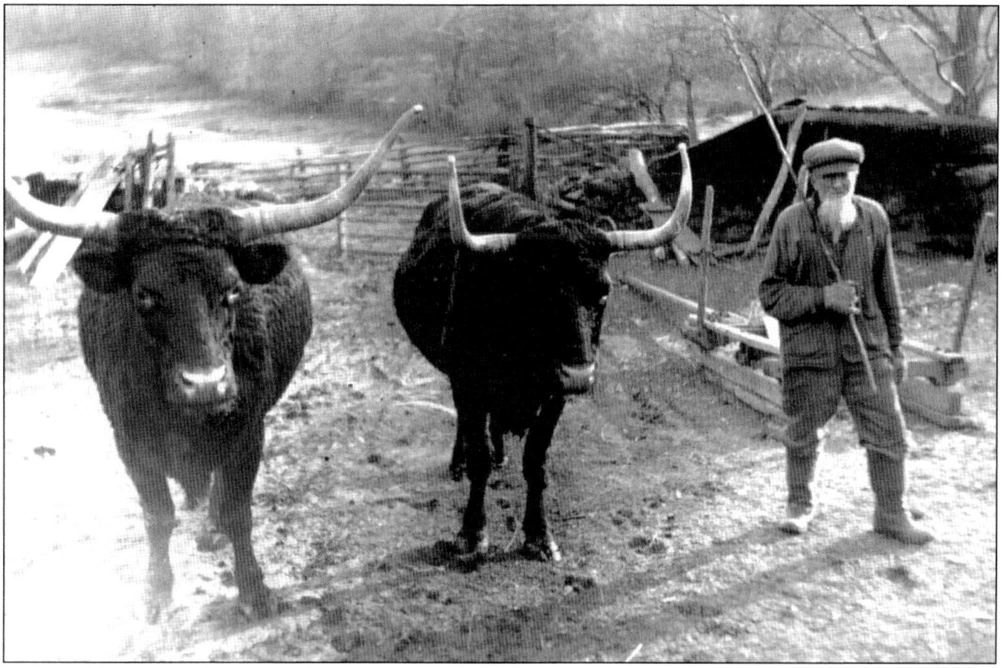

AARON LEWIS WITH THE OXEN TEAM c. 1908. Early settlers utilized ox power more than horses to get around and continued to use them for work such as mowing in the 1900s. In 1781, when Rochambeau marched through the town, the modes of transportation included a few carriages, riding horses, and many oxen-pulled vehicles. (TL.)

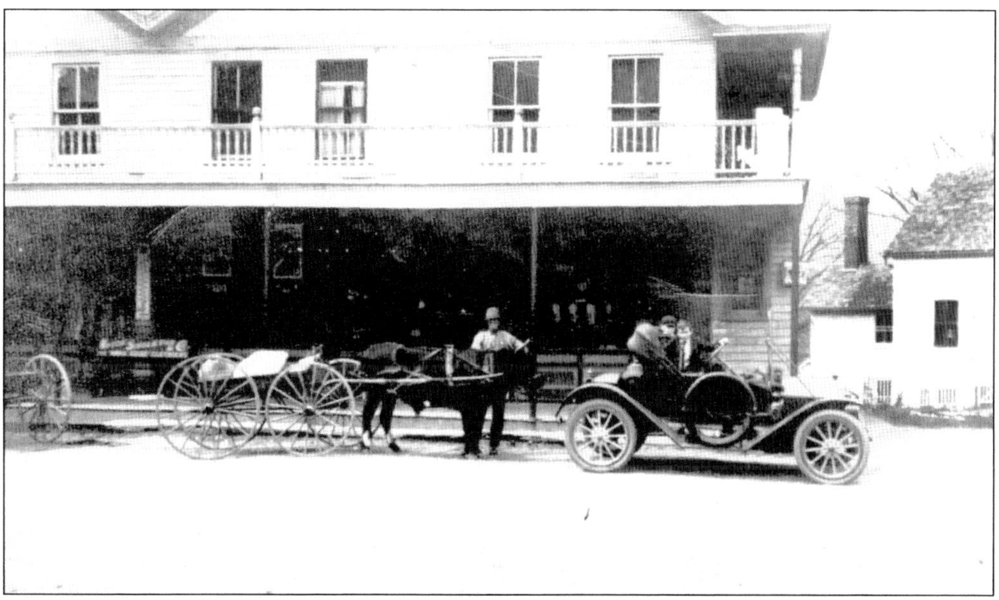

THE OLD WORLD MEETS THE NEW. Seen is an automobile parked near an older form of transportation in front of the South Britain general store. (ET.)

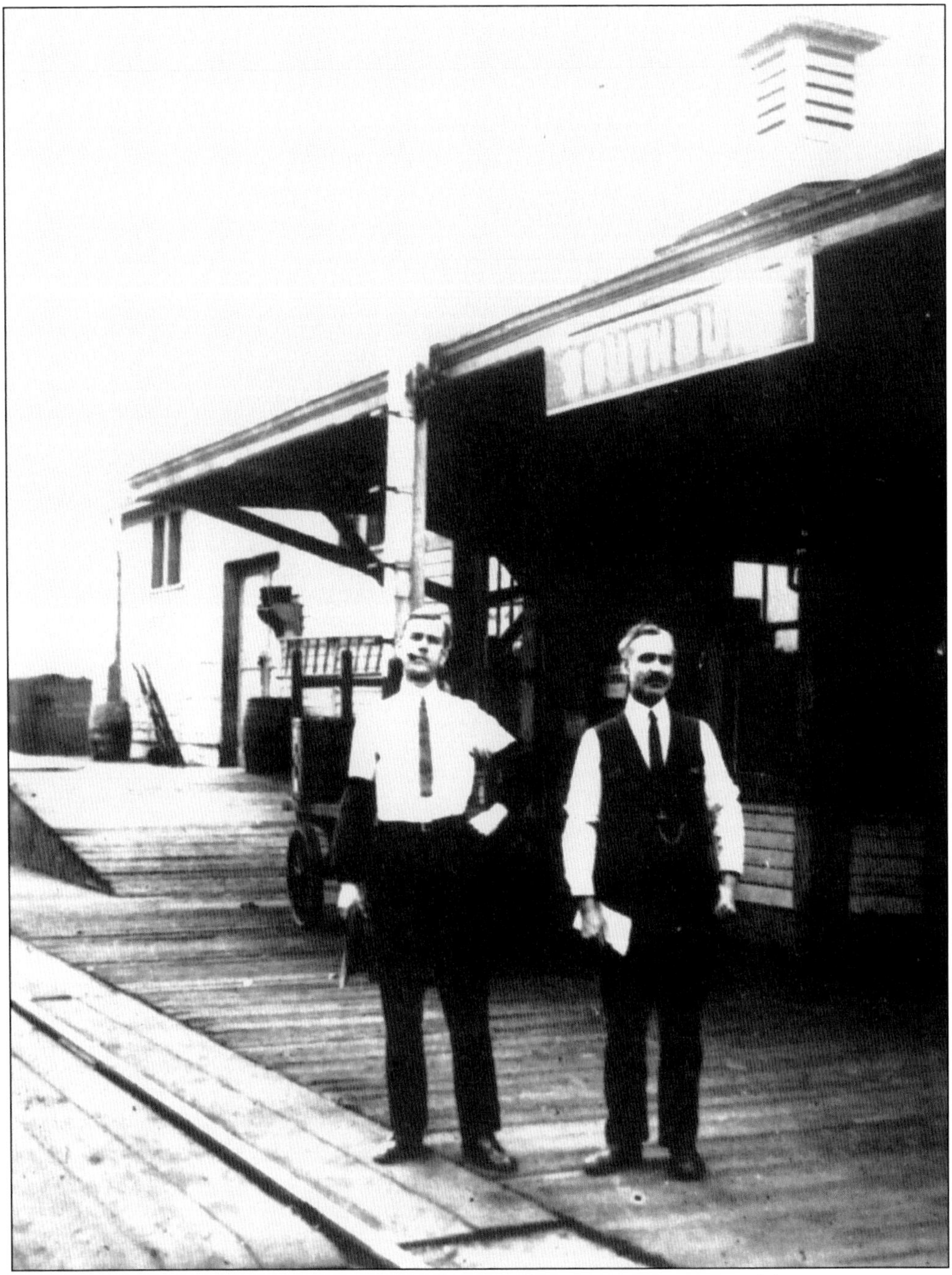

Meeting the Arriving Train. George Brewer, the station master, and his assistant wait for arrivals of passengers and freight. In the 1930s, the railroad stopped carrying passengers to Southbury, and Brewer finished his career off at the Thomaston station. Railroads started somewhat later in Connecticut than in other states due to favorable water transportation routes and the use of steamboats. Rivers provided somewhat convenient transport for about two-thirds of the year. Early railroad routes were developed based on geography. (ET.)

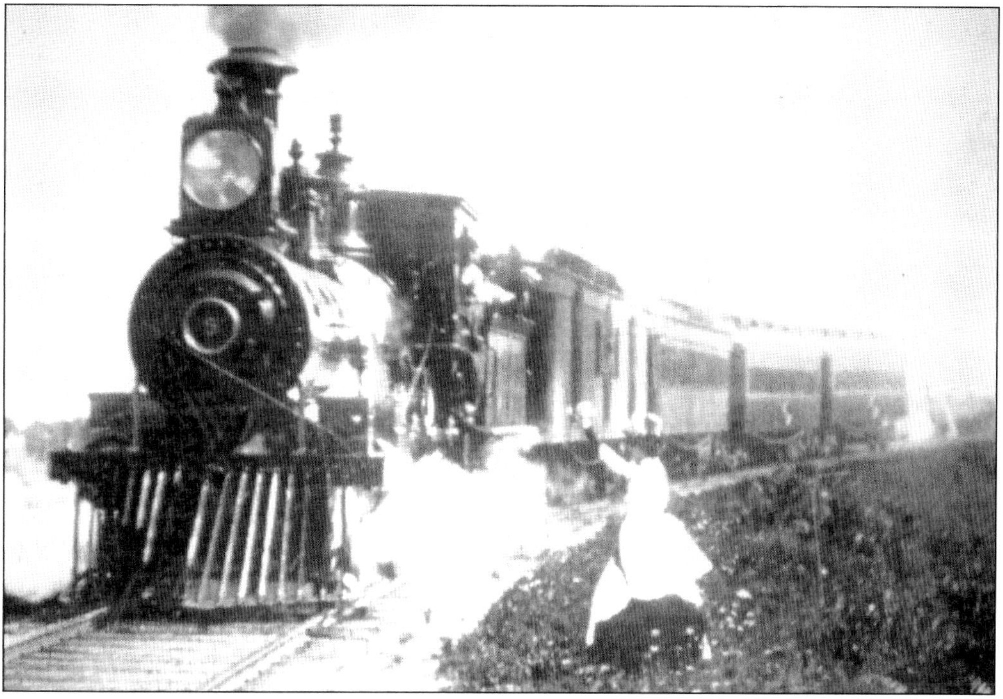

RUNNING TO MEET THE TRAIN. This photograph shows a lady anticipating an arrival of someone, who will receive a bouquet of flowers. Railroads began to be built all over the country after the Civil War. The Boston, Hartford, and Erie Rail Road Company began purchasing rights-of-way through Southbury, from Southford to the center of town, then to Newtown across the Housatonic River after the survey of 1845. Building started in 1869. The New York & New England Railroad completed the job and started operations in 1881. (ET.)

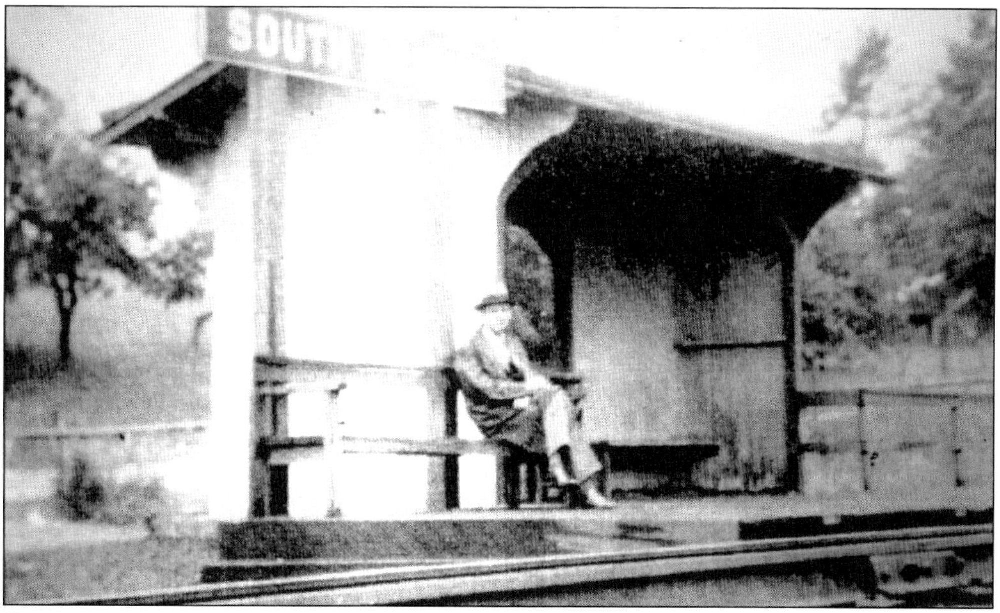

THE RAILROAD STATION IN SOUTH BRITAIN IN THE EARLY 1900S. This gentleman awaits the train to go to work or conduct trade. This was a flag stop near Ichabod Road. (SHS.)

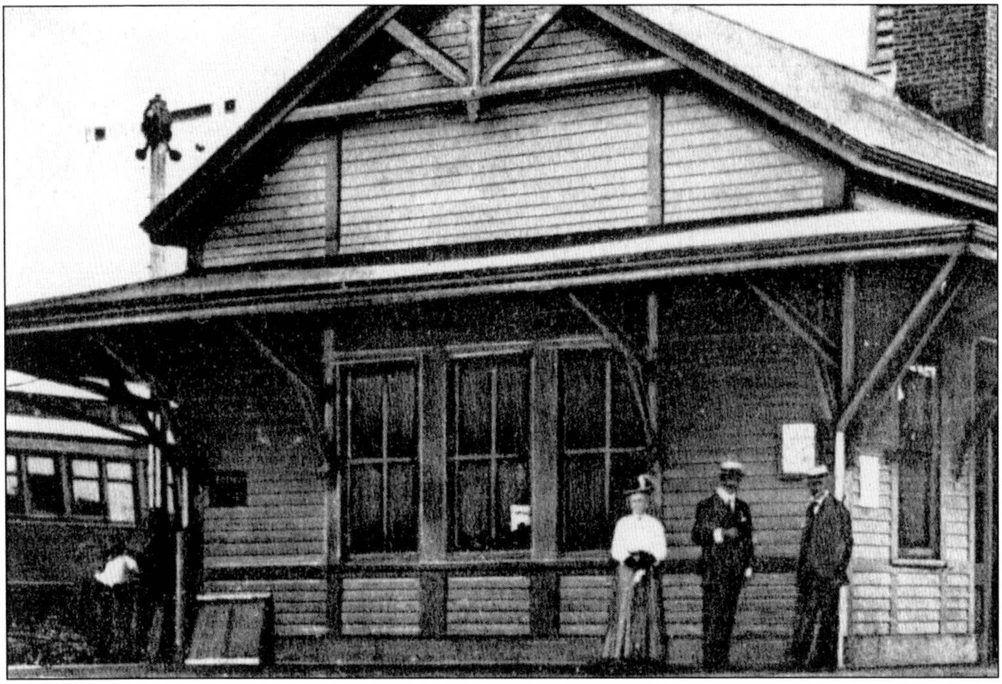

WAITING WITH THE STATIONMASTER. It took about an hour to get from Waterbury to Danbury, with seven stops on the way. The east-bound trip was longer due to the upgrade between Sandy Hook and Towantic, which required a second engine. At Sandy Hook, the pusher service was maintained, and a pusher would get behind the train to help it over the hill. The Southbury station was a full-service station and included a freight room, ticket booth, waiting room, and schoolhouse clock. (MCW.)

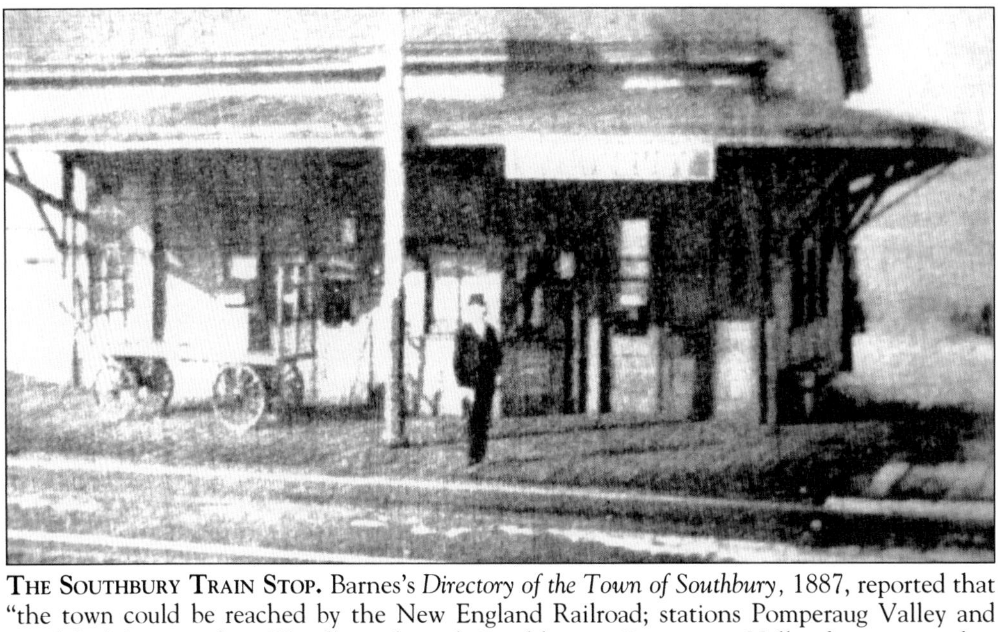

THE SOUTHBURY TRAIN STOP. Barnes's *Directory of the Town of Southbury*, 1887, reported that "the town could be reached by the New England Railroad; stations Pomperaug Valley and Southford, by stage from Woodbury through Southbury to Pomperaug Valley four times a day, from South Britain to Pomperaug Valley one time a day." (ET.)

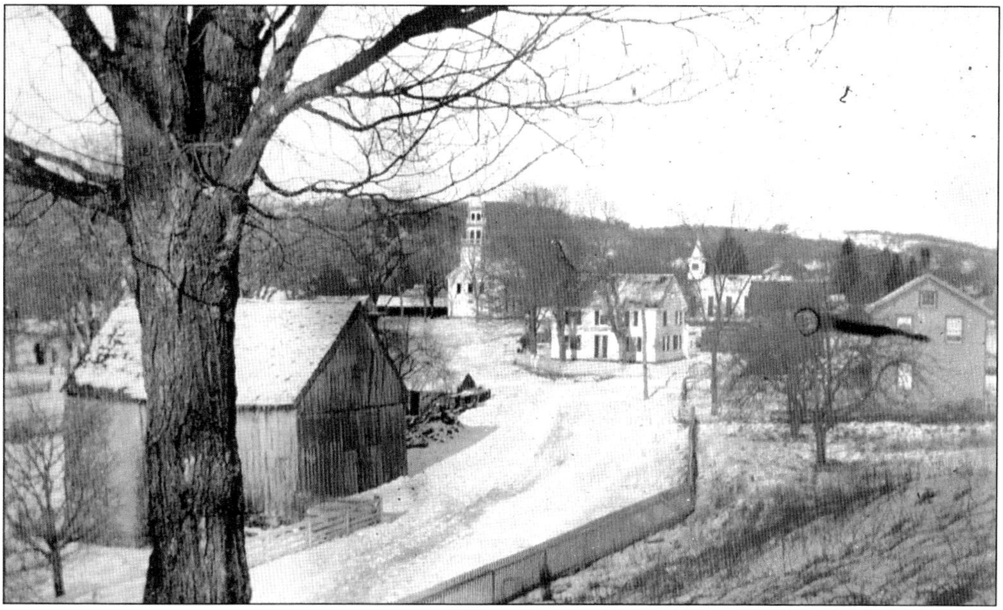

MIDDLE ROAD. This picture is of Middle Road, heading toward the South Britain Church and Moses Down's house. (AM.)

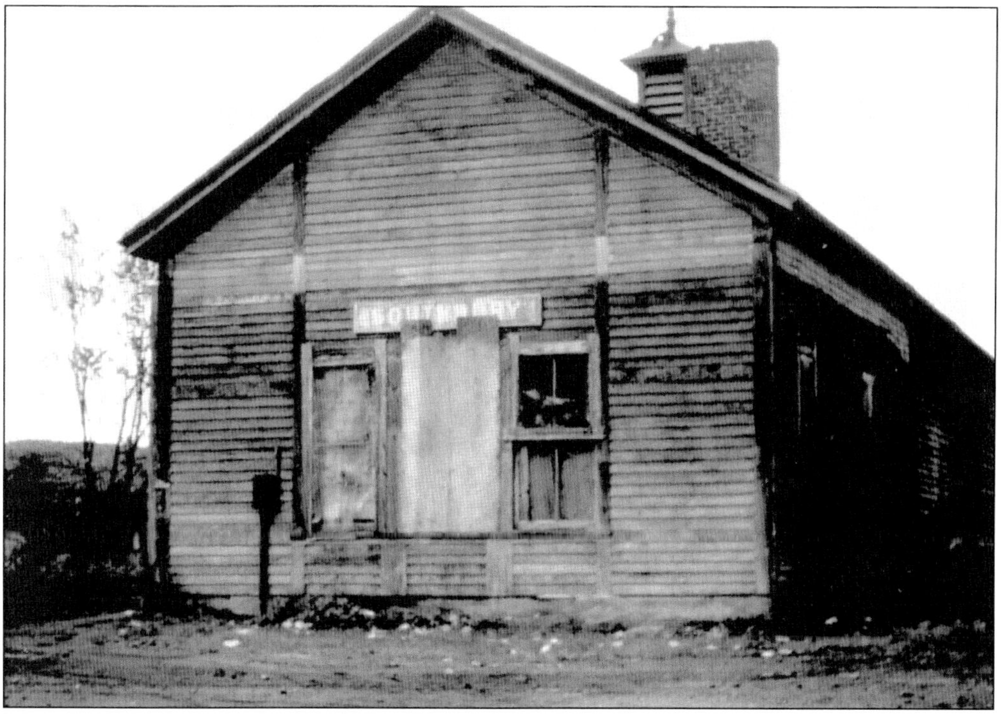

NO MORE TRAINS TODAY. In this c. 1960s photograph, Southford station is boarded up. In 1948, the railroad closed as cars, trucks, and buses became commonplace. Interstate 84 now uses part of the railroad's right-of-way, as does the gas company for its pipeline. Part of the track is also used as a bridle path. (MCW.)

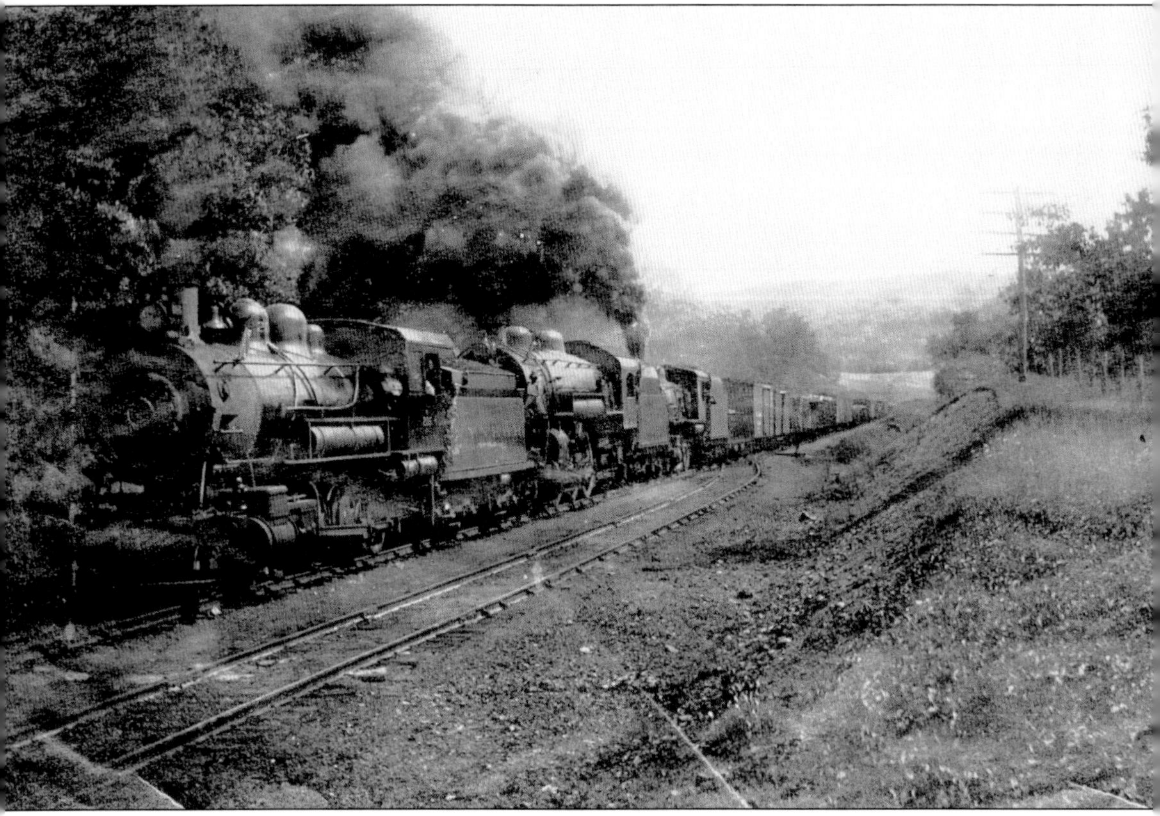

UP THE HILL TO SOUTHBURY STATION. In December 1892, a serious accident happened that injured three men and killed two others. Instead of stopping at Pomperaug, Engine No. 155 left Sandy Hook and tried to make it to Southford station. On the heavy upgrade at the second milepost, it encountered No. 83 coming downgrade at full throttle. The engineer of the train, William Beebe, blew his whistle, braked, and threw the engine into reverse. It was too late, and the trains met head on. Freight, which included doorbells, cotton cloth, oil cans, barbed wire, silverware, flour, and tea, was thrown everywhere. The boilers of the two trains were telescoped, one inside the other. (ET.)

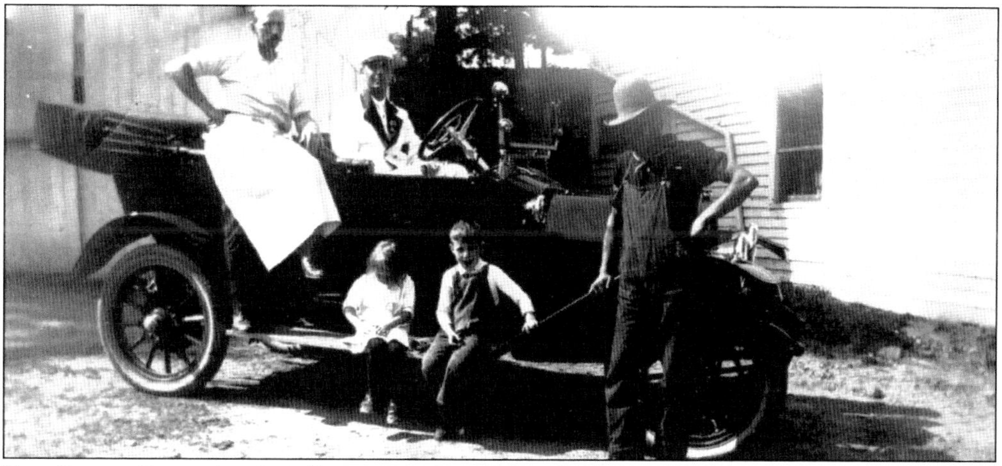

THE OLIVER FAMILY'S 1919 OVERLAND CAR. According to J. Edward Coer in his *Fifty Years of Southbury*, 1962, there were practically no cars in town *c.* 1912. Some early car owners were John Mitchell, a Ford owner; Harvey Stone, a Kelly-Springfield truck owner; Edward Scoville, a Stanley Steamer owner; ? Hawkins, a Reo truck owner; George Hine, a Locomobile owner; and Judge William Waklee, a one-cylinder Cadillac owner. Cars were used from May to November. (DM.)

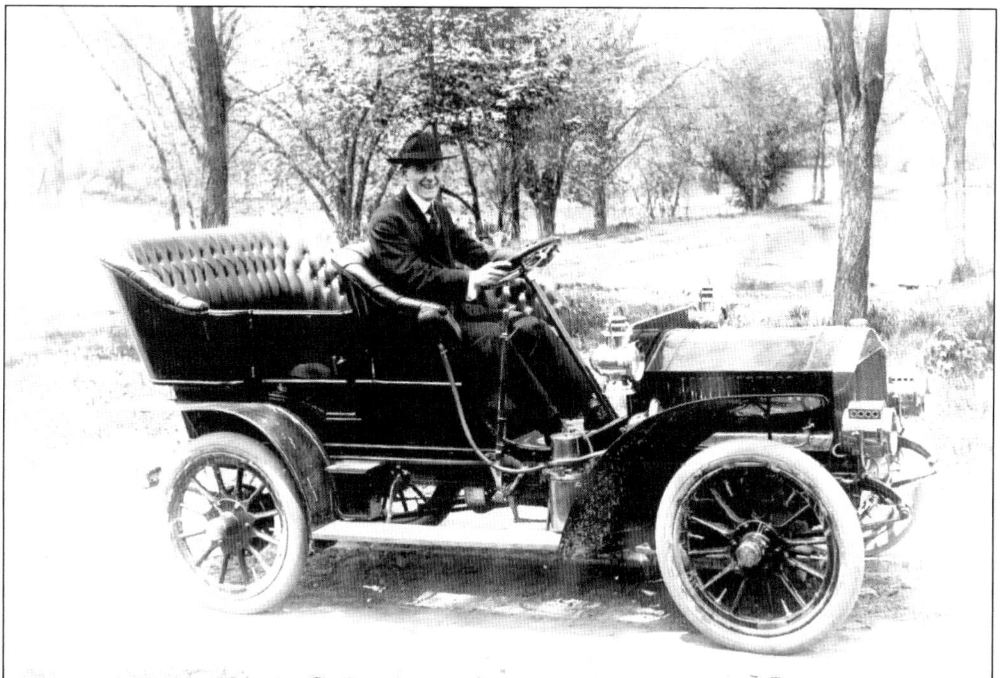

ELLSWORTH HINZE. Here, Hinze proudly sits behind the wheel of his car. This view exemplifies the story of the love between a man and his car. (SHS.)

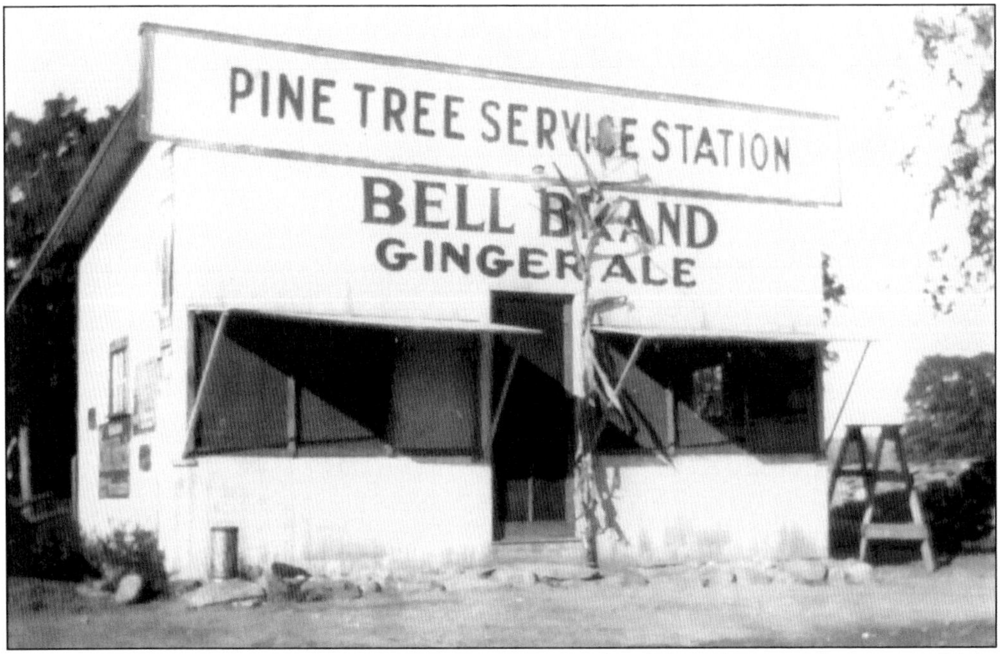

The Pine Tree Service Station. At this station, gas and Bell-brand ginger ale were available. The station was at the corner of Transylvania and Route 67. (TL.)

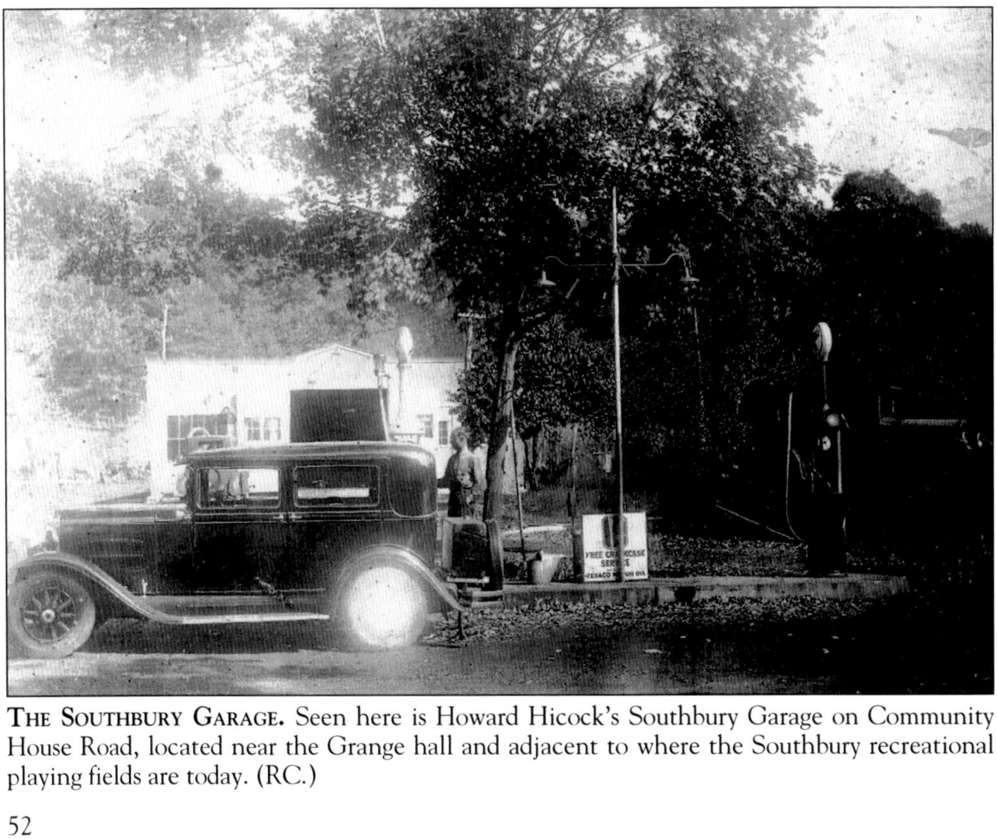

The Southbury Garage. Seen here is Howard Hicock's Southbury Garage on Community House Road, located near the Grange hall and adjacent to where the Southbury recreational playing fields are today. (RC.)

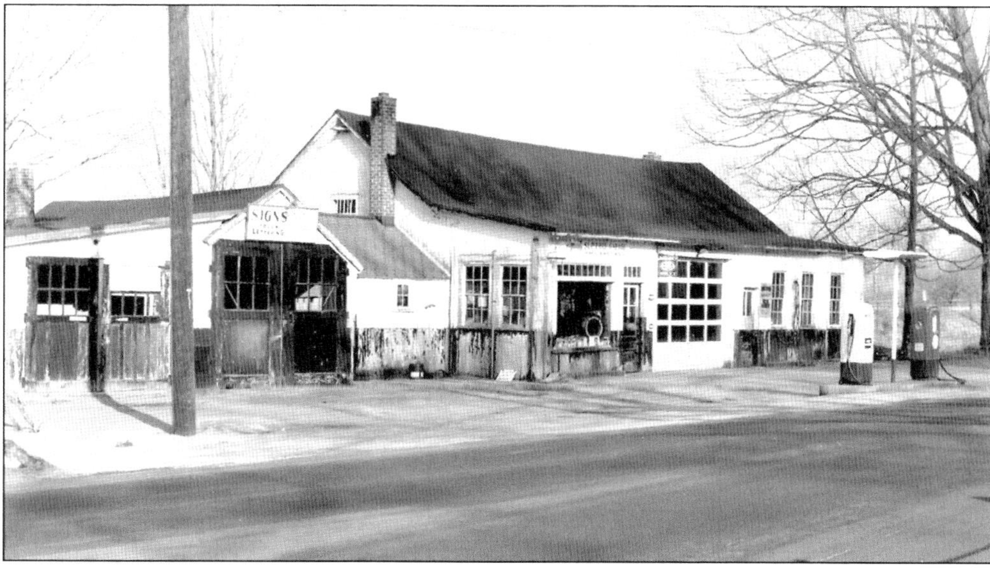

St. Pierre's Garage. Seen here is the garage run by Arza Bennett Sr., which was located on Main Street in the area of the former Southbury Primary Care office. It was the first place the fire department housed a fire truck. The local siren was located there. (RC.)

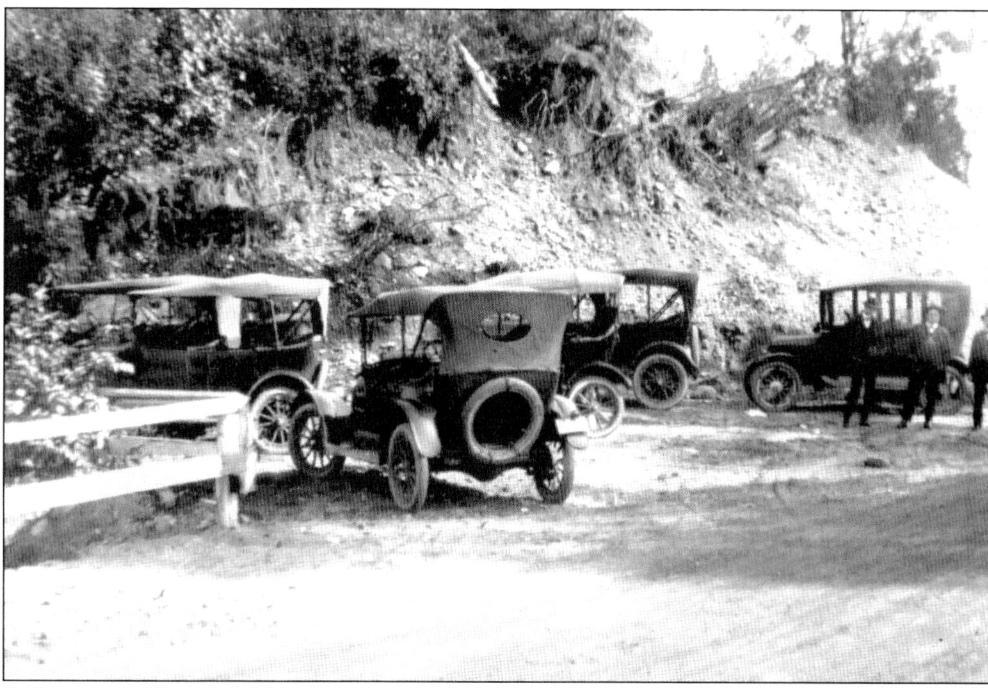

The First Parking Lot. An event creates one of the town's first parking lots. Here, cars are seen at the entrance of the Berkshire section of town. (SHS.)

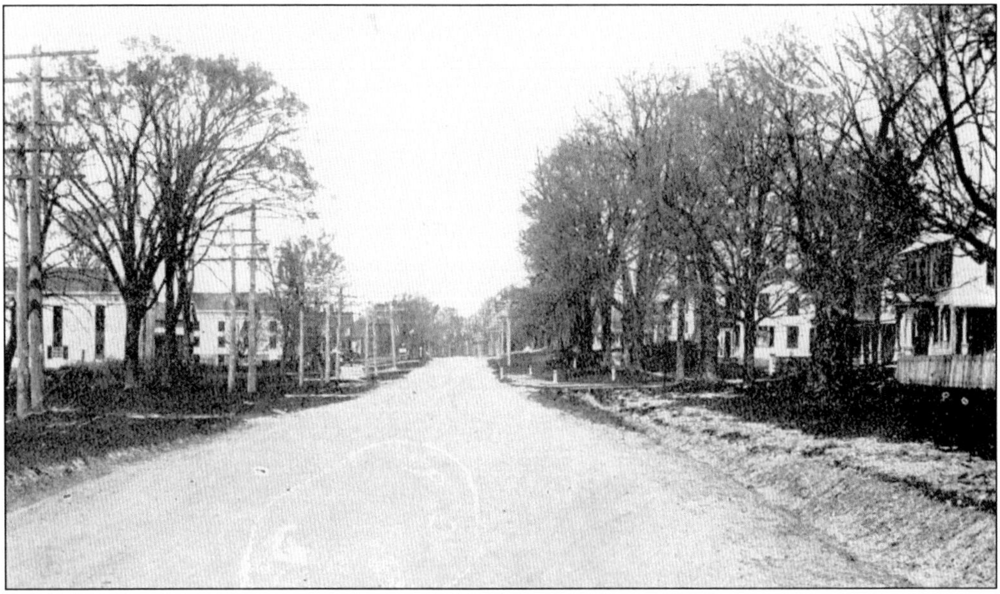

DOWNTOWN SOUTHBURY'S DIRT ROAD. Seen here is Main Street North in Southbury prior to 1916. The major roads used today were the principal routes used when the area was first settled. Rochambeau's army followed the path from the Woodbury town line to the crossing of the Housatonic River, today's site of Lake Zoar, in his 1781 march to Yorktown. Early Native Americans traveled between the Pootatuck and Nonnewaug villages on trails following similar paths. (TL.)

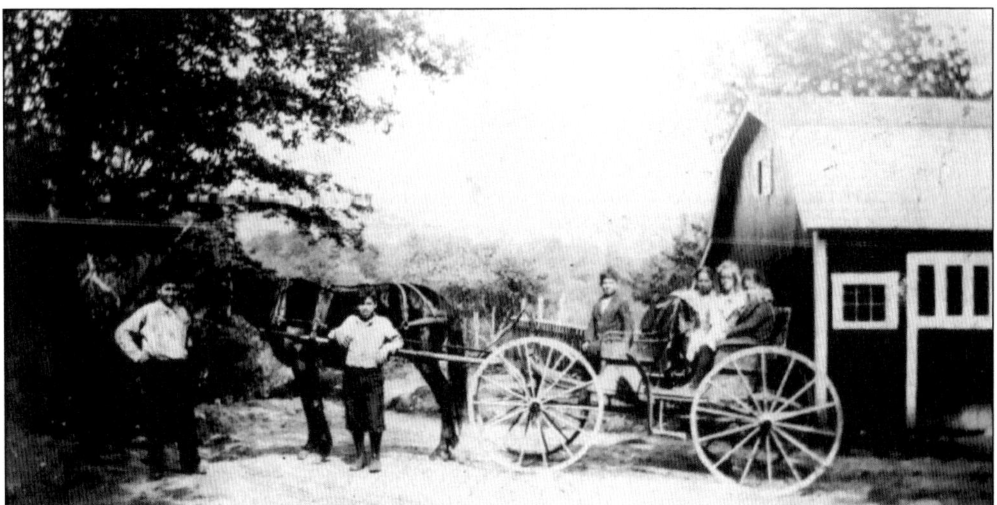

GILLOTTI'S TRANSPORTATION. Sometimes, parents used buckboards, horses, horse-drawn carriages, or private cars to transport children to and from school. Rides were also often hitched. (SHS.)

Three

The People

My father dear then owned this land
By him these shops and mills were planned
For him the large and rugged rock
Were drilled and blasted into blocks,
And each one made a place to fill
In building shop or yard or mill,
Or road or bridge or dam or race,
Till he had filled up this place,
And made it pleasant, fresh and new
So picturesque and useful, too.

—Nancy Marie Abbott. (SHS.)

The community of Southbury has attracted people for many reasons. It started as an outpost for religious freedom when dissidents from Stratford came a mere 50 some years after the Pilgrims landed in Plymouth. Through the years, many people have been beckoned by the local beauty and charm and what the area has offered in terms of jobs and inspiration. At times, undesirables such as the the Bund came to town. Artists and writers have been drawn by the bucolic countryside of farms and fields surrounded by beautiful stonewalls. Several well-known actors still reside in the area. Families are drawn to the town in droves as the community is part of one of the highest rated school districts in the country. Some interesting residents have included Ed Sullivan, Barbara Hershey, and Victor Borge. One former resident, Ann Winterbotham Stephens is credited for inventing dime-store novels. Four of her novels were *The Wife's Struggle; Silent Struggles; Fashion and Famine*; and *The Homestead*. She lived in South Britain in the early 1800s. South Britain also had a consul to Greece, who was appointed by President Lincoln, named Henry Monroe Canfield. His life is described in a book written in 1920, *From South Britain to Bagdad*. He was born here in 1841.

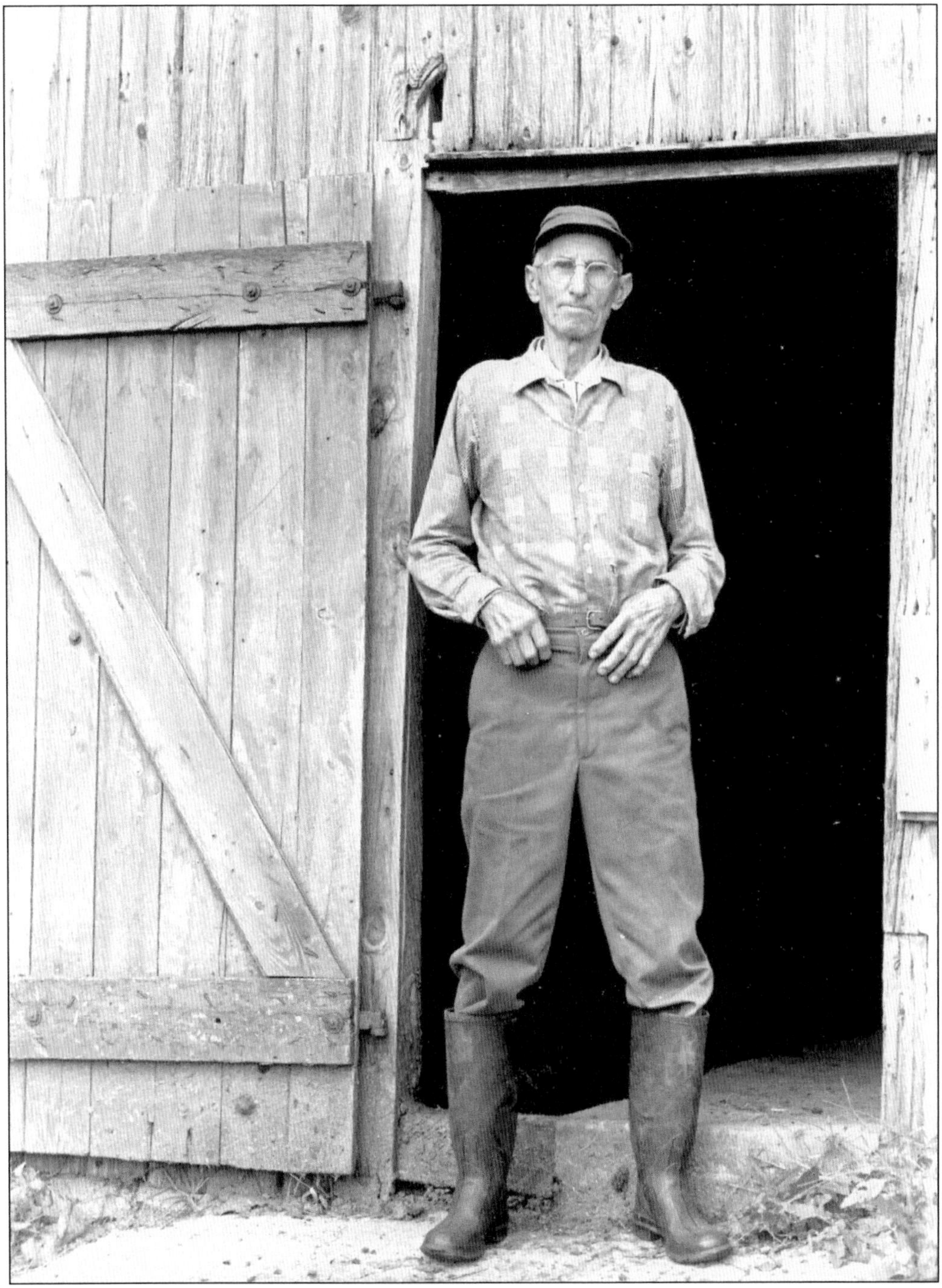

John Ludorf. This local farmer lived in the Purchase area. He was a farmer, despite the area's rocky terrain. Born in 1897, he played the fiddle at dances in town and lived almost 100 years. An article was written about him in *Yankee Magazine*. Award-winning photographer Georgia Sheron took many photographs of Ludorf, including this photograph, published here with her courtesy. Another local character was the bee man "Himie," a hermit who lived between Community House Road and Route 67.

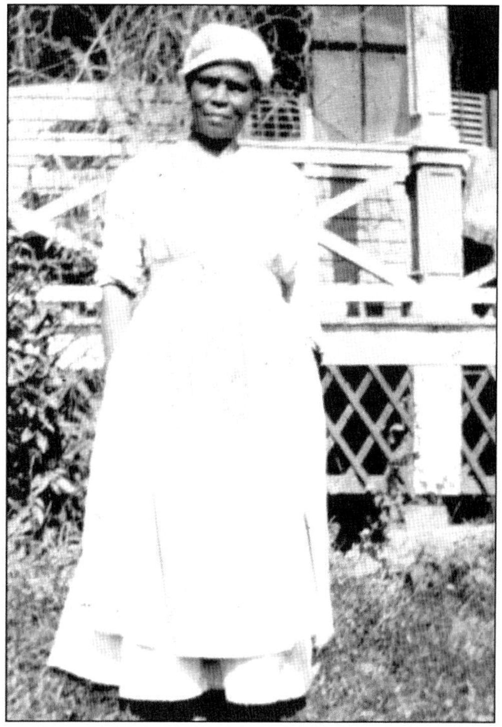

Susan Jackson. Jackson played an important role in town in the late 19th and early 20th centuries as a woman who brought many skills to a small community. She was born into slavery *c.* 1850 and was brought to Southbury as a domestic in 1875. She was a midwife. Her husband served in a Black regiment in the Civil War under the name of George Starr. Although African Americans were living in neighboring Woodbury at the time, there were very few in Southbury. (SHS.)

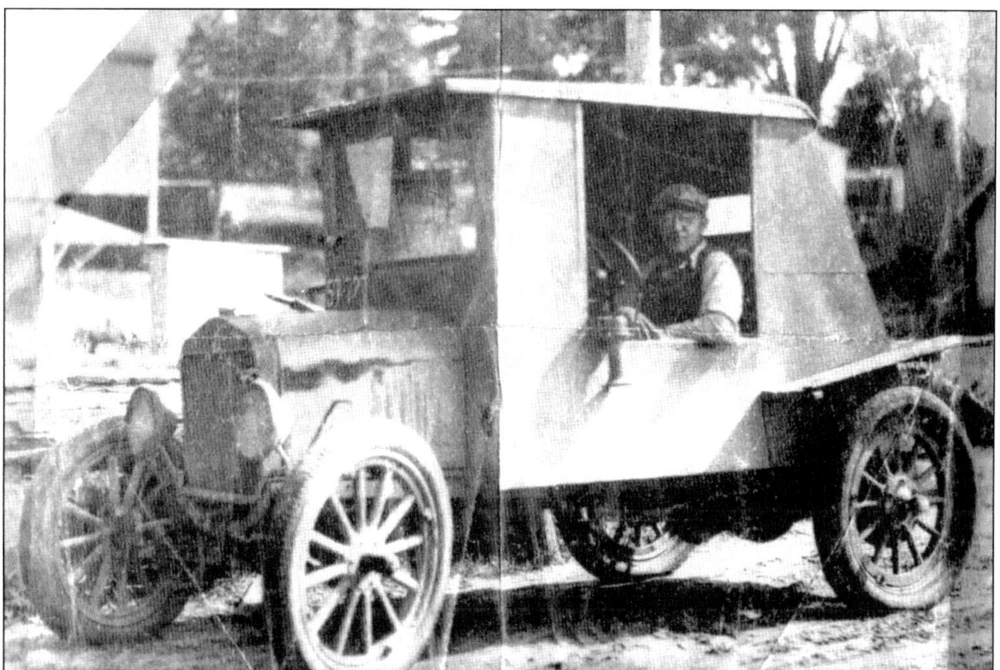

Delivering the Mail with Fliver. Ely P. Hicock delivers mail *c.* 1921. Hicock delivered mail around town in his custom-built car, Fliver. Prior to the development of railroads, *c.* 1840, a four-horse coach made three trips through Southford per week, on the turnpike, on a post-office route. Within 10 years, the railways took over the duty. (AM.)

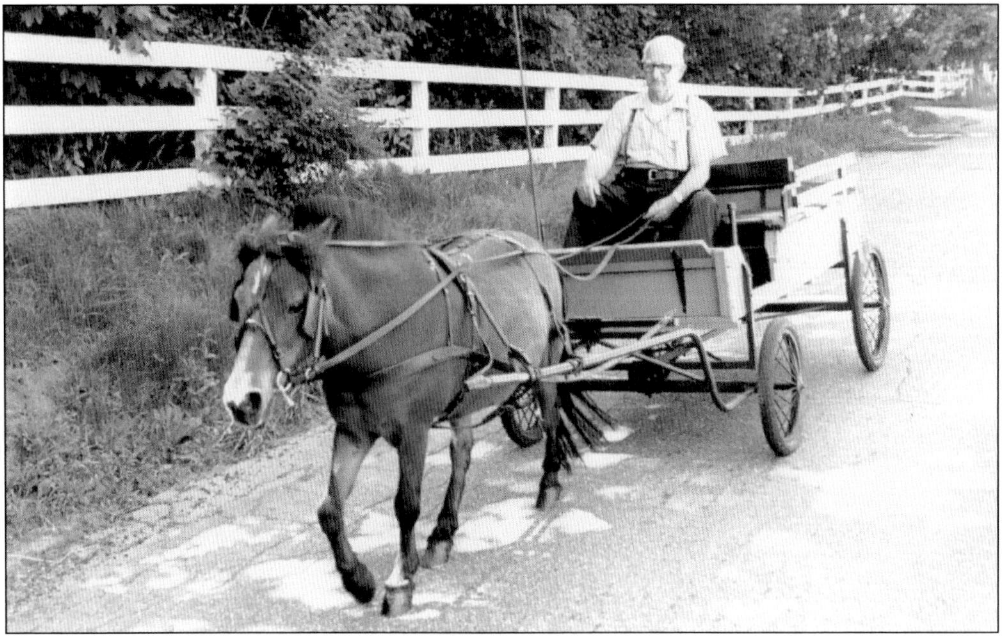

Delivering the Mail with Bucky. Bill Brandt makes rounds in Cedarland with a horse cart. He delivered interschool mail from the post office to Rochambeau School (presently Gainfield School), Pomperaug Elementary School, and Southbury High School (the current location of Rochambeau Middle School). In the 1800s, Carrie Manville drove the mail stage to Waterbury daily. She charged 25¢ per passenger until she upgraded to a Model T Ford car. (SHS.)

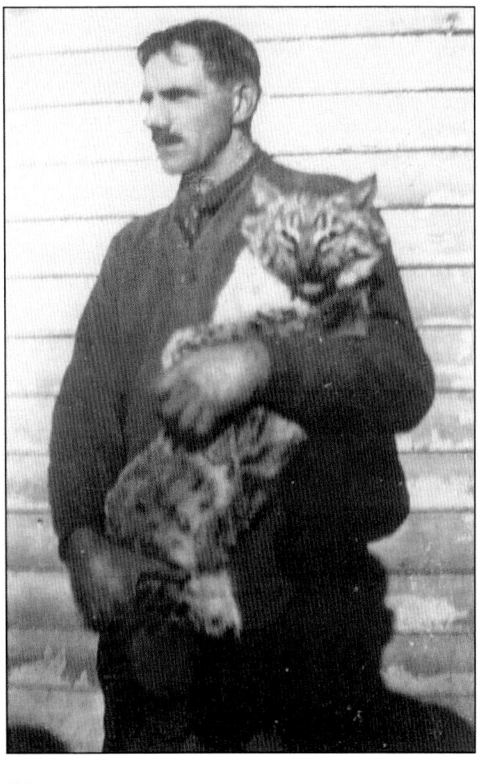

An Unusual Pet. This picture shows Nate Everts holding his bobcat. Nate was a big hunter and trapper in the area. (PH.)

PLAYING DOLLS. Here, Doris Hotchkiss is four years old. She became a beloved school teacher in the Southbury school system and taught at many of the district schools, including the Bullet Hill School. When she married, she was known as Mrs. Solosy. (PH.)

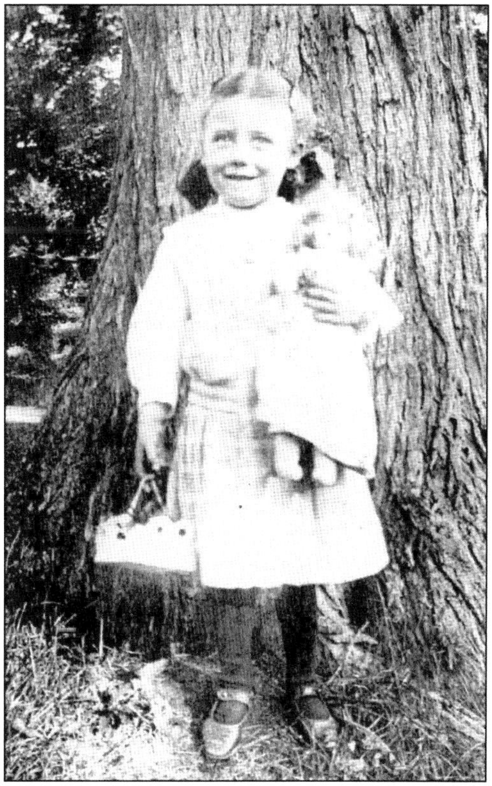

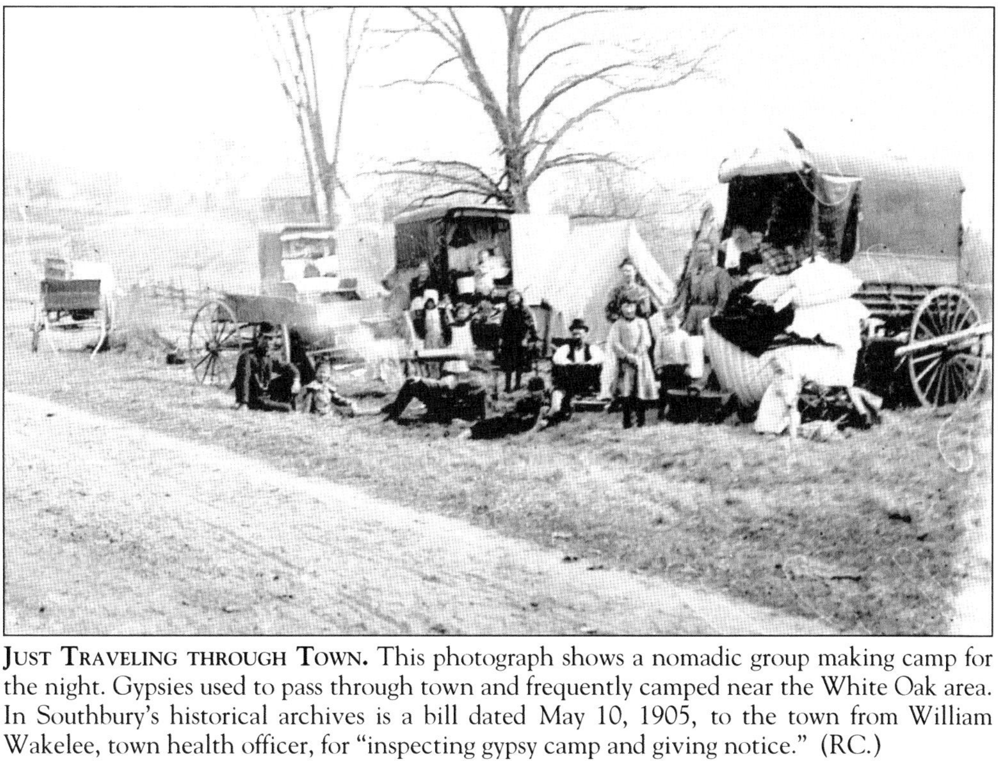

JUST TRAVELING THROUGH TOWN. This photograph shows a nomadic group making camp for the night. Gypsies used to pass through town and frequently camped near the White Oak area. In Southbury's historical archives is a bill dated May 10, 1905, to the town from William Wakelee, town health officer, for "inspecting gypsy camp and giving notice." (RC.)

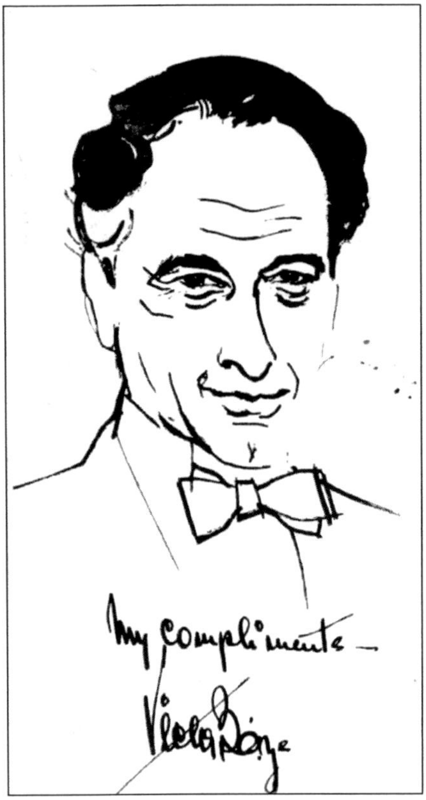

AN AUTOGRAPHED CARD FROM VICTOR BORGE. Victor Borge, the famous comedic pianist, lived in the area of Heritage Village. Borge telecast a Christmas Eve production from Southbury. He called his home, built by Truman Wheeler, ViBo Farms. A tower was erected on the nearby Russell Warner property to broadcast the 11.5-minute program. Southburians formed a group of carolers that included Lorraine Chase, Betty Moeller, Jean Smith, Meta Willenbrock, William Carlquist, Bernard Gracy, Fred Green, and Don Mathison. (SHS.)

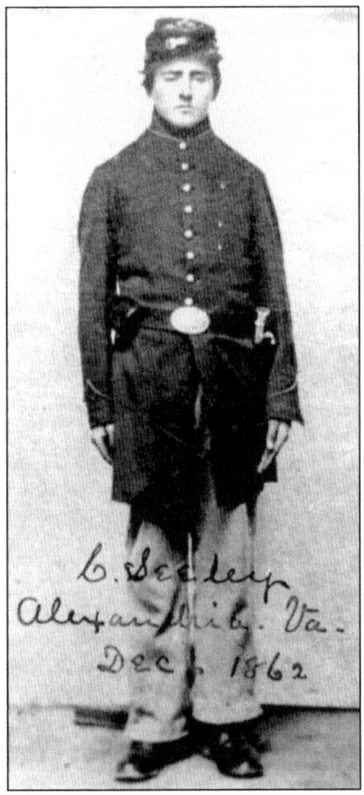

FIGHTING FOR THE UNION. Seen here is young Civil War soldier Chauncey Seeley in December 1862. Southbury contributed to the success of the Union army in "the great war for the suppression of the rebellion." Many local businesses economically benefited from the war. In 1865, Ira Bradley reactivated his fulling mill and produced uniforms for the Union army, along with satinet and woolen goods. In 1864, The Union army received many ship supplies in straw-board boxes made in Daniel Abbott's converted paper mill. (BI.)

AFTER YEARS OF SERVICE. In this 1910 photograph is an older Chauncey Seeley, from Wadham's Grand Army of the Republic. At the time of the Civil War, there were more than 40 men who served from Southbury. The town population at the time was 1,300. Southbury's expenses for the war totaled about $12,000. An additional $8,500 was spent for bounties for draftees, volunteers, and pay for substitutes. A $300 bounty was approved for anyone who would volunteer for the home guard, which would defend Connecticut in case the Confederates invaded.

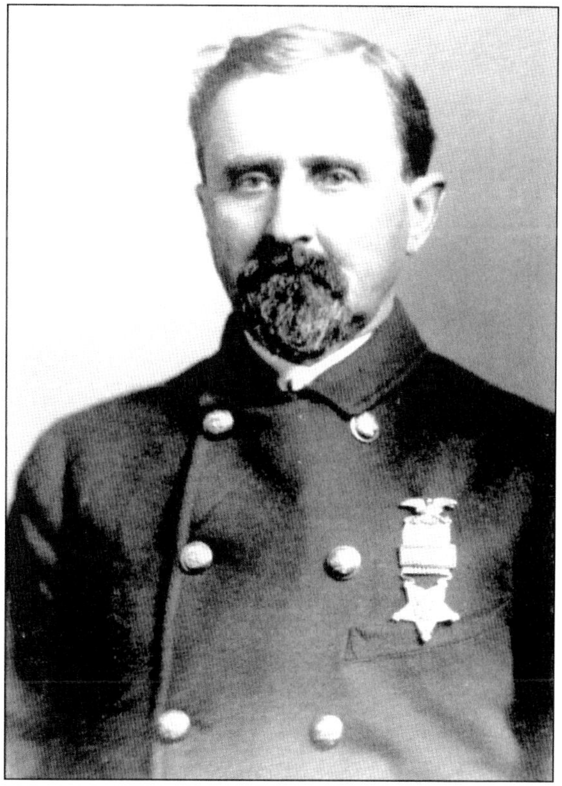

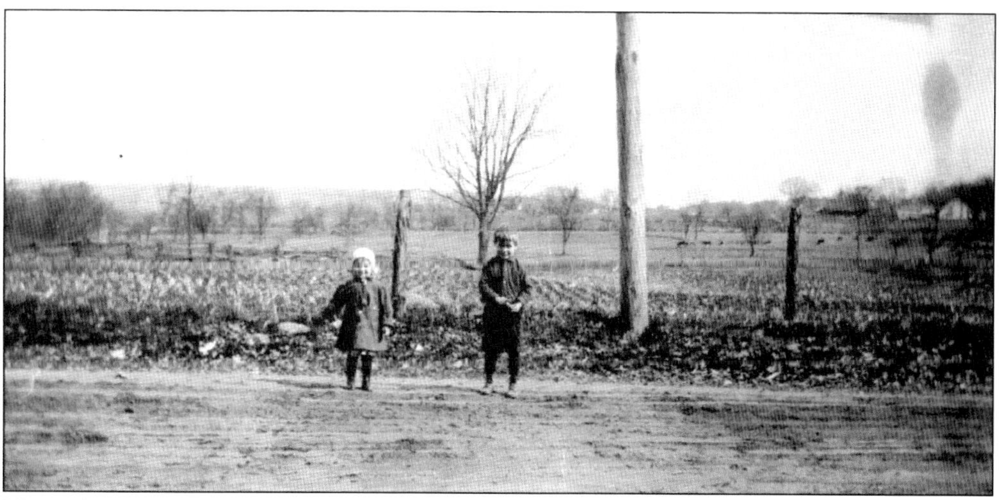

HINES CORN FIELD. Irene and Sidney Oliver stand in front of the Hines corn field. This is the present site of Hines garage in Southbury Center. (DM.)

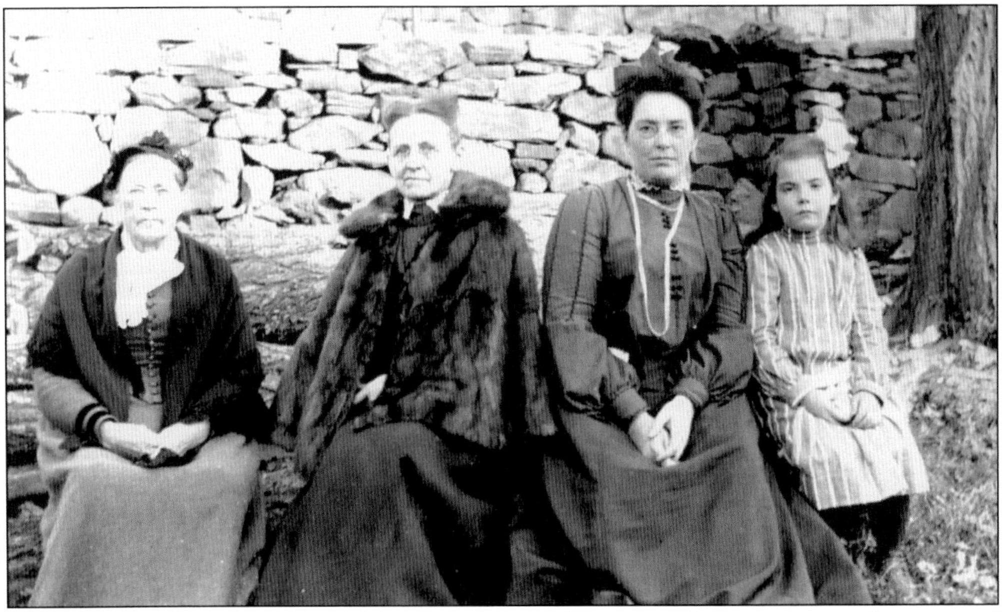

Four Generations of Women. Four generations of women gather together in the spring of 1904. Included are Jane Platt, J. Eliza Mitchell, Abbie Mitchell Williams, and Evelyn Williams-Hicock. (AM.)

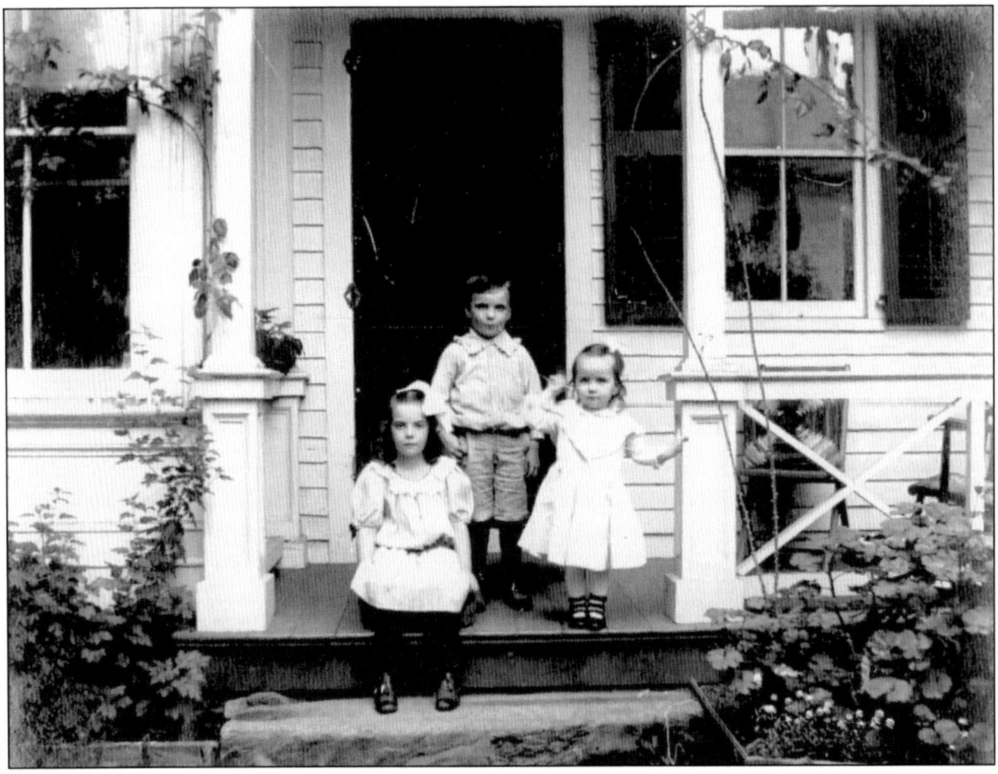

On the Front Porch. Evelyn Roger and Winifred Williams pose on their grandfather's porch in South Britain. The third child is unidentified. (AM.)

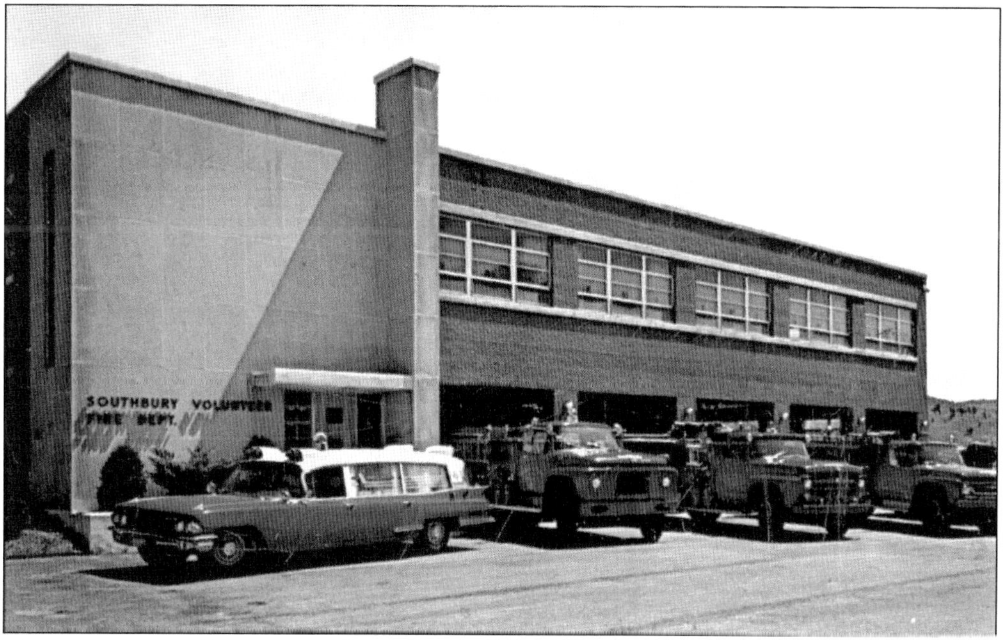

The Southbury Volunteer Fire Department c. the 1970s. The Southbury volunteer fireman's association was organized in the early 1930s. Initially, the Southbury ambulance was run by the Lion's Club. (DM.)

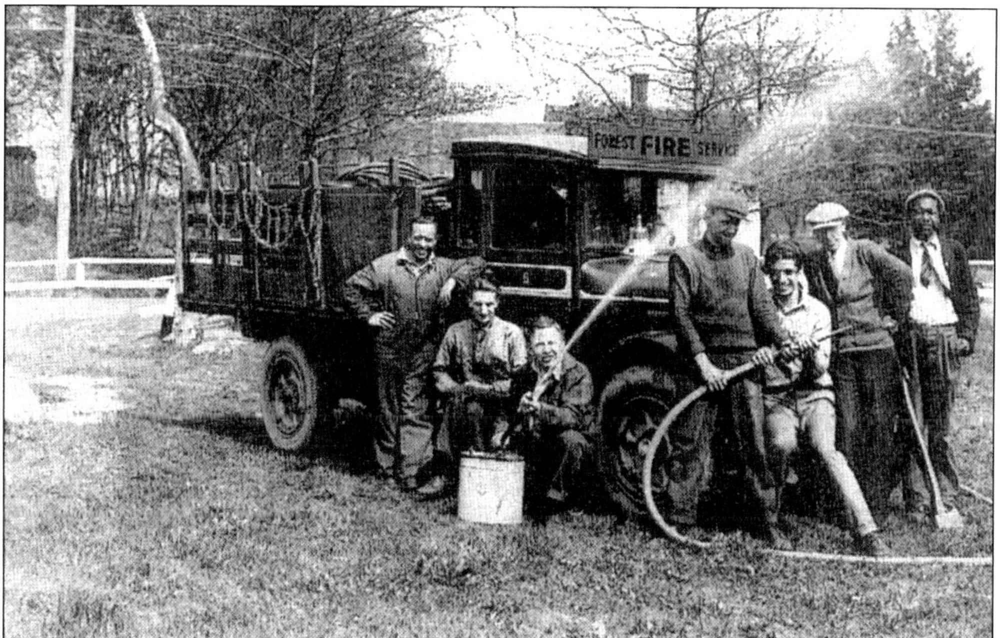

Members of the Department. Included in this mid-1930s, fireman's association photograph are Rip "Bunny" Cahill, L.C.W. Tyler, John Reynolds, and Chief Arza Bennett. (AB.)

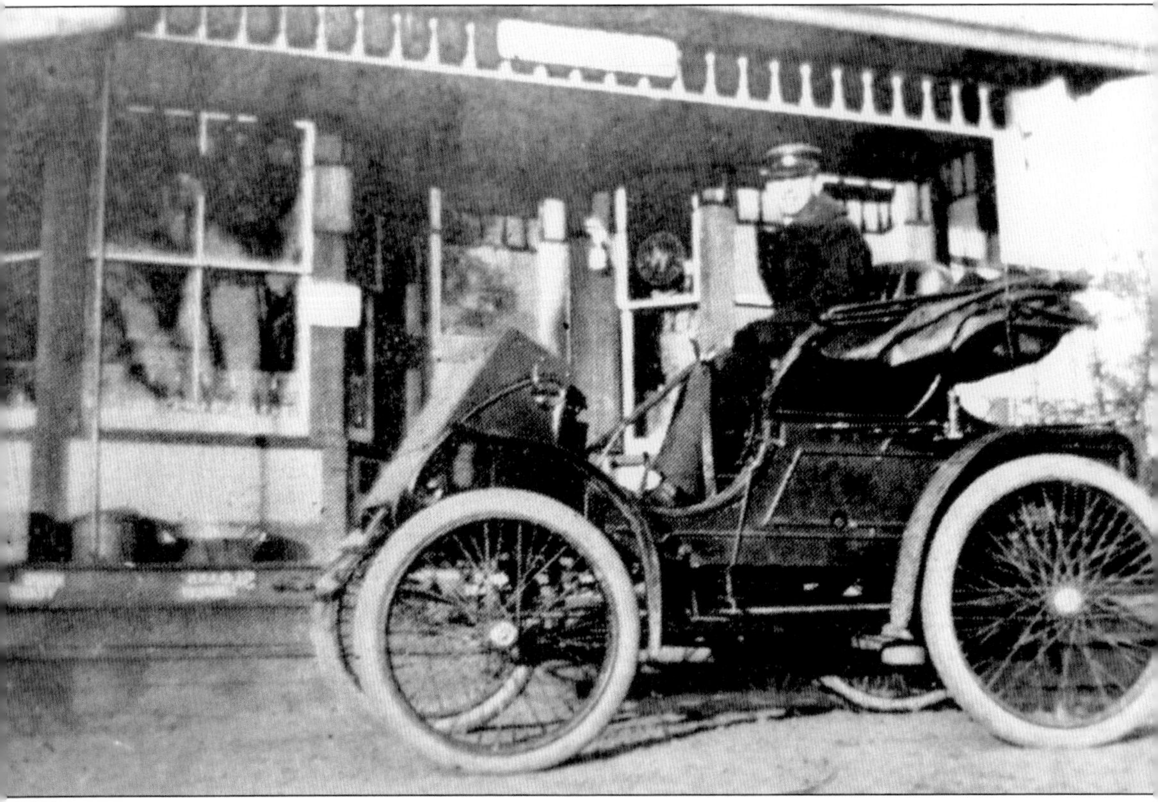

A Man Sitting in His Seven-Horsepower Car. The photograph shows H.H. Brown in front of his store, where, among other things, he was the town postmaster. He is believed to have been the nation's oldest dealer of Cadillacs. He began selling Cadillacs in 1904 and was chairman of the Brown and Thomas Automobile Agency in New Haven. He was born in 1873. (SHS.)

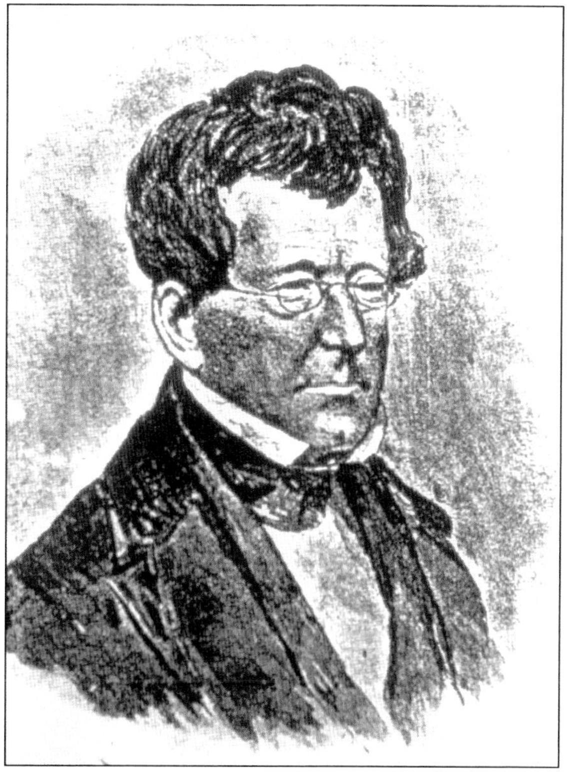

PETER PARLEY. This is a sketch of the children's book author Samuel Goodrich. Peter Parley was his *nom de plume*. He was an author in the early 1800s, and he lived in Southbury between 1857 and 1860. He wrote over 100 books in a series of tales about Peter Parley and America, as well as many textbooks. His home is now the site of the Lutheran Home He is buried in the White Oak Cemetery. (SHS.)

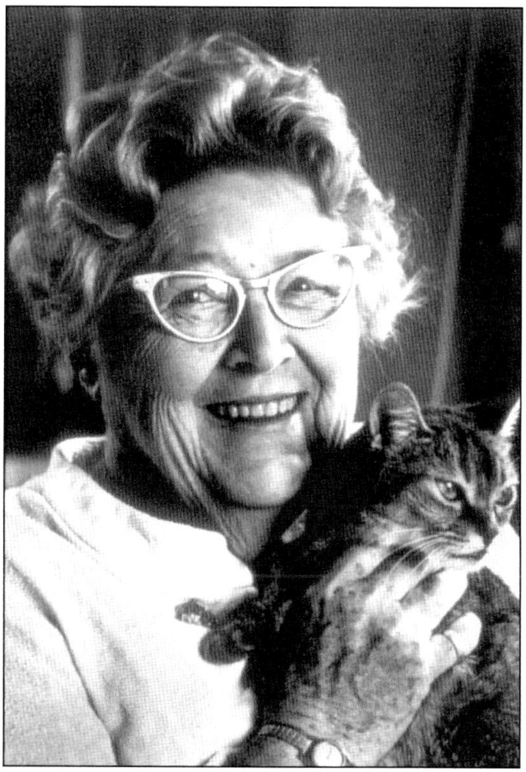

GLADYS TABER. Seen here is Gladys Taber, a famous writer and novelist who lived in a home known as Stillmeadow in Southbury. It was located on a dirt road across from the Phillips farm. Her writings included detailed descriptions of the rural countryside she lived in. She was fascinated by the effects that seasonal changes brought on nature and farming. She wrote more than 50 books, including cookbooks, novels, short stories, and books about cats, dogs, flower arranging, and cooking. (SHS.)

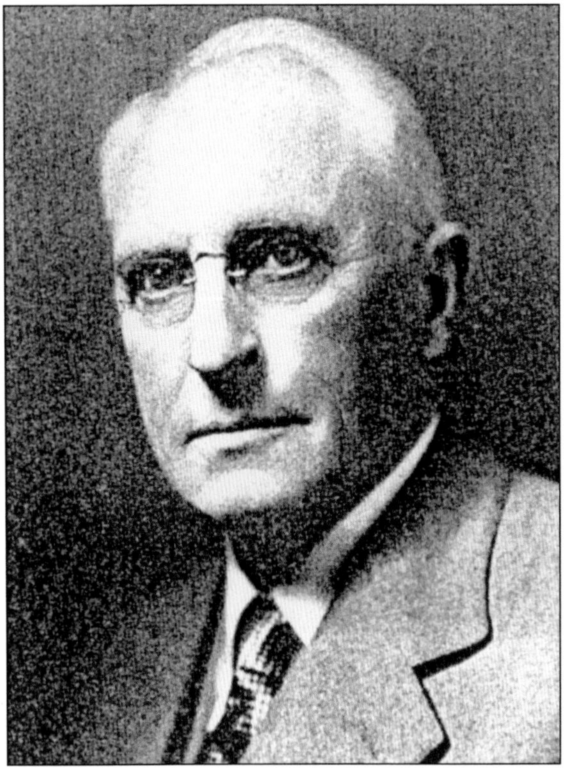

WALLACE NUTTING. This picture shows Wallace Nutting, an author, photographer, reproduction furniture maker, and antique collector. (SHS.)

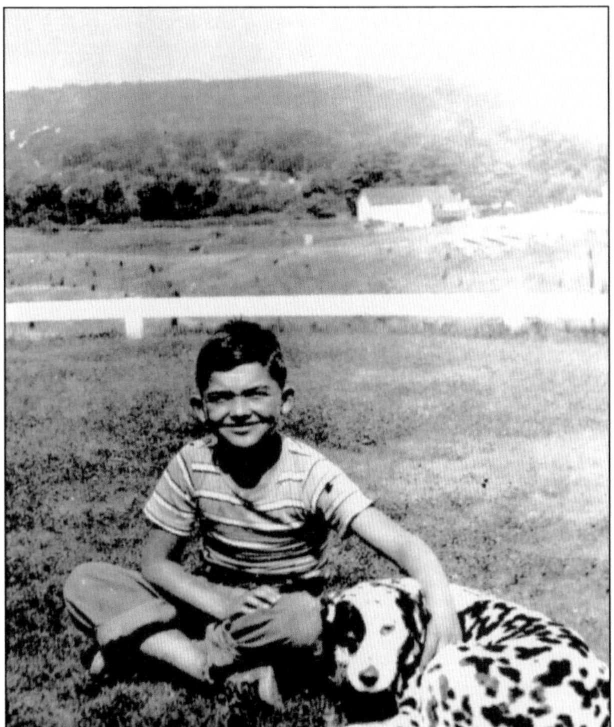

GARY WHEELER. Gary Wheeler is pictured with his grandfather's dog Spotty at the Wheeler house in Southbury. In the background are both of the Nettleon's mink cages and Ely Hicock's big barn. The lawn of the property shown is now the site of the CVS store on Main Street North. (MCW.)

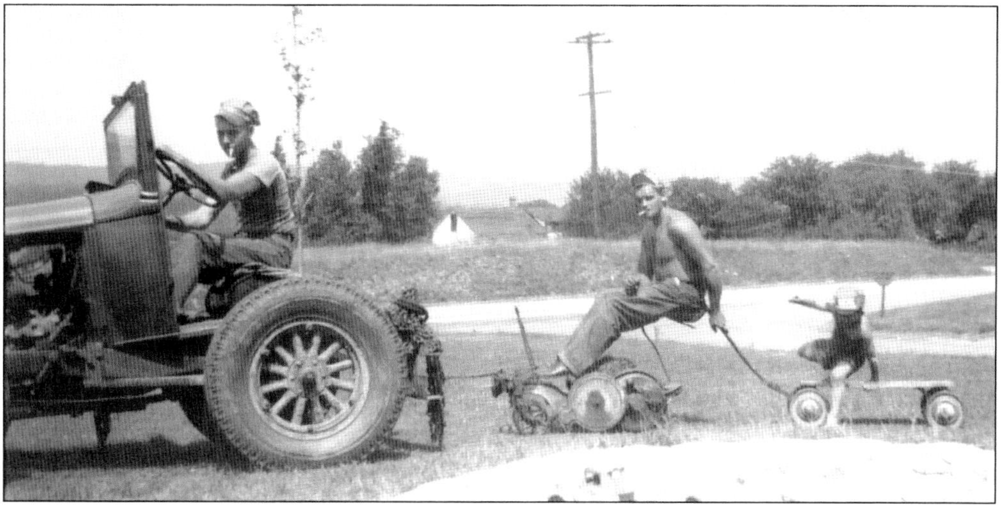

The Wheelers. After a long day, Harvey Stone and Mel and Gary Wheeler pull each other along. (MCW.)

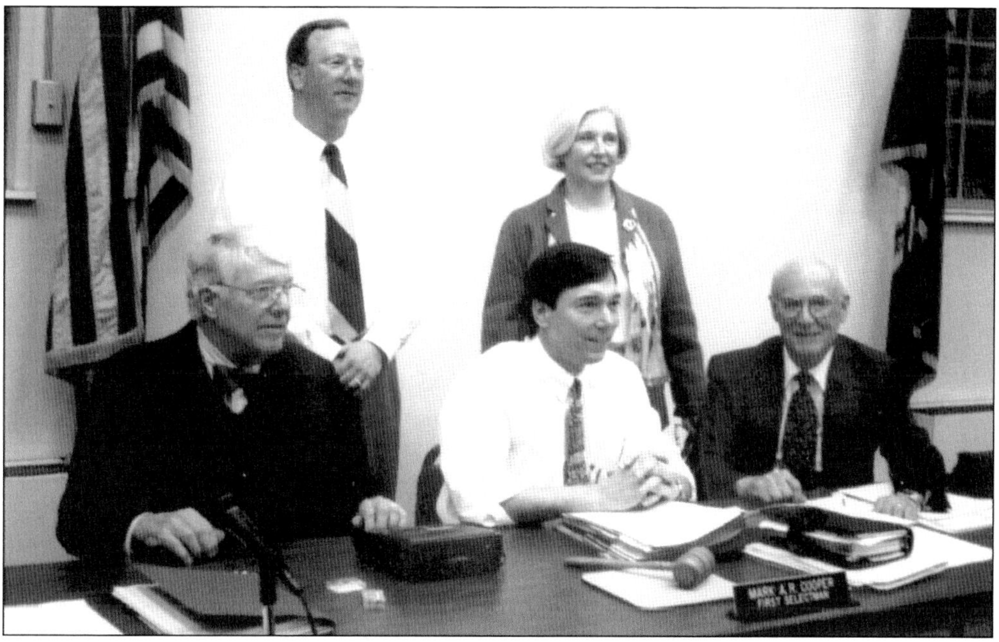

The Southbury Board of Selectmen. In this photograph are the current town selectmen, including the author's father. Seen here are, from left to right, the following: (front row) Donald Briggs, first selectman Mark Cooper, and Paul Palmer; (back row) Jeffrey Hughes and Carol Hubert. Missing from the photograph is David Mathieu. Southbury operates under a traditional New England town-meeting form of government. It functions under the guidelines of the town charter, revised in 1997. Executive authority rests in a six-member board of selectmen. Numerous boards and commissions are made up of volunteers who are either elected or appointed. These commissions determine policy for planning, zoning, inland wetlands, economic development, conservation, and parks and recreation. (CPP.)

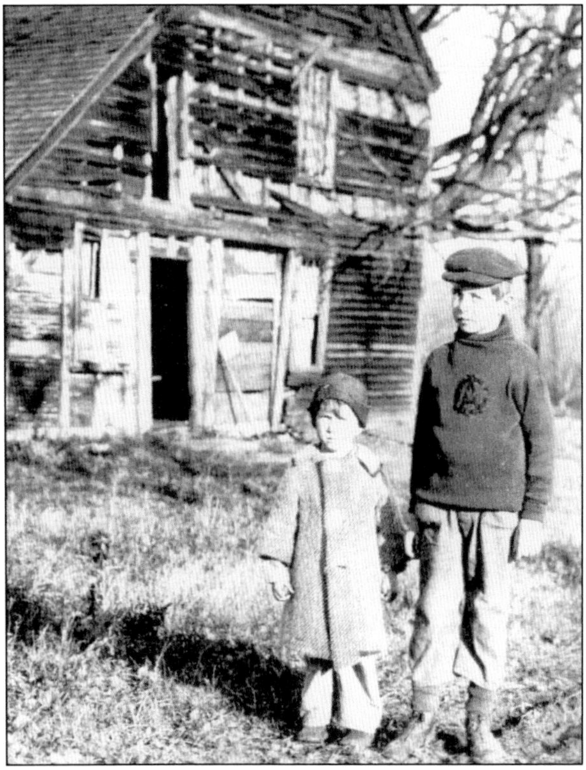

BILL AND BOB LAUTENSCHLAGER. This photograph shows brothers Bill and Bob Lautenschlager in front of the Hicock house on Transylvania Road c. 1926. (TL.)

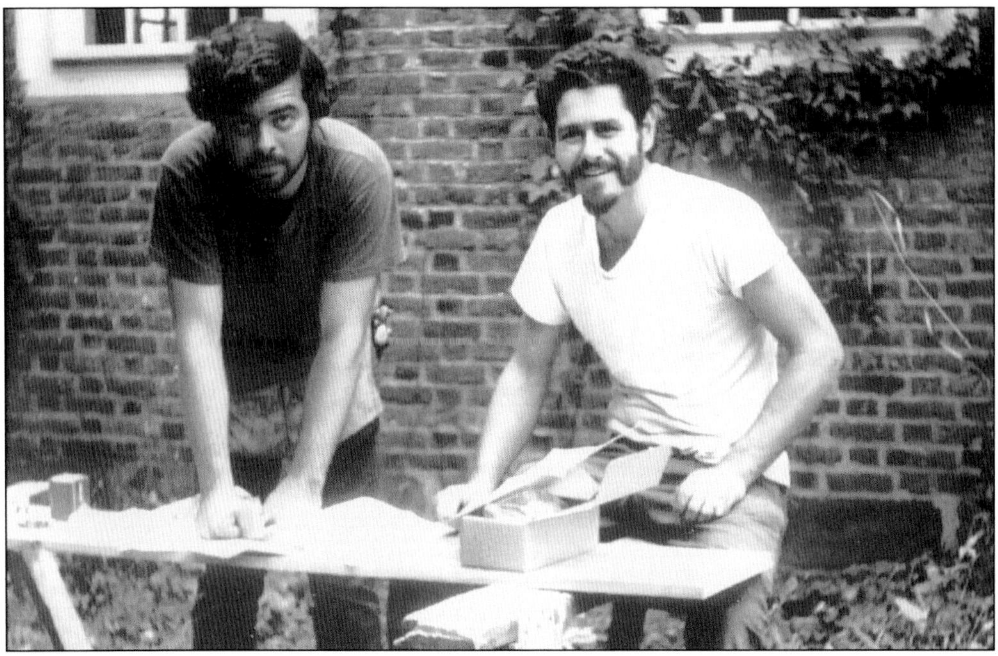

THE BULLET HILL SCHOOL RESTORATION. Seen here are two of the many people who value historic buildings and wish to maintain their integrity. Richard V. Patrick and Tom Lautenschlager help make historic restorations to the Bullet Hill School. Many people were instrumental in either planning or facilitating this preservation effort. (TL.)

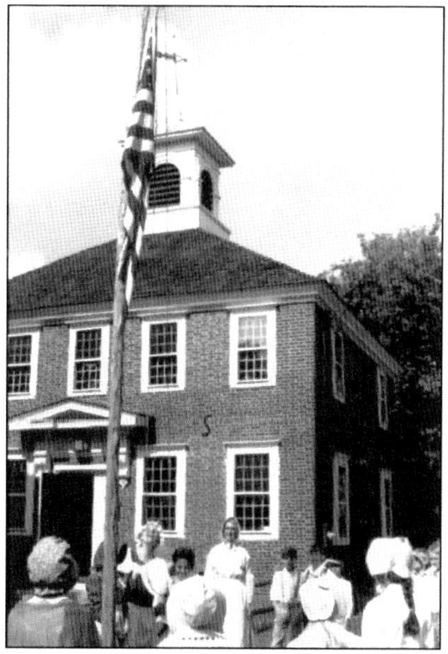

A Living Museum Program. The Bullet Hill School living museum program is a reenactment of a typical 1800s school day for children. It was initiated in 1989 by Catherine Palmer, who is the founder and director of the program. Sylvia Forbes has also been a important part of the program and its development. Although flags were usually not present in the schoolyards of the 1800s, a flag is present in this photograph because the Bullet Hill School is a public building. Children did not have the Pledge of Allegiance in 1850. It did not exist until 1892 and was not used in schools until 1942, when Congress made the pledge part of its code for the flag. (CPP.)

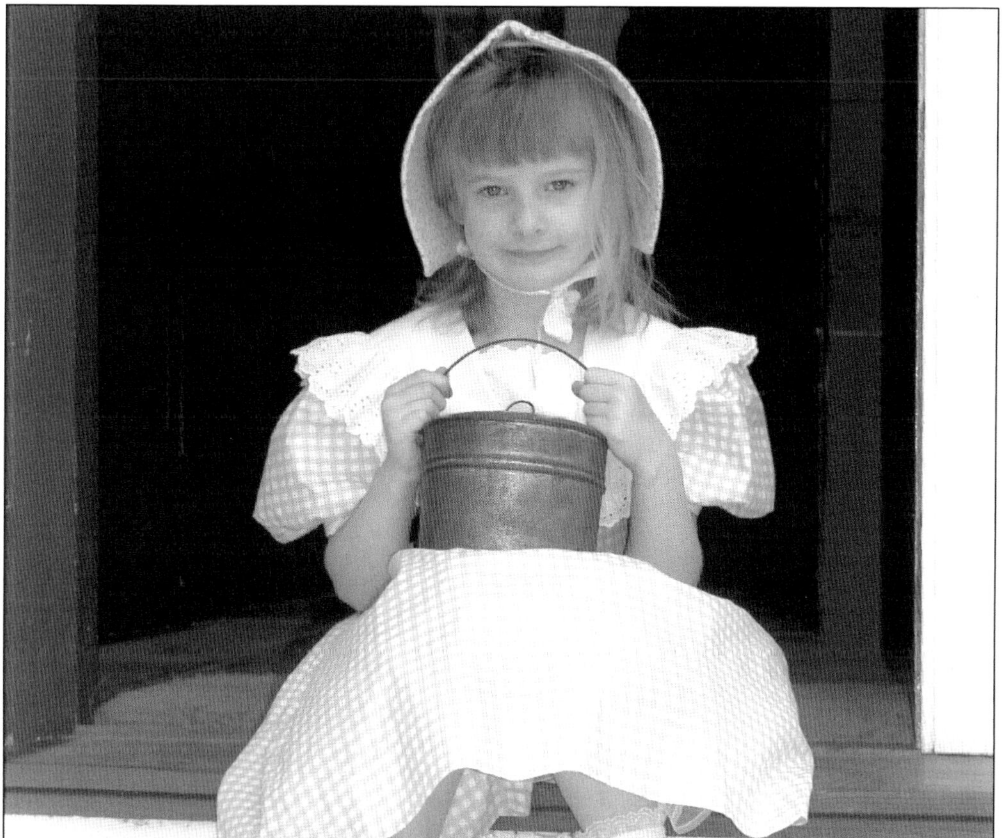

Abigail Manville. This little girl is at the Bullet Hill School with an old-fashioned lunch pail. The Bullet Hill school open house brought Abigail in a reproduction 1800s-period dress and bonnet. (AS.)

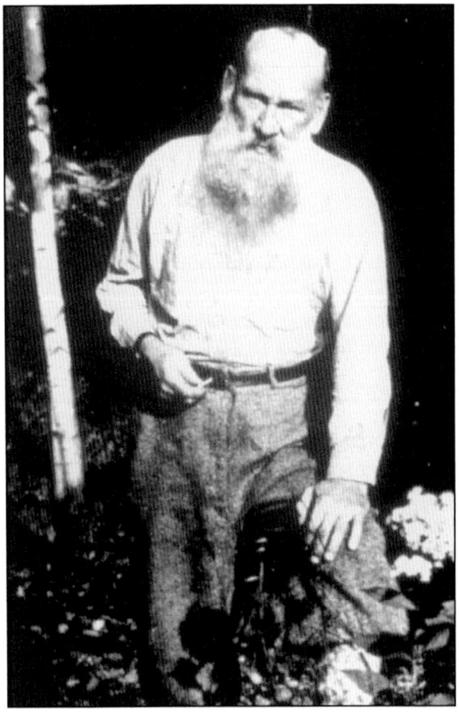

Ilya Tolystoy. Seen is the son of Leo Tolstoy, the author of *War and Peace*. The Russian Village groundwork was laid down by Ilya Tolystoy. He had visited Woodbury frequently to see an English translator. He fell in love with Southbury's scenic quality, which resembled Russia. It made him think of his family's summer home, Yasnaya Polyana, outside of Russia. He purchased 16 acres of land from local resident Edward Scoville. Many people of notoriety visited, including Igor Sikorsky, Sergei Rachmaninoff, and Pearl Buck. Many Russian expatriates joined Tolystoy as they fled political persecution in Russia. Today, only a few Russian families remain, keeping with Ilya Tolstoy's dream. (SHS.)

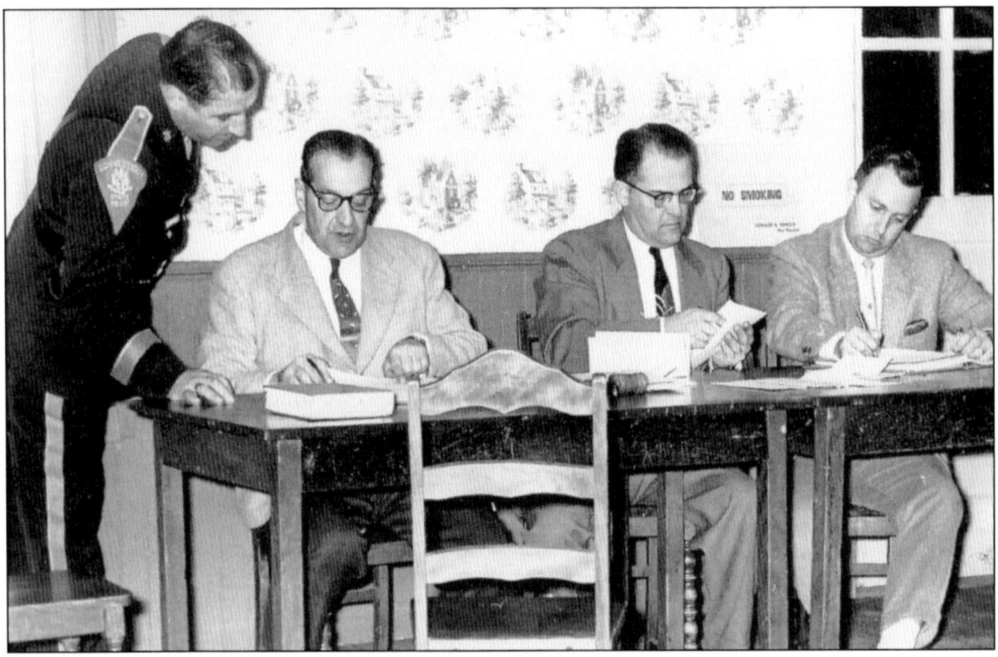

The Old Town Hall in South Britain. This photograph shows members of the last court session meeting, including resident state trooper John Lombardo, prosecutor Ralph Hoxie, trial justice Wesley F. Rouse Sr., and assistant justice Samuel Green III. Lombardo was the first resident state trooper. Green also served as a Southbury first selectman. The town used to operate with a trial justice court system. The selectman appointed a justice of the peace to serve as a trial justice, and this person appointed a grand juror as a prosecutor. (SG.)

Four

AT WORK

Southbury now constitutes a beautiful, fertile farming town, well watered by the Pomperaug River, its branches and other streams. There are 4 grist mills, ten saw mills, 1 paper mill, 1 manufacturer of edged tools, several wool hat manufacturers, one satinet manufacturer, shears, tin and 7 stores.

—William Cothren, 1850.

Local occupations have changed with the times. Townsfolk originally made their livings through an agrarian society. With the advent of water power, industry grew in little pockets, which created more jobs and had a direct impact on the number of inhabitants. At one time, it was said that you could not find a fur trap in Canada that did not have the label of a South Britain manufacturer on it. The famous Wakelee plow was also invented here. Other manufactured products included buttons, bustles, spoons, scythes, shoes, wools, and more. Forges and mills sprung up along with paper mills. A popular site that is visited today is the Southford Falls Park that sits on the original burned-out foundation of the Diamond Match factory, a paperboard manufacturer. More recently produced items include ice cream and small screw machine parts. A Southbury ice-cream manufacturer is accredited for the availability of ice cream in supermarkets, today, due to early marketing efforts. Today, the Telenor national satellite-monitoring site is located near the Shepaug Dam. This area attracts visitors who want to view nesting bald eagles.

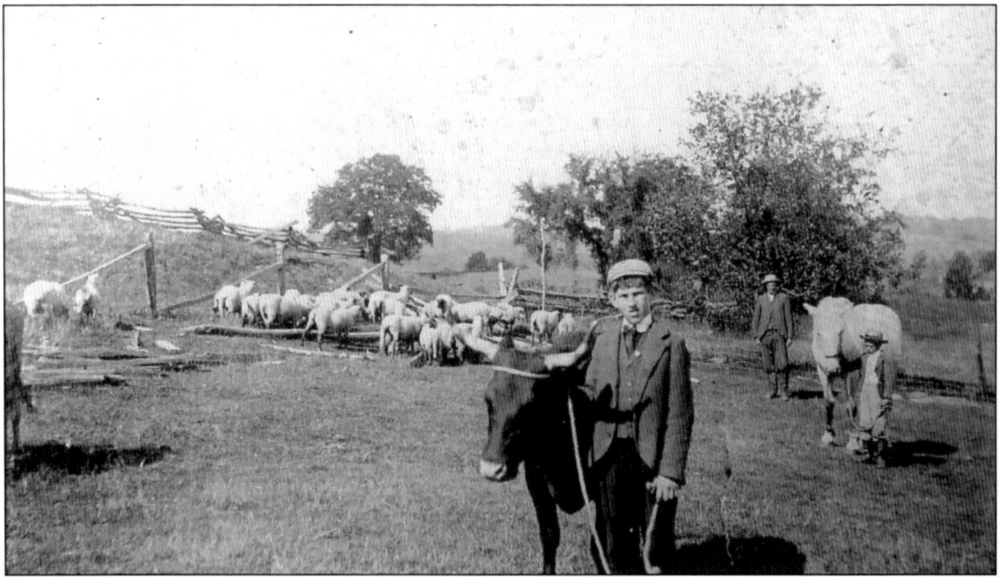

The Henry Russell Farm. Shown here is the Russell farm. The town provided some subsidies to encourage the development of mills. In 1673, taxes were set on rye, corn, flax, and buckwheat. Because there was little currency, taxes were paid with pork, wheat, corn, and other farm yields. As early as 1691, John Mitchell and Samuel Stiles entered an agreement with four citizens to run a corn mill with a dam for all of the town's inhabitants. The town compensated the miller with payment. (TL.)

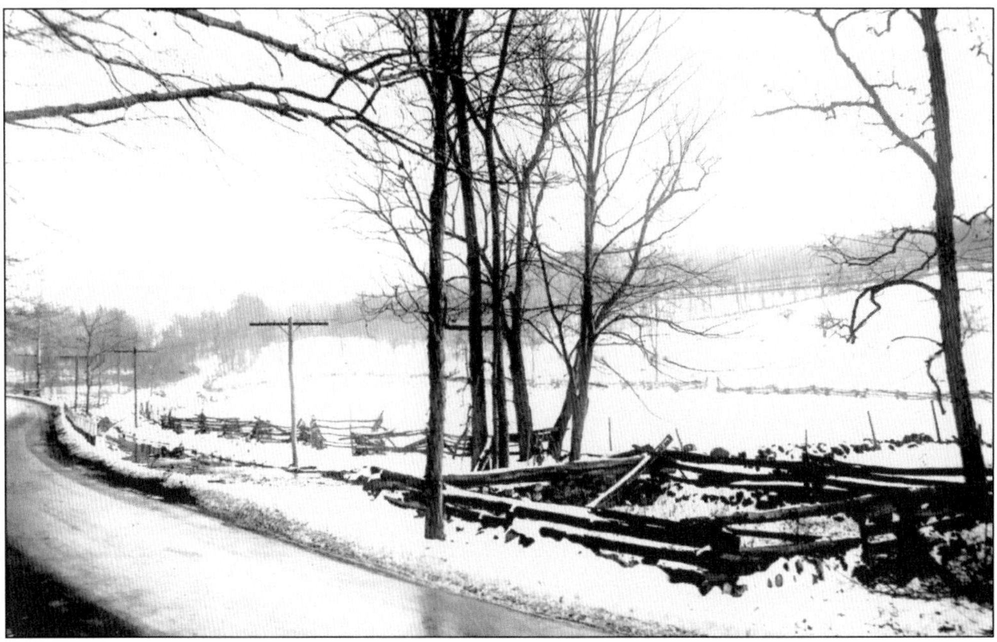

The Animal Pound. Cattle and loose animals were kept in this pound, located along Route 67. In later days, people would to take their cars to the area and drive them into the brook to wash them. The pound in South Britain was at the buttonball tree on East Flat. There was also a horse pound just east of today's Interstate 84 and south of Peter Road. Owners could get their impounded animals with payment and a promise to keep them within fences. (SHS.)

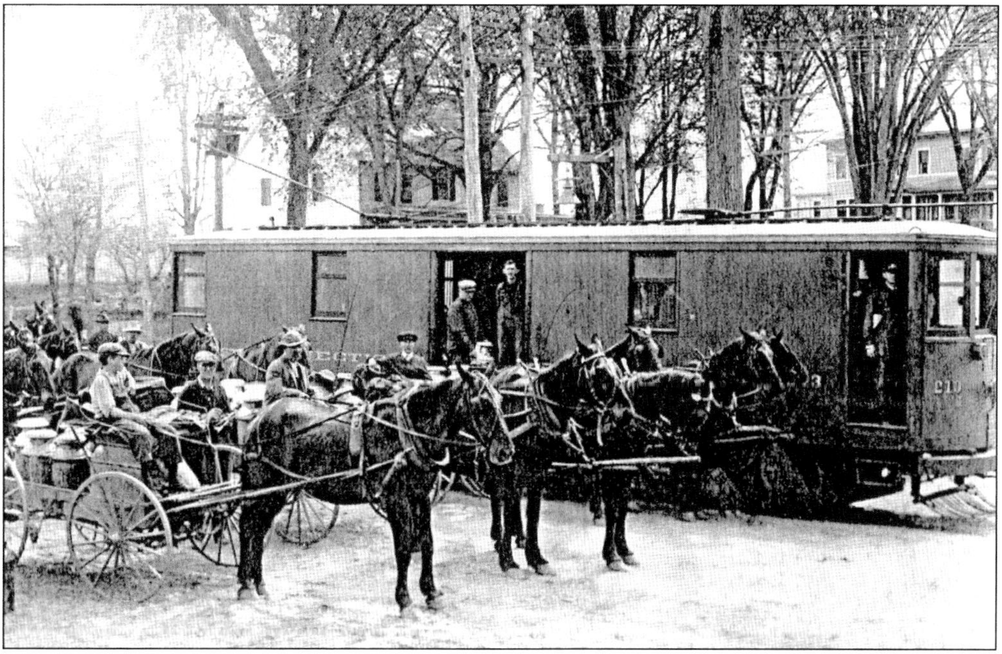

Delivering Milk. This photograph shows a milk route. Early on, trips were made by horse teams to New Haven and Derby to deliver produce on one day and bring back merchandise on the next day. (MCW.)

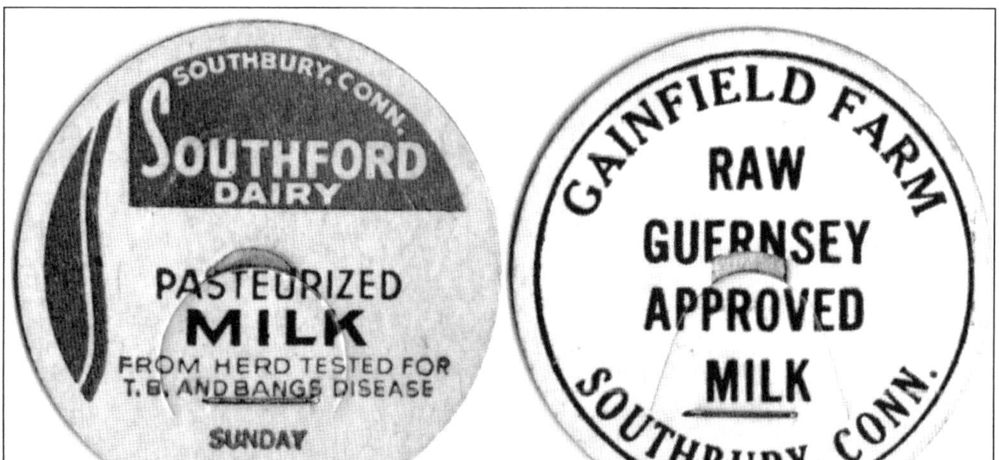

Bottle Caps. This picture shows milk bottle caps from both the Southford Dairy and Gainfield Farm. Today's Gainfield School sits on the location of its namesake. Before World War II, Southbury was always an agricultural society, and dairy farming was a large part of the economy. Many farmers had prize Guernsey and Holstein herds. In 1870, dairy cattle began replacing sheep. (TL.)

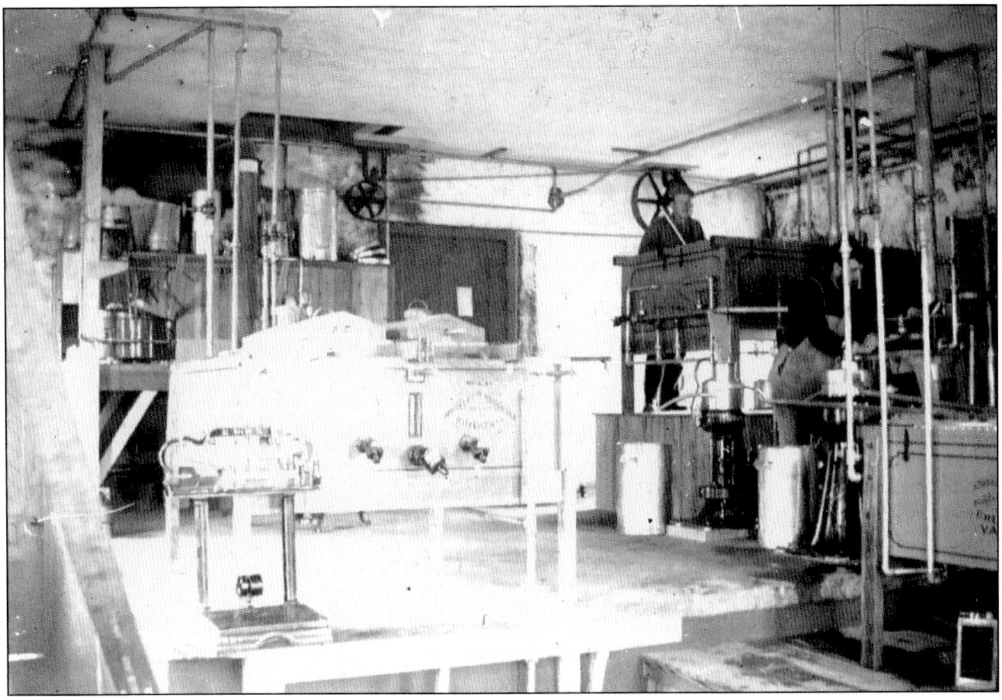

Inside the Creamery. The South Britain Creamery was managed by Mr. Sage. It also served as a cannery. (SHS.)

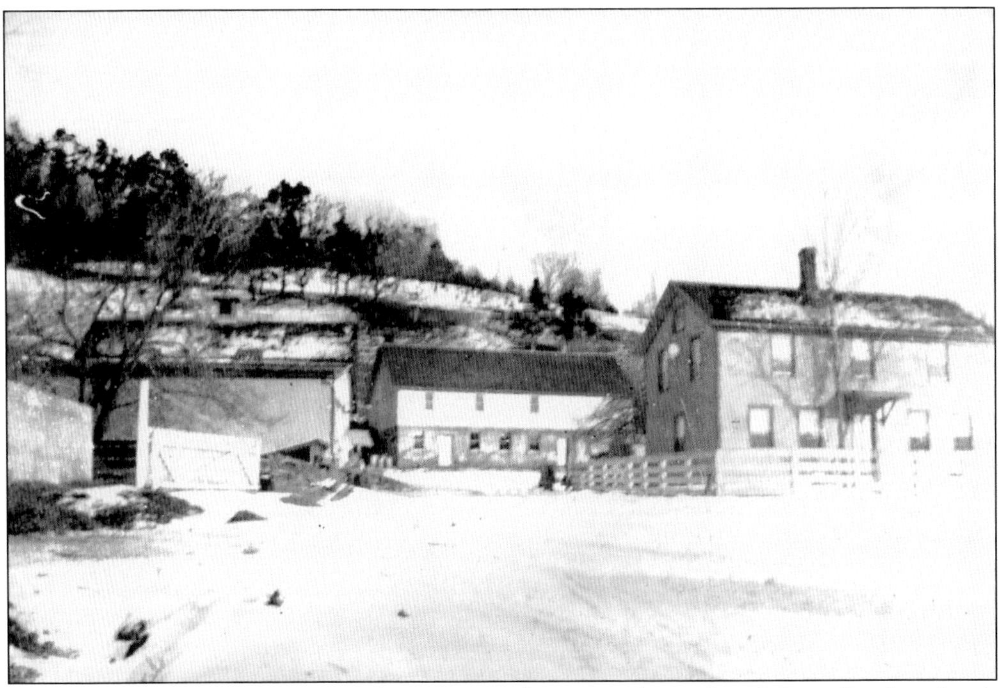

The South Britain Creamery. The creamery shown was located on Library Road in South Britain. (AM.)

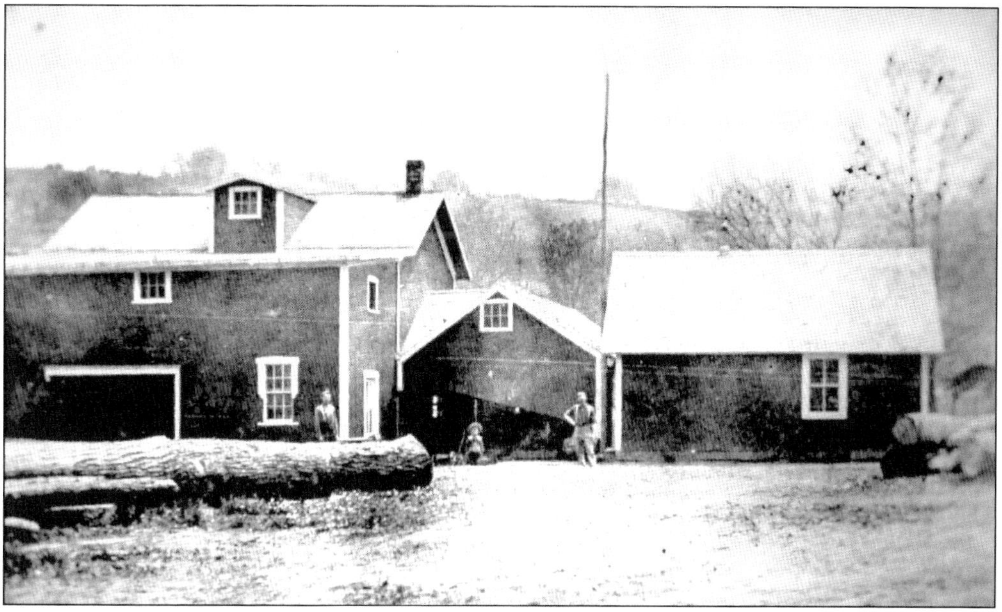

The Lumber Mill. This is a photograph of an early lumberyard. In 1783, the Curtiss family had built another sawmill along Eight Mile Brook. Two of the early sawmill operators were Charles Hine and Ed Scoville. Two active timber men were John Mitchell and Merwin Mitchell. One sawmill, run by a Hines family, made its own branded railroad ties. (SHS.)

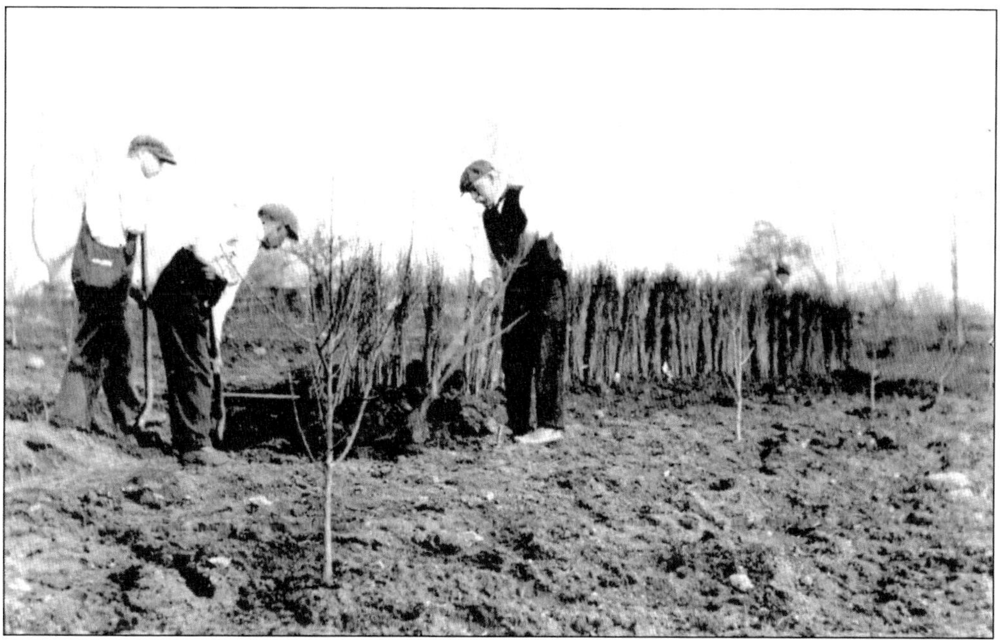

A Peach Orchard. This orchard was on Peach Orchard Road and was established like an early co-op. Peaches were taken to a cannery that was nearby in South Britain. The town was concerned that some of the people did not pay taxes on the small lots. Another agricultural venture was a mulberry plantation, located in the Purchase in Mulberry Corners, that attempted to raise silk worms, but the trees failed. Mulberry Corners is at the intersection of Purchase Brook and Gilbert and Brown Brook Roads. (TL.)

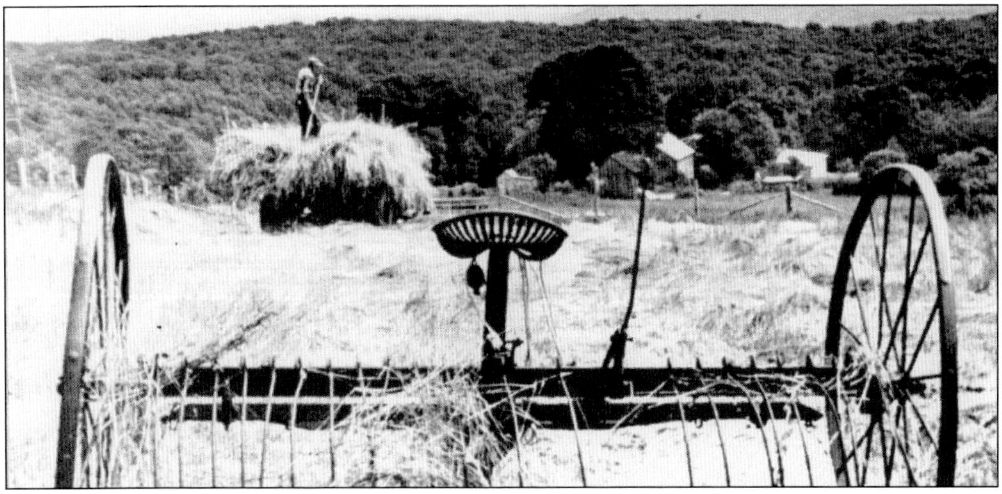

A Hay Rake. This is a photograph of a common farm implement. The late John Ludorf, a respected Southbury farmer, is pictured in the background, forking the loose hay onto the hay wagon. When the mowing machine was invented in 1870, horses replaced slower oxen in the fields. At the same time, sheep were being replaced by dairy cattle. (Courtesy of Georgia Sheron.)

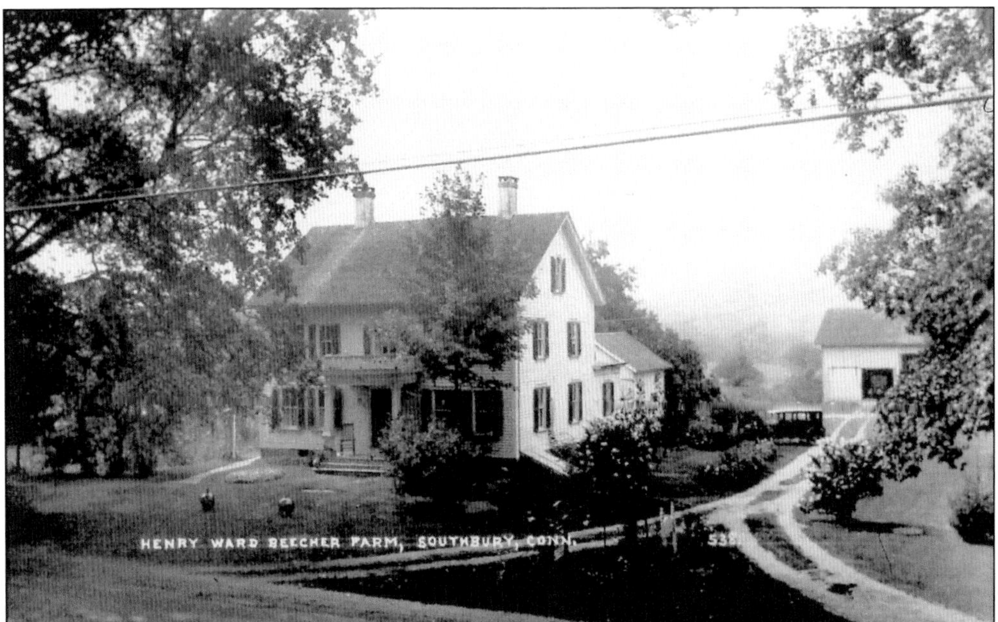

Henry Ward Beecher Farm. Agriculture was the main industry in the first 100 to 150 years after settlement. Farming contributed to the local beauty with the building of stonewalls, which were constructed so that farmers would not break their plows. Pastures existed along main roads. The original inhabitants, the Pootatucks, were also agrarian. They raised beans, corn, squash, tobacco, and apples prior to the establishment of the white settlers' community. The prominent Indian Chief Tummasute even owned an apple orchard. (SHS.)

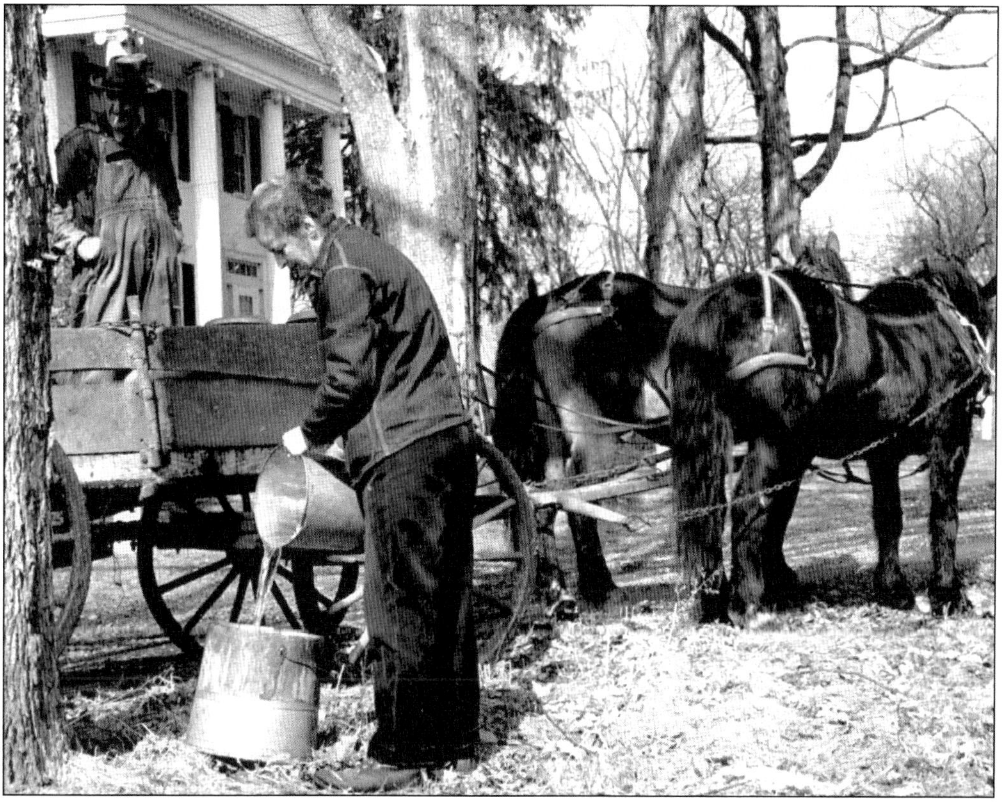

MAPLE SYRUP HARVESTING ON KINGSLAND. A woman collects syrup on Kingsland, the green across from the Lutheran Home. Some people have referred to it as "Queensland." When the second ecclesiastical society was formed, in the White Oak district, a log-cabin meetinghouse was built at the southern end of Kingsland. For more than three centuries, ownership of the small parcel of land has shuffled from community to private ownership to state ownership. (RC.)

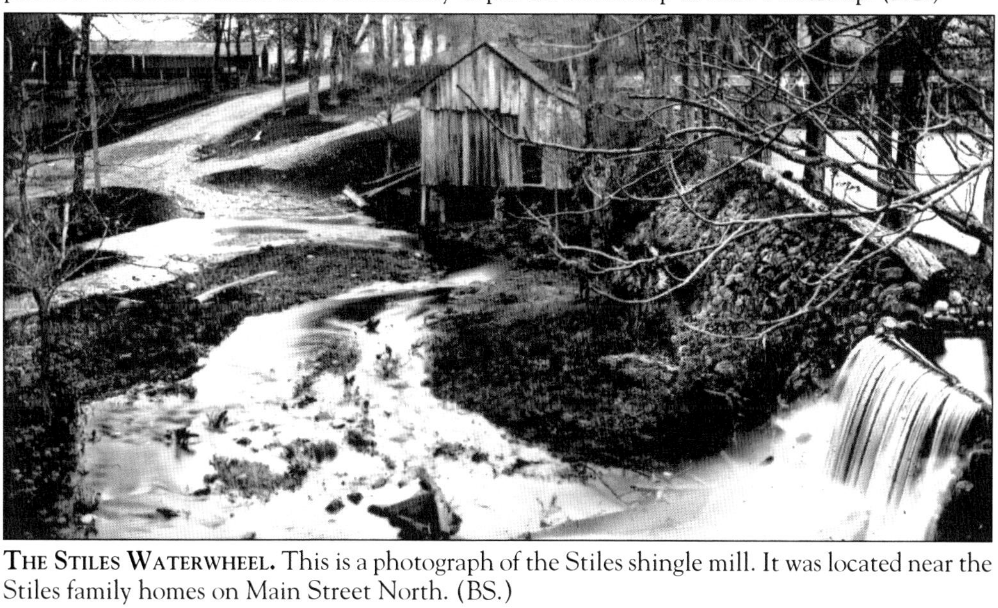

THE STILES WATERWHEEL. This is a photograph of the Stiles shingle mill. It was located near the Stiles family homes on Main Street North. (BS.)

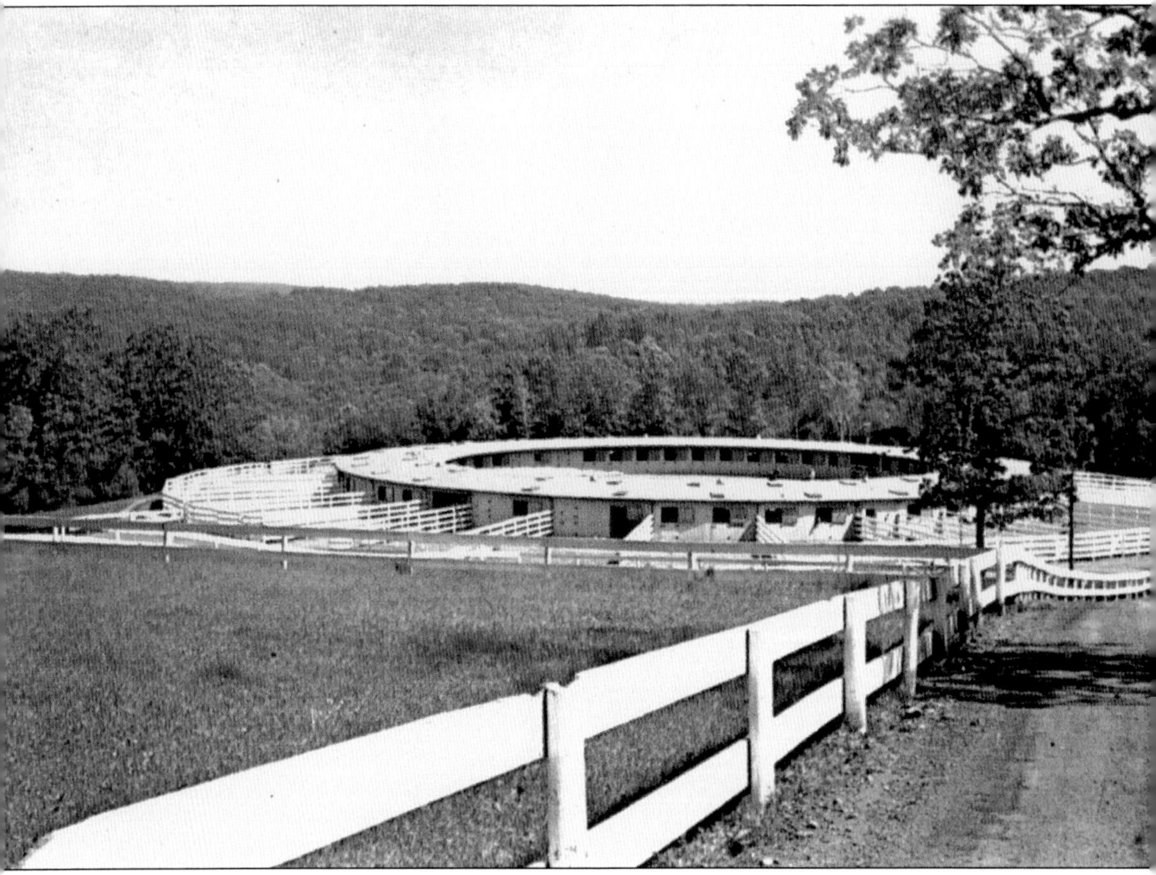

Westonhook Farm. Miles of white-washed fence surround this horse farm. This beautiful, sprawling horse farm is situated on North George's Hill. The early Kettletown district school is across the road and is still standing today. (DM.)

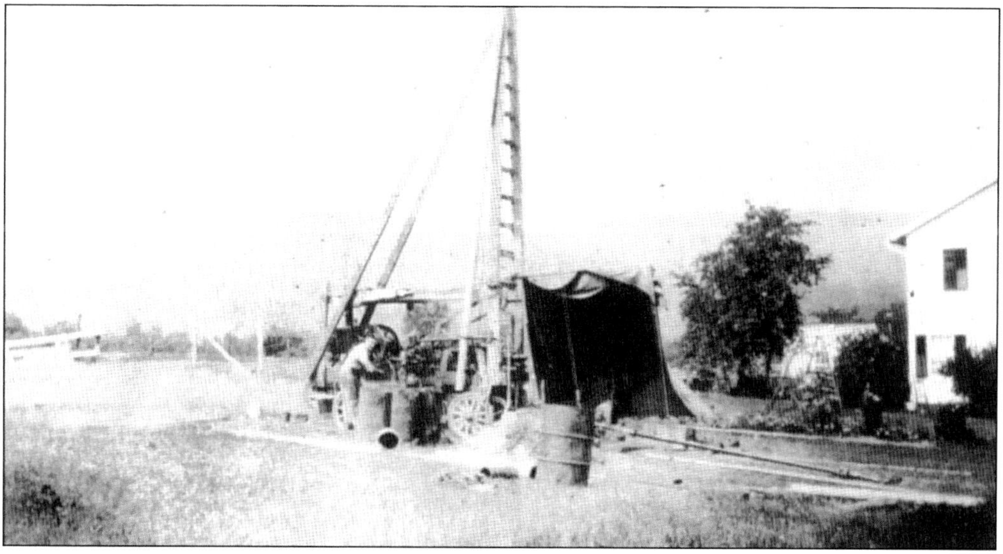

DRILLING FOR WATER. Water is being drilled for at the Hotchkiss house on Bradley Hill. In 1888, the Southbury Company drilled another well on Poverty Road. The company drilled to 1,400 feet before giving up. At one time, residents even searched for both coal and oil. In 1830, a shaft was sunk to develop coal but was abandoned. In 1831–1832, an English speculator, Charles Cleveland, invested in an oil derrick to drill for oil on Main Street, near the Congregational church. (PH.)

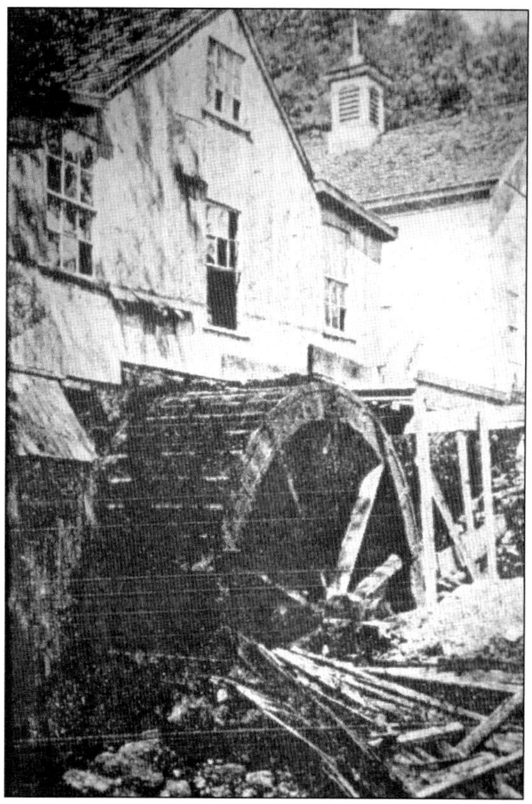

A GRIST MILL. This is one of the early mills in town. Some incentives were given to both tradespeople and artisans. Abraham Falford, a clothier, was given a 10-acre accommodation by the town. Seven years later, Joseph Hurd was given a fulling mill. In 1837, Daniel Abbott started a feed mill to grind corn and other grain. (SHS.)

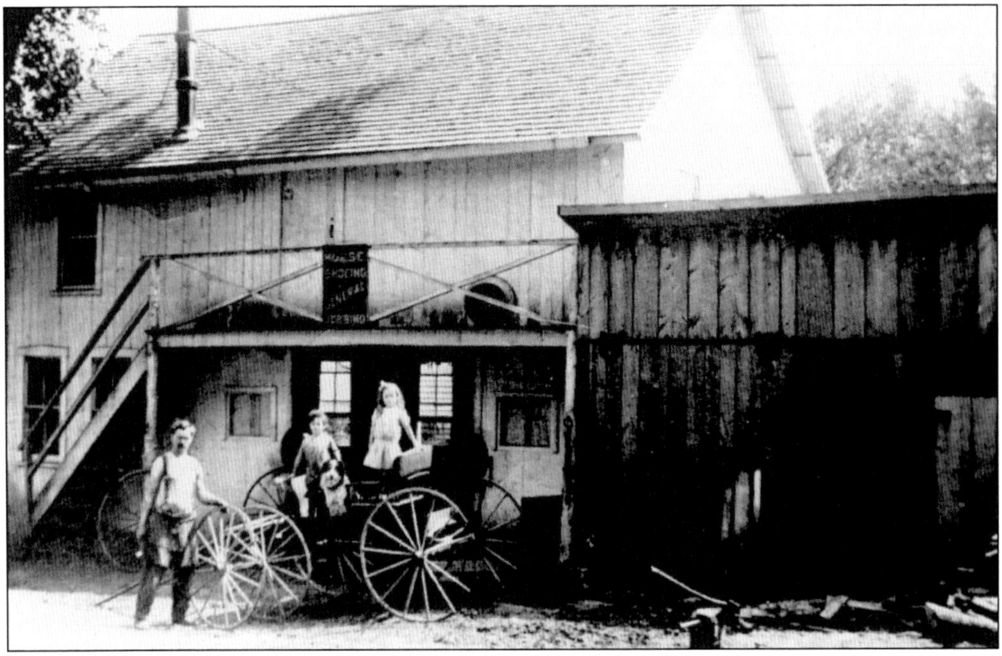

TIP HALL'S BLACKSMITH SHOP. Seen here are Tip Hall's daughter, Dorothy, and son, Gerald. Hall was a blacksmith in South Britain. The sign advertised horse shoeing and general "jobbing." In 1865, R.G. Squires had a wagon shop in Little York, which also included a wheelwright, sawmill, hat shop, and cider mill that operated in season. Wagon wheels were made from hickory trees found in local forests. The shop was on the east bank of the Pomperaug River. (ML.)

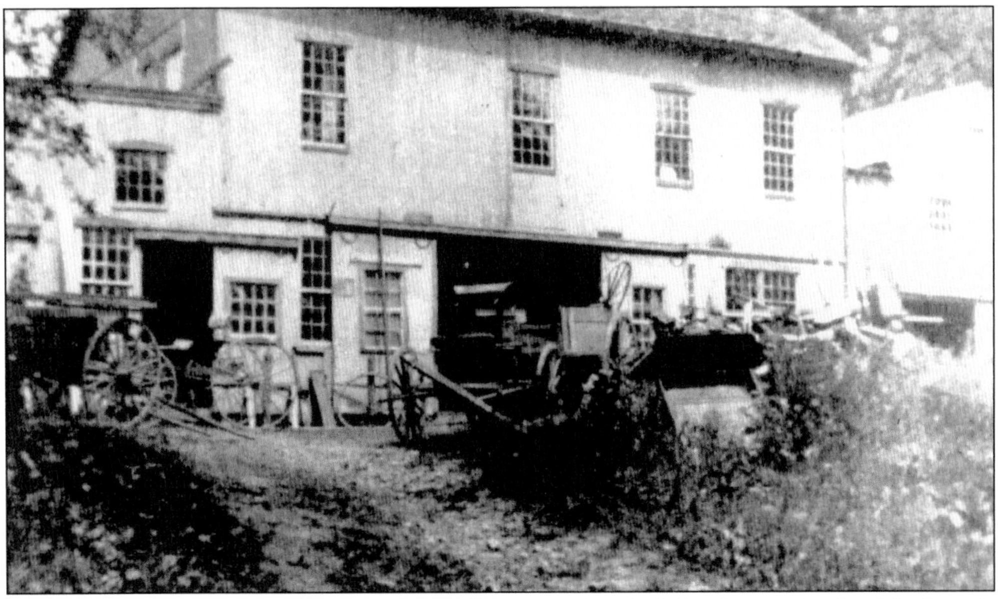

THE MUNSON BLACKSMITH SHOP IN SOUTH BRITAIN. The Bull family ran the first blacksmith shop in town. In the mid-1800s, a forge was operated for a short period of time on the Shepaug River for manufacturing iron. Difficulties were encountered because the iron ore had to be transported a long distance. Art McDonald also had another blacksmith shop, which was located on Main Street next to the funeral home. It was still operating in the 1950s. (SHS.)

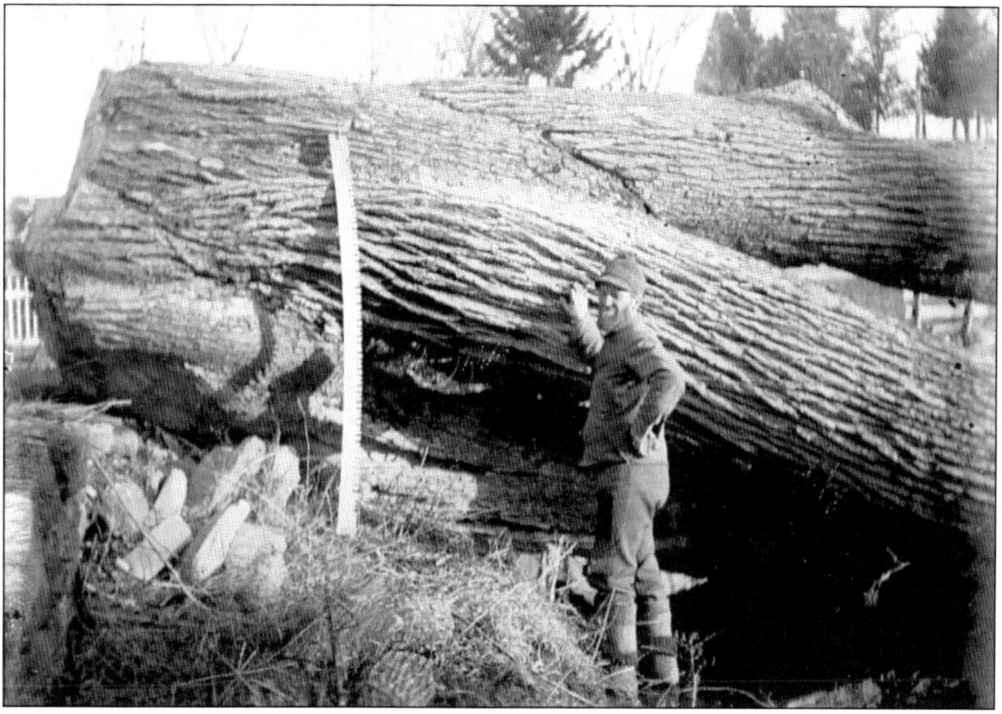

RAYMOND STILES. This photograph shows Stiles cutting wood *c.* 1900. In those days, there were no power tools, and everything was cut by hand. The elm tree in the picture was said to be more than 200 years old and was written about in New Haven *Register*. Farmers were paid $5, by the power company, for each chestnut tree they cut. The trees were used for electric poles, as chestnut trees were noted for their rot-resistant qualities and were often used as a sturdy, long-lasting building resource. In the early 1900s, there was a chestnut tree blight.(RC.)

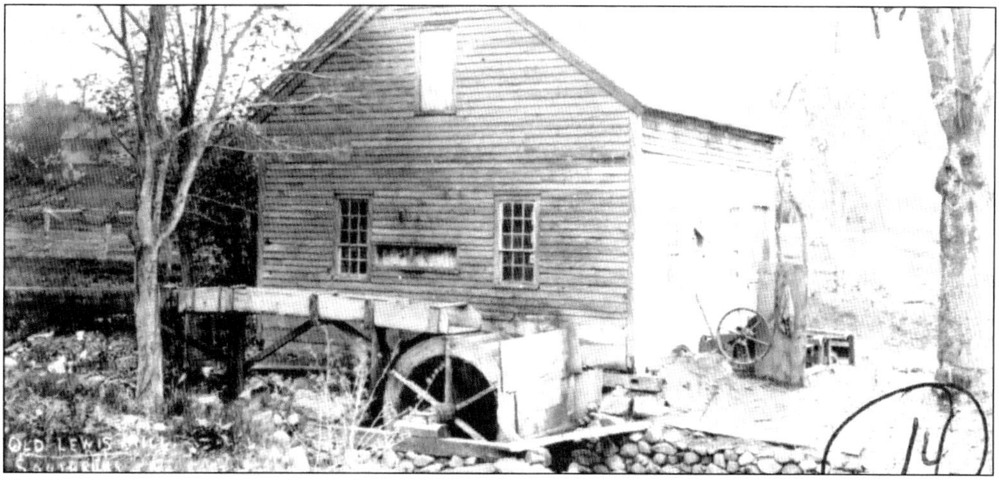

THE LEWIS-PERRY MILL. This mill was located where the current entrance of the Kmart plaza is. When the mill was dismantled, the wheel was sent to Sturbridge Village, Massachusetts. This mill (the Issac Lewis mill) was probably working as early as the 1830s. Its specialties included "yokes, also sawing, turning and general repairs to order." From the mid-1700s, the Lewises had a large farm on Kettletown and George's Hill Roads, including both a sawmill and charcoal pits. (SHS.)

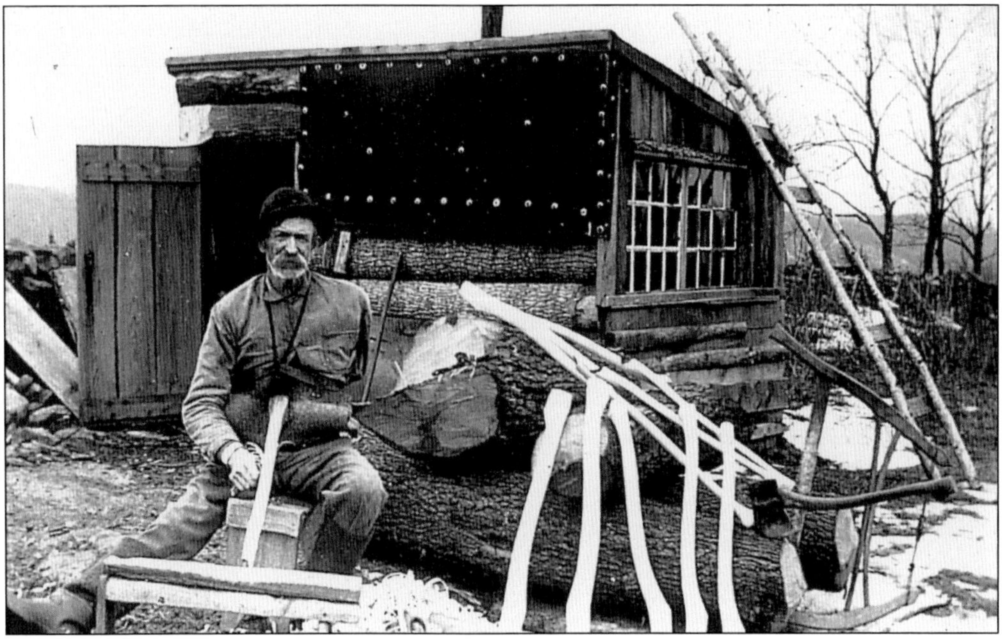

Wales Warner. Warner fashioned axe handles with a jack knife. Farmers needed to be farmers, builders, and repairman. Old tool inventories include a gouge, an old square, a narrow ax, a broad ax, timber chains, a nailing hammer, scythes, spades, riddles, cards, and iron wedges. Carpenters used what were called jacks—planes that they would take with them to their jobs. Since the plane was slapped on the surfaces that were being smoothed, the tool acquired the name "slapjack." (SHS.)

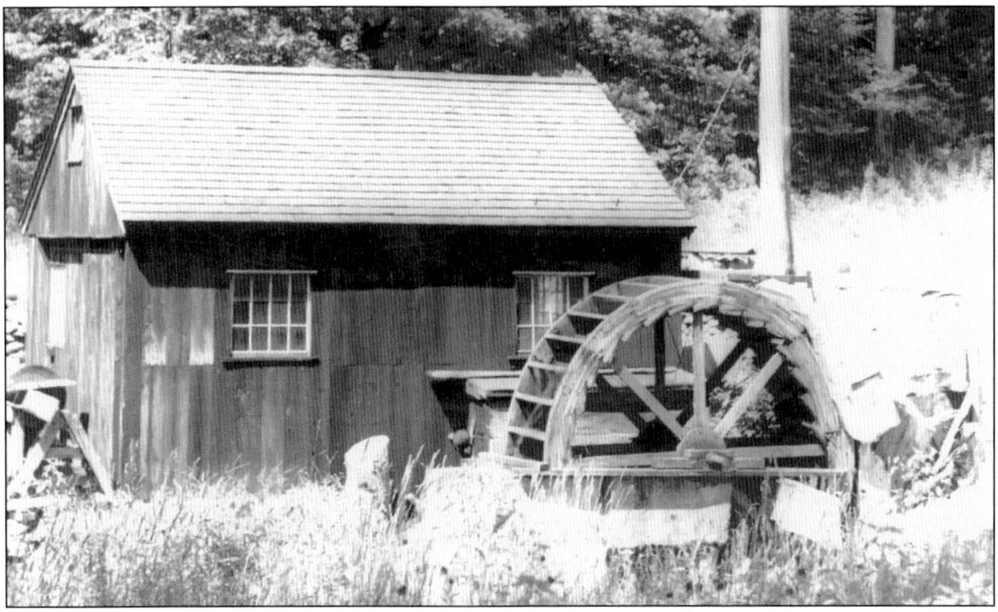

The Waterwheel on Community House Road. The town's focus on agriculture began to shift toward manufacturing in the 19th century. Waterpower helped to give birth to a series of manufacturers, which had a direct impact on the town's needs for service industries such as stores. (SHS.)

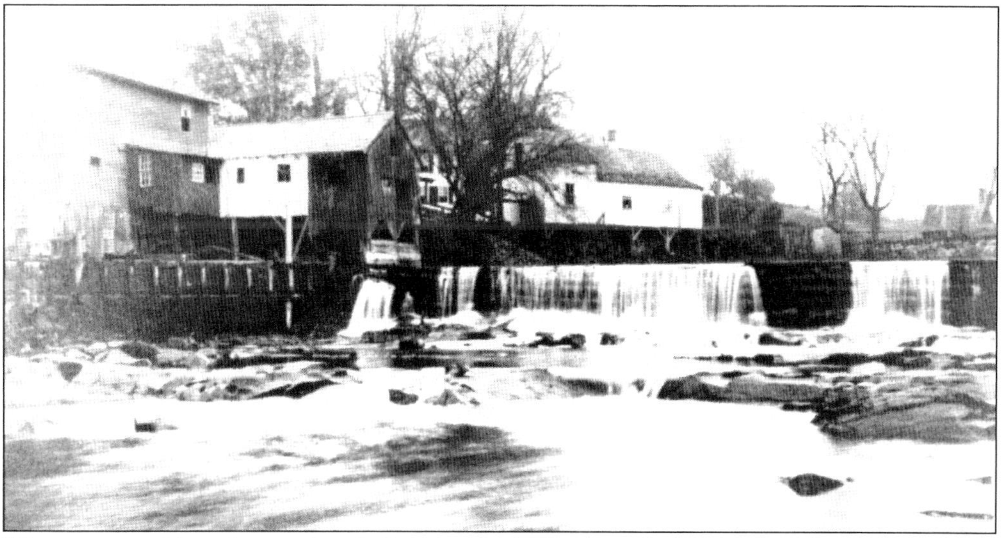

WATERPOWER. This dam in South Britain was located on the Pomperaug River. Water was diverted through the sluiceway. A nearby red-sandstone quarry was used for headstones and building stones. (SHS.)

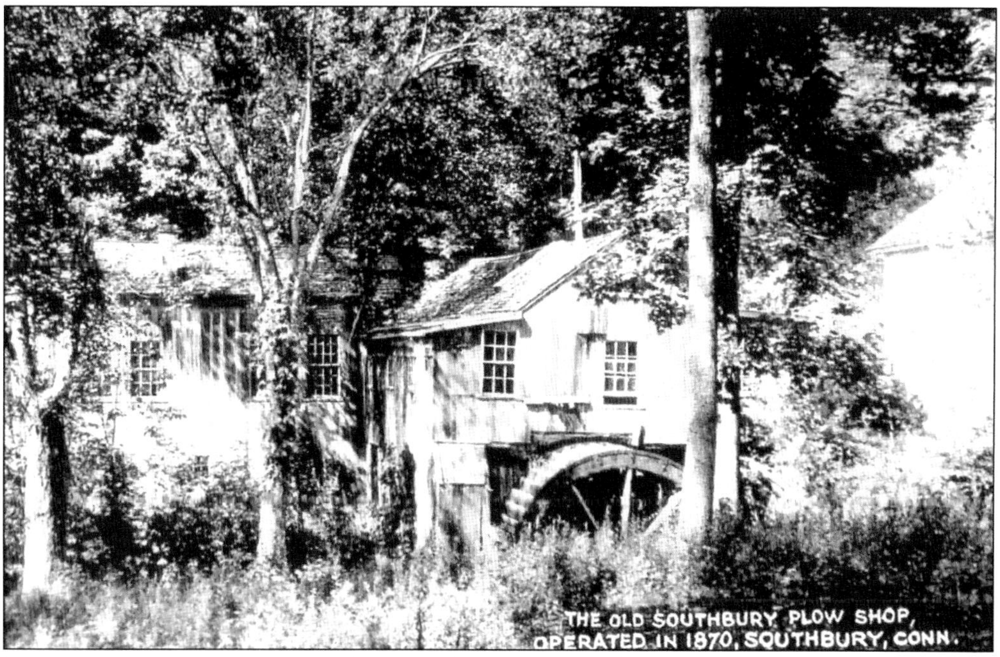

THE WAKELEY PLOW SHOP. The Wakeley Plow Shop was built next to Bullet Hill Brook. The shop made customized plows and included cultivators and other wrought-iron utensils. After the death of Charles Wakeley, the Wakeley Plow Shop became Charles Hine's shingle mill. It is still standing on Community House Road. From 1860 to 1870, Aaron Shelton operated both a sawmill and threshing mill here. (SHS.)

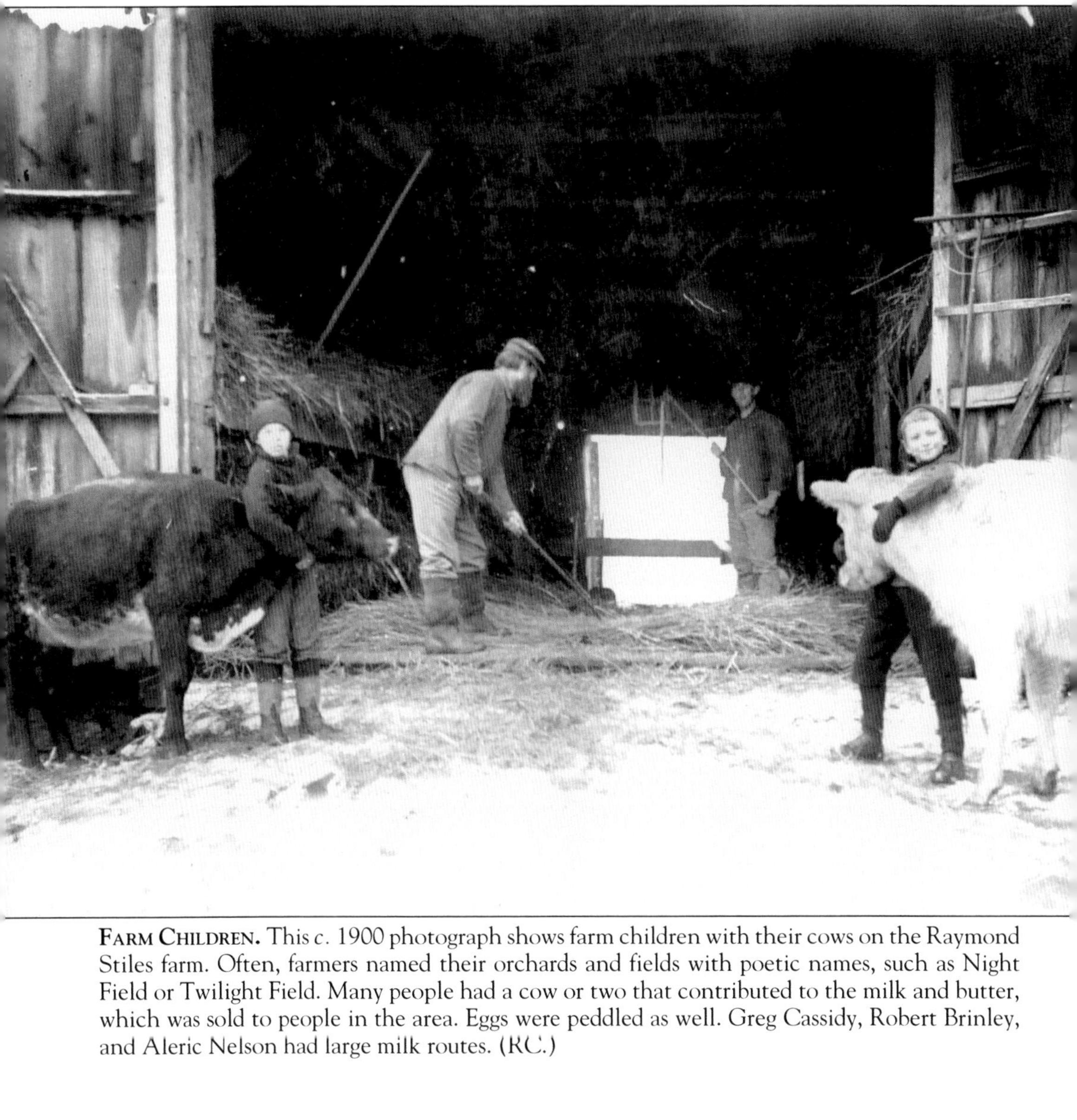

Farm Children. This *c.* 1900 photograph shows farm children with their cows on the Raymond Stiles farm. Often, farmers named their orchards and fields with poetic names, such as Night Field or Twilight Field. Many people had a cow or two that contributed to the milk and butter, which was sold to people in the area. Eggs were peddled as well. Greg Cassidy, Robert Brinley, and Aleric Nelson had large milk routes. (RC.)

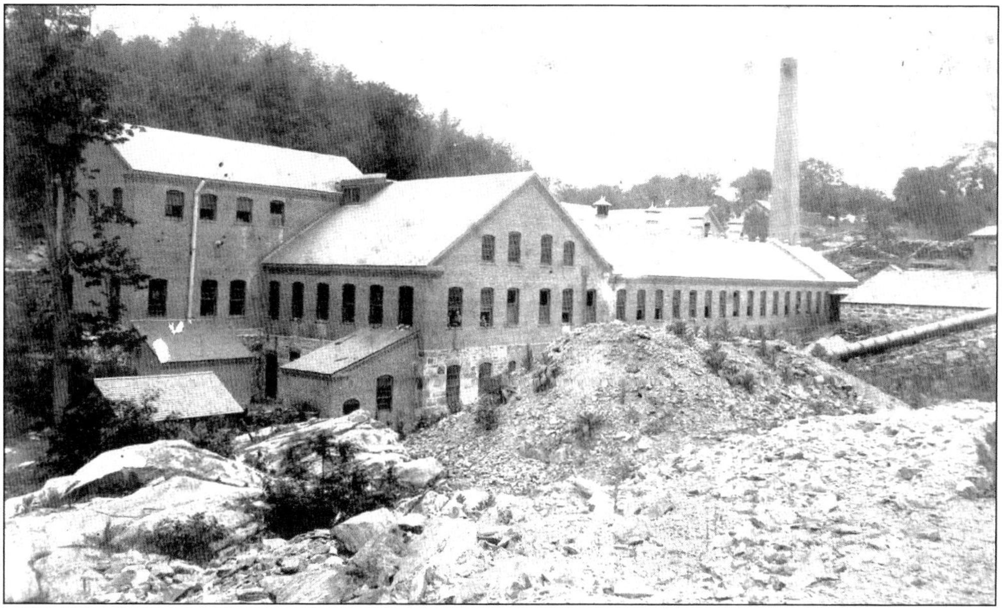

The Diamond Match Company. The Diamond Match Company's superintendent's house was the first in the surrounding areas to have electricity. The nearby dam powered it. The Diamond Match Company received supplies at the Southford station. Adam Lumm had a trip-hammer shop one-quarter mile downstream from the Diamond Match factory. (SHS.)

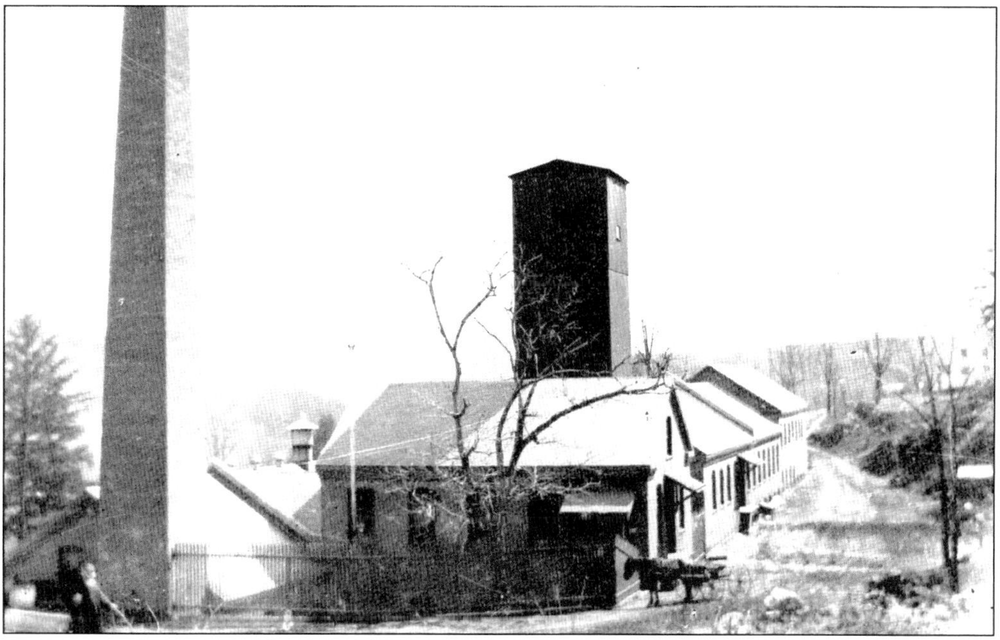

The Paper Company. The Southford Paper Company was started in 1882 with a new brick mill, slate roof, and modern equipment. The cost was $200,000, which was a very large sum at the time. Plain board was produced for use by several match companies. The company went bankrupt and was closed for 13 years, until the Diamond Match Company purchased the property. After making some improvements to the plant, they manufactured paperboard for matchbooks until 1923, when the building burned down. (SHS.)

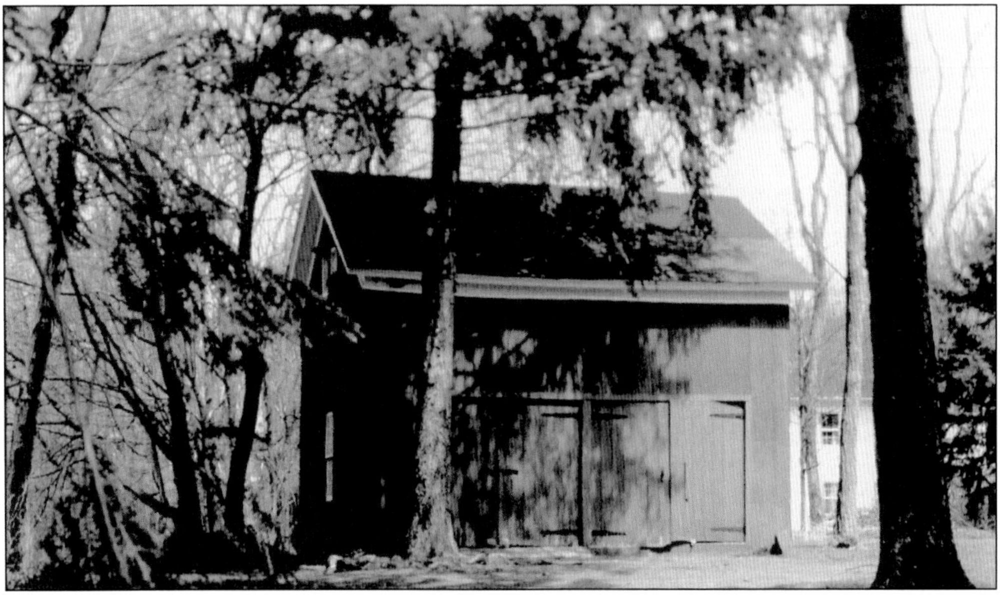

The Hat Shop in South Britain. Danbury was not the only town that made hats. Following the War of 1812, hat shops started to spring up many places. Judson Manville had a shop in Kettletown. He moved the shop to South Britain on the Pomperaug River. Working in a hat shop was dangerous. The chemicals used in the tanning process were absorbed through the workers' skin. Many workers were poisoned in this industry and became "mad as a hatter." (SHS.)

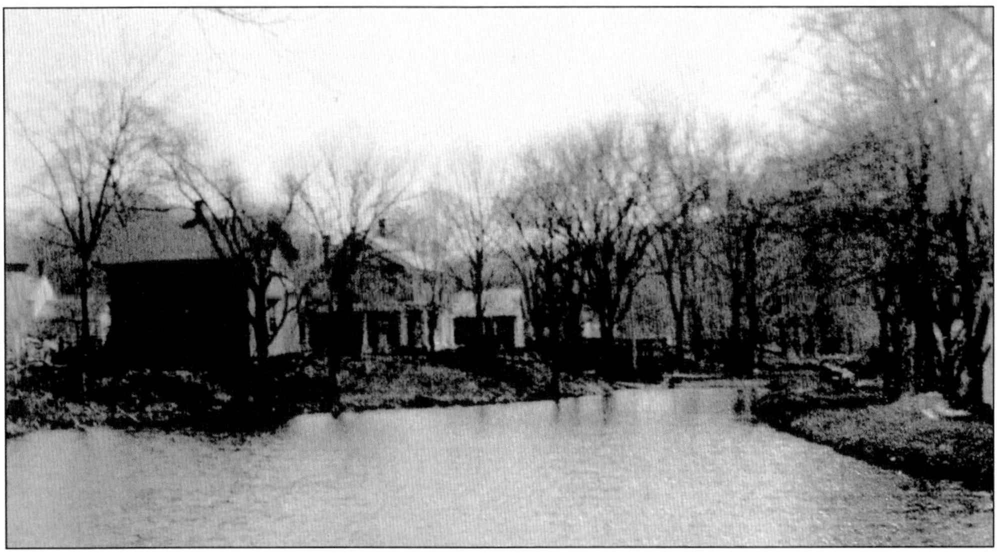

The Pond in South Britain. In this photograph is the pond, which no longer exists, and the ice house behind the South Britain School. In 1833, the South Britain Water Company started, hoping to attract more companies to the area. The water company was established to provide electricity and waterpower with a 40-acre lake and canal system. Chief owners Erastmus and Sidney Pierce renamed the project Lake Disappointment, as a questionable leak made an embankment give way when the lake was being filled. (SHS.)

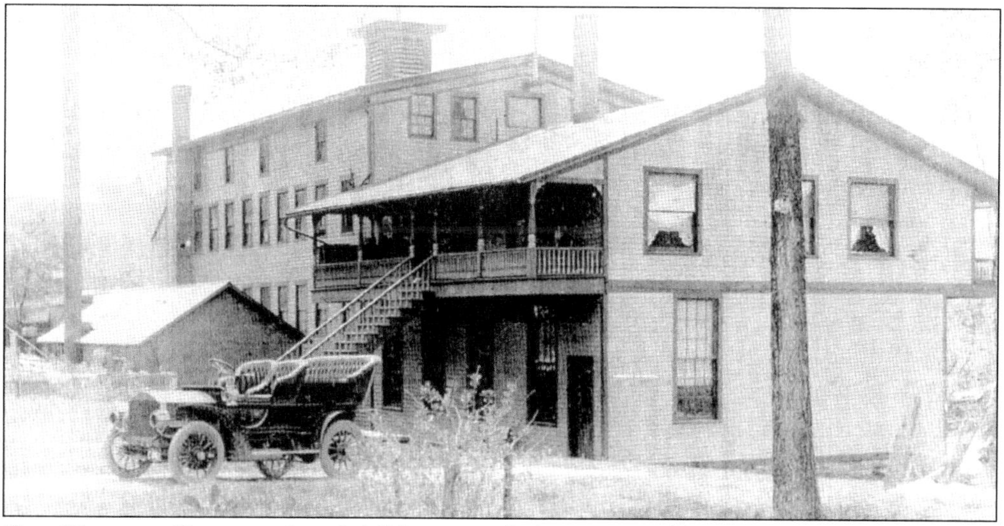

The Hawkins Factory. Local folklore stated that you could not find a trap in Canada that did not have South Britain written on it. The Hawkins Company was incorporated with $9,000 capital. Trapping animals was a source of income to many settlers. The animals were skinned for their fur, which was then processed by clothing manufacturers for coats and hats. Beavers, in particular, were in great demand for the male top hats that were fashionable at the time. (SHS.)

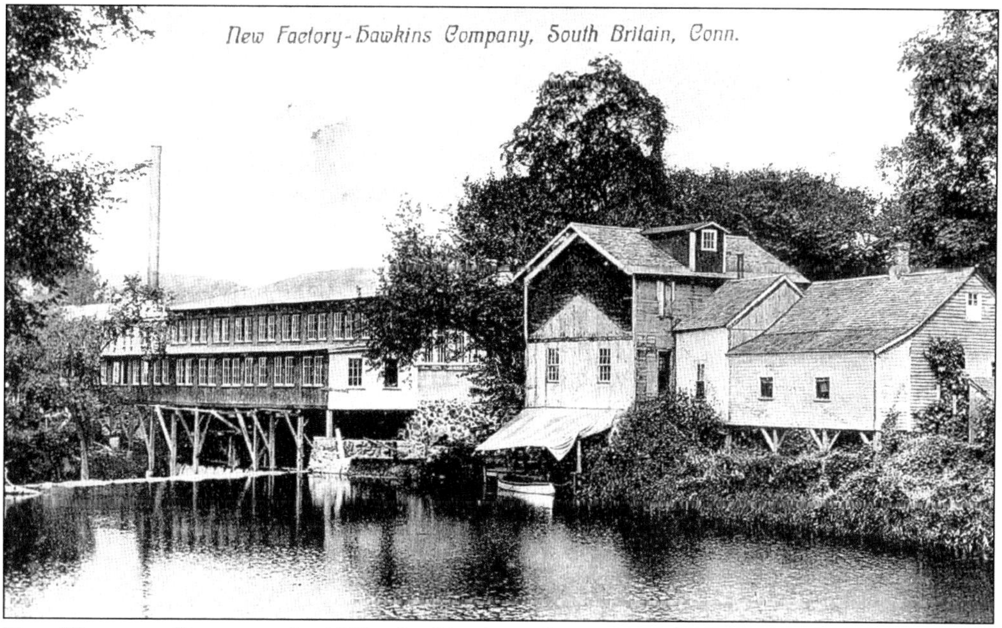

The Hawkins Company. In 1895, the Hawkins Company, which made tacks and buttons, merged with the Blake and Lamb Company. A new home was created in the Bradley woolen mill in South Britain. Initially, it was water powered with a canal system. In 1899, Hawkins co- bought the Bradley and Hoyt woolen mill in South Britain with the idea of having adequate waterpower rights. Hawkins also purchased the bankrupt South Britain Water Company property. The floods of 1955 destroyed the canal system. (SHS.)

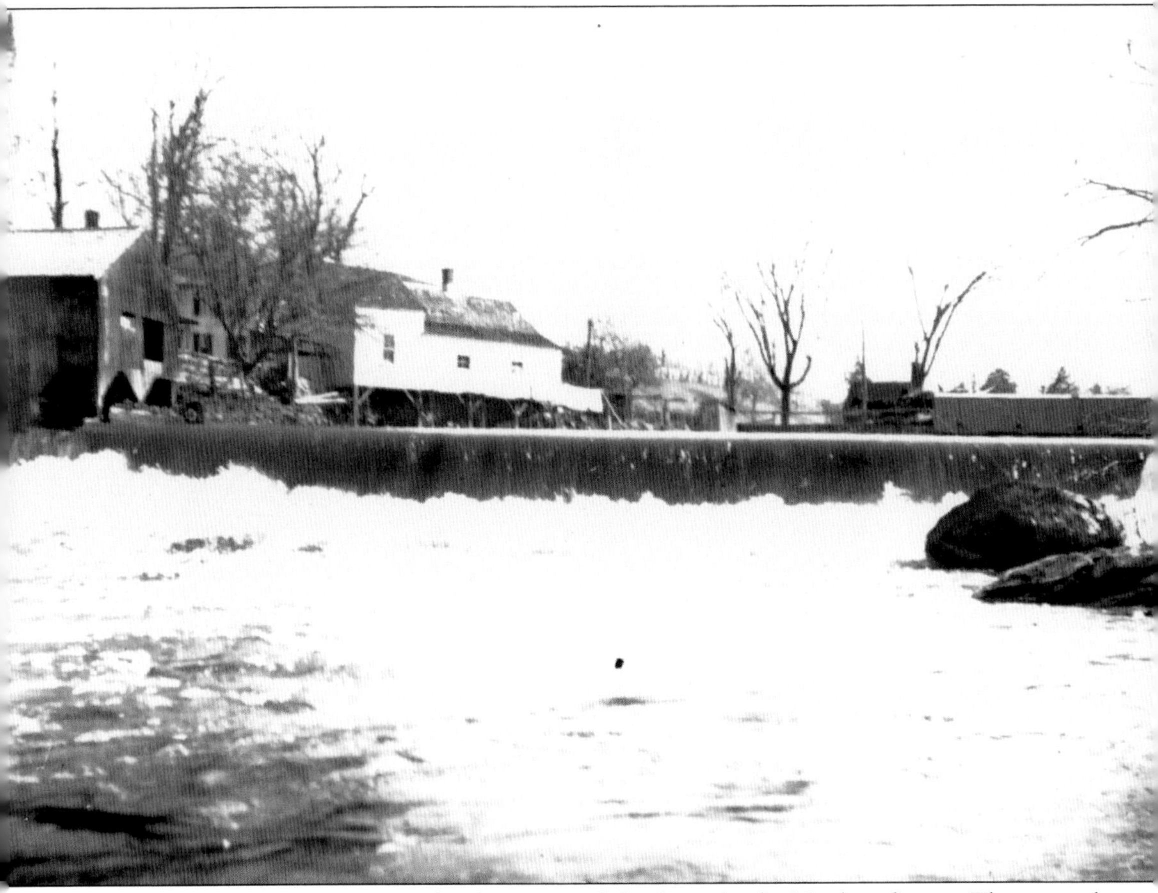

The Dam in South Britain. This dam powered the flume for the Hawkins factory. The original dam was wooden, and a stone dam was built in front of it later. The dam had a sluiceway to power factories and led into a pond that later fed Lake Disappointment. In 1955, a flood knocked down part of the dam. (RC.)

Five

At Play

I finished my dress and washed and ironed it with my other things. . . .
At seven I dressed for the dance and a little later J. Mitchell
came over with Sarah Osborn and I went in the carriage with them to Woodbury
to the ball. I danced thirteen or fourteen times. . . . The ball was over at two.
—the Julia Evelina Smith diaries, October 1814 to February 1817. (CHS.)

Southbury has always made time for leisure, from activities and sports to simply enjoying the many natural sites.

Today, there are many scenic local and state parks and recreational areas that attract visitors. Some of these include Southford Falls, Lake Lillinonah, Lake Zoar, Kettletown Park , the Bent of the River Audubon Center, and Waldo State Park.

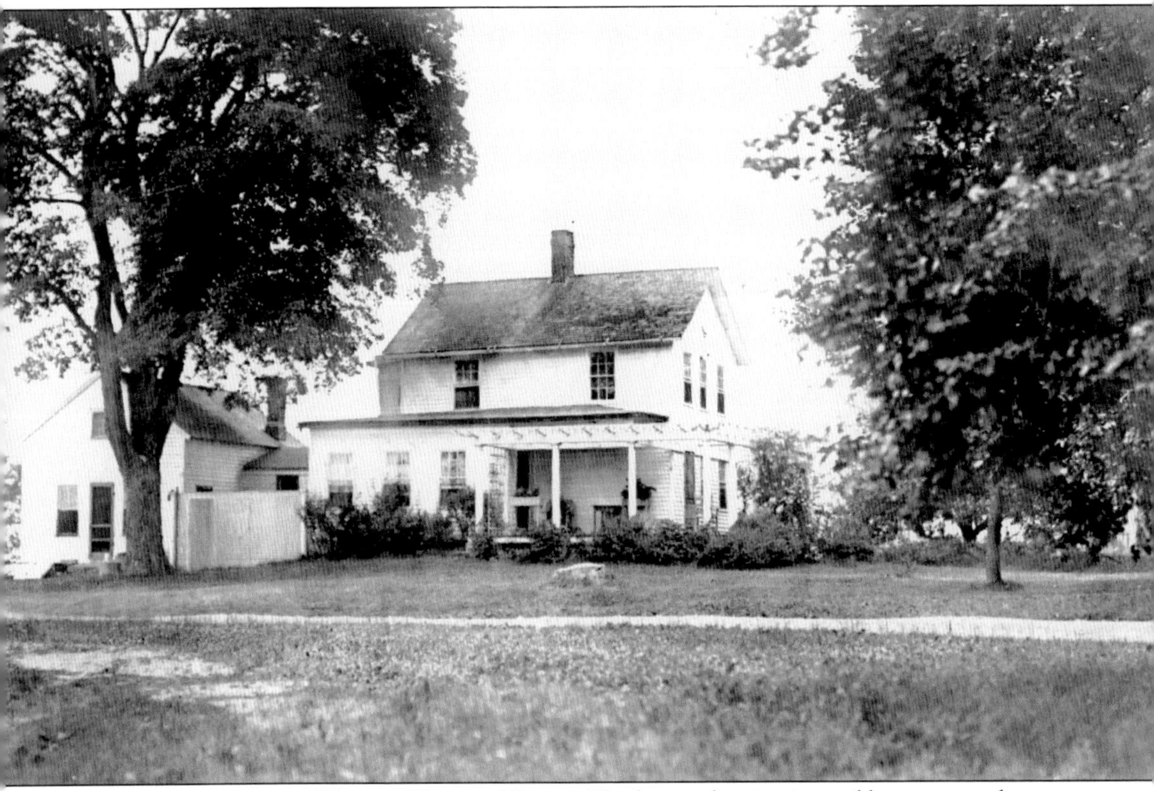

THE ADELAIDE AND HAROLD HICOCK HOUSE. The house that is pictured here sat on the corner of Pine Hill Road and Main Street, where the United Church of Christ Green is today. It was the location of the Pergola Tea House. Adelaide Hicock was an independent businesswoman who ran the business herself. When men were arrested from the Bund, they were taken here to see the town prosecutor, Harold Hicock, who owned the home at the time. Guests came from around the world. It is said that a dignitary from Canton, China, made a stop here. Maypole dances were also held here. The house is now gone. (SHS.)

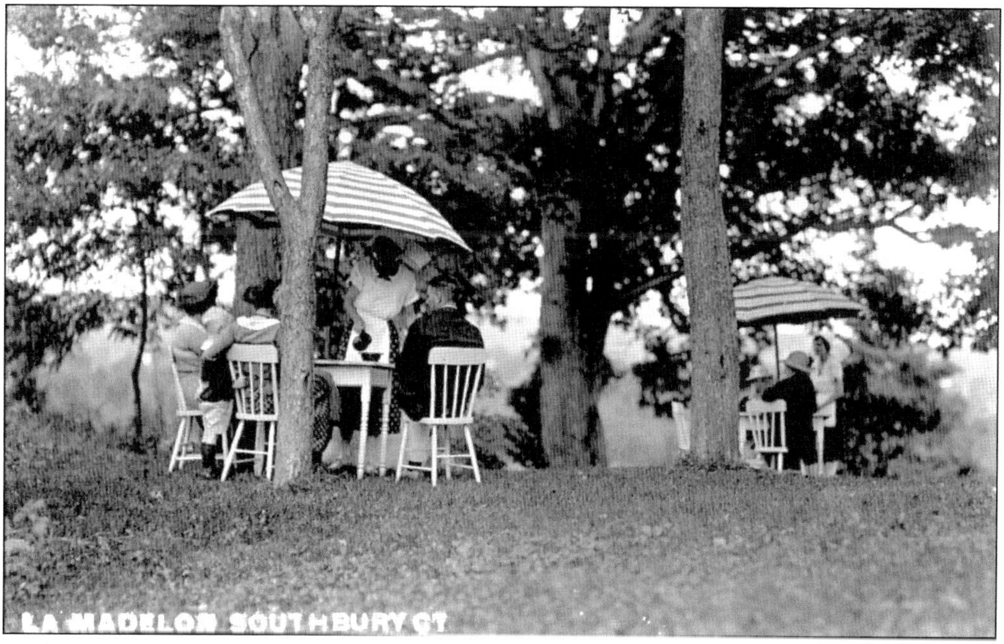

LA MADELON COFFEE RESTAURANT. The picture shows a sophisticated coffee restaurant of yesteryear. It was open from June 19 to October 1. Patrons were offered afternoon tea and cool drinks, as well as dinner by appointment. The restaurant advertisement featured it as a perfect stop between Danbury and Waterbury. (TL.)

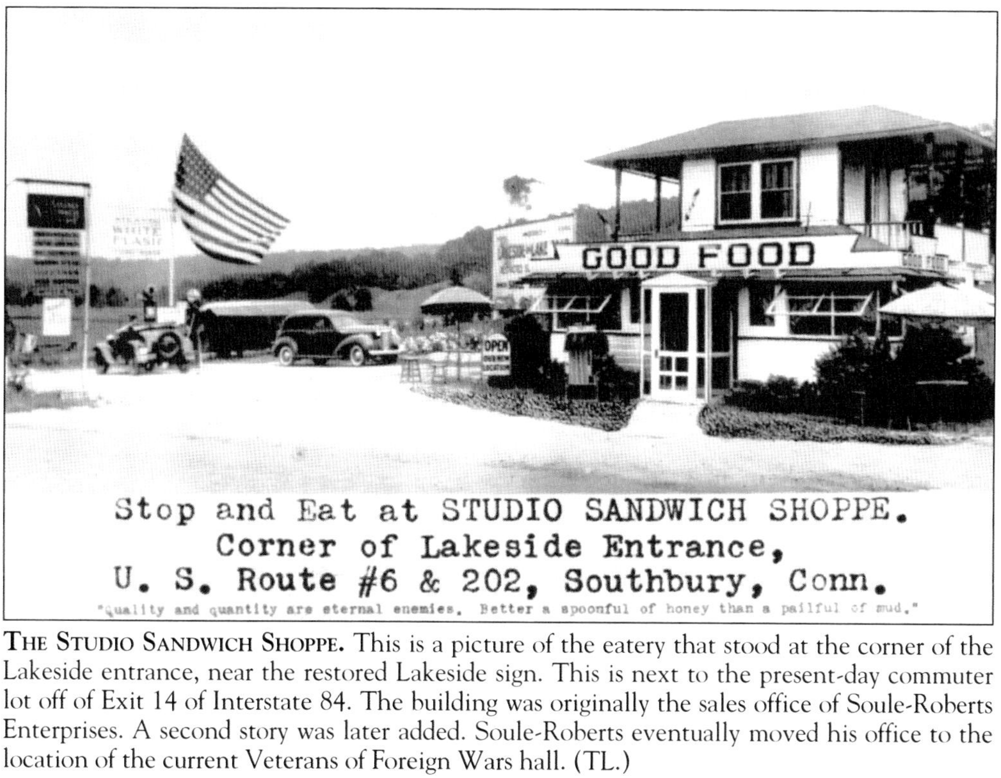

THE STUDIO SANDWICH SHOPPE. This is a picture of the eatery that stood at the corner of the Lakeside entrance, near the restored Lakeside sign. This is next to the present-day commuter lot off of Exit 14 of Interstate 84. The building was originally the sales office of Soule-Roberts Enterprises. A second story was later added. Soule-Roberts eventually moved his office to the location of the current Veterans of Foreign Wars hall. (TL.)

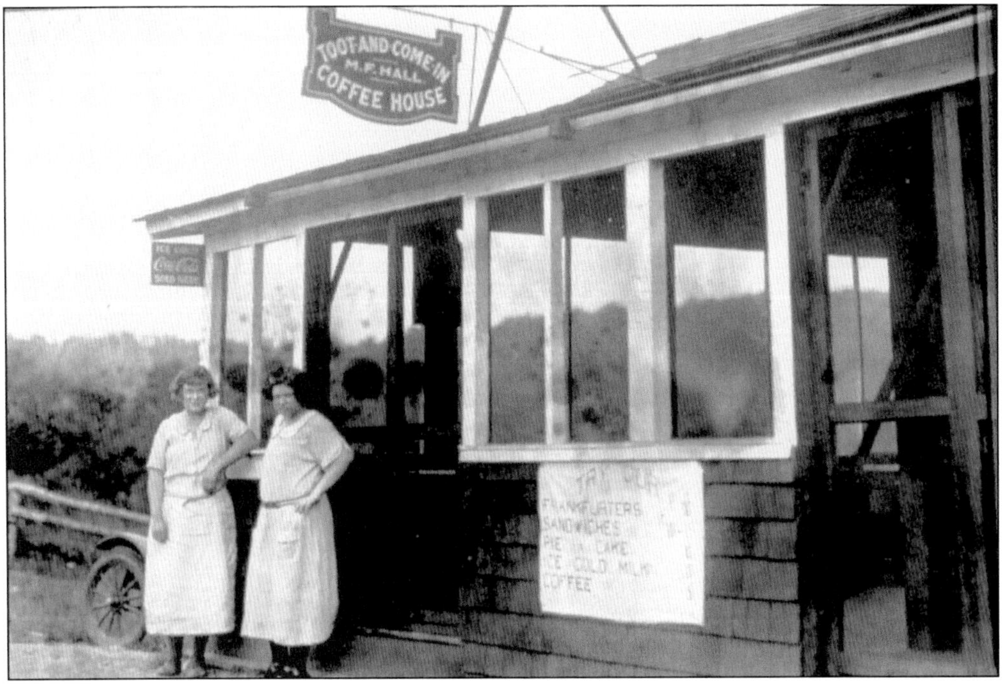

Ma Hall's Toot and Come In. This picture shows the local bar run by Ma Hall on Route 6 by Lake Zoar. It was closed in the 1940s. The sign indicates that frankfurters were 10¢, sandwiches 10¢ and 15¢, milk 10¢, and coffee 5¢. The building is currently a private home. (SHS.)

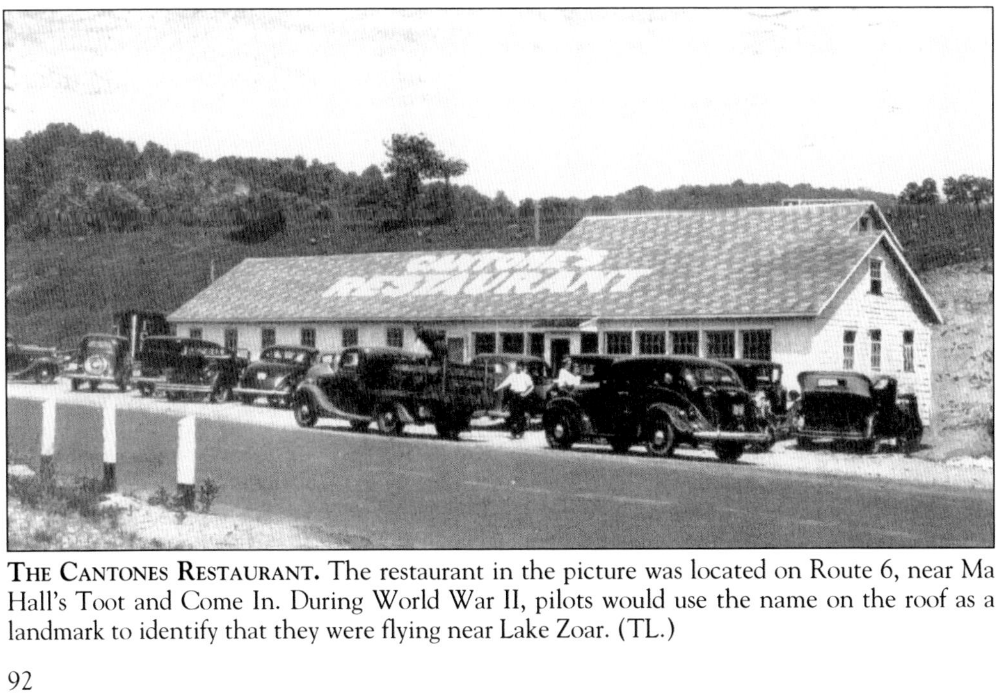

The Cantones Restaurant. The restaurant in the picture was located on Route 6, near Ma Hall's Toot and Come In. During World War II, pilots would use the name on the roof as a landmark to identify that they were flying near Lake Zoar. (TL.)

AN ADVERTISEMENT. The picture shows an advertisement for the Oak Tree Hotel and Restaurant. It states that the Oak Tree is "a smart restaurant" with "popular prices" and serves "choice wines and liquors." (TL.)

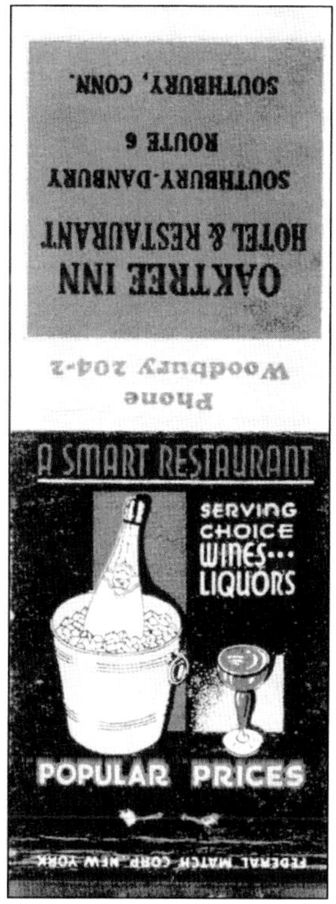

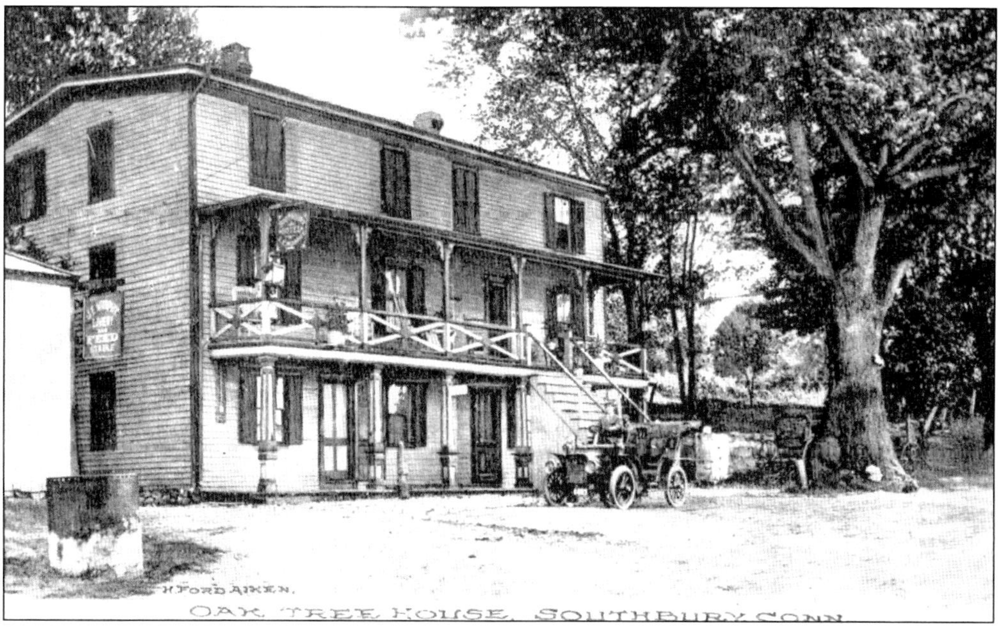

THE OAK TREE INN. During World War II, gas was rationed, and townsfolk frequented the inn because it was within walking distance. At that time, the Kelly family owned the inn. Meals featured included "Seafood in season, steaks and chops, chicken and Welsh Rarebit." Prior owners included Sidney Oliver, in 1912. A livery was also housed here. (SHS.)

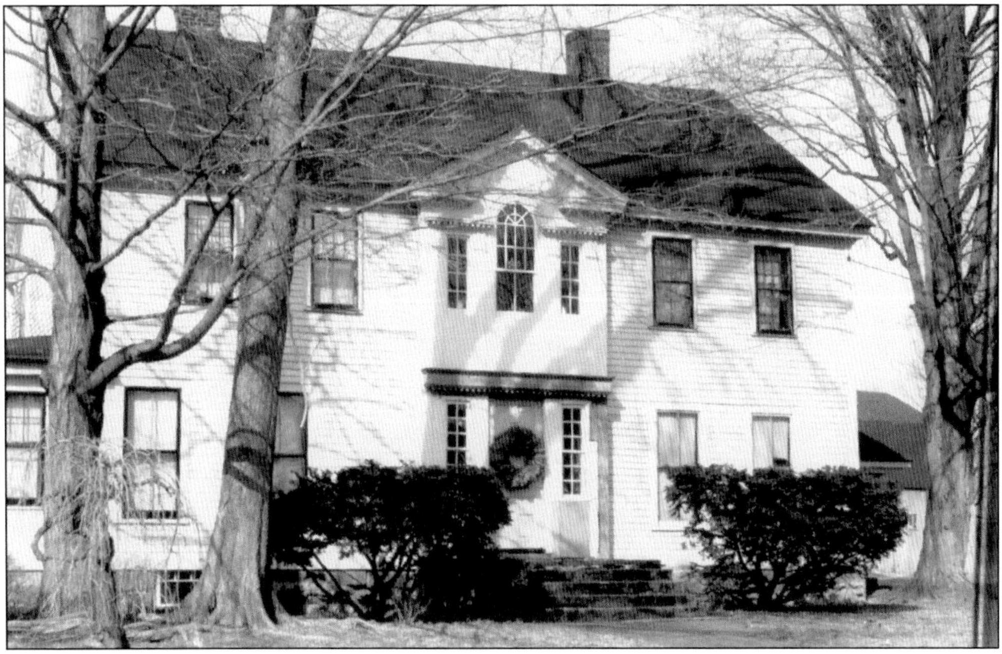

THE OATMAN HOTEL IN SOUTHFORD. This picture shows the old Oatman Hotel. Southford served as a midway stop on the turnpike between New Haven and Litchfield. Because of this, hotels were built there and well utilized. George Thompson built the Oatman Hotel in 1806. It was used as stagecoach stop for many years. Later on, it became the Fenn-Brock Dairy. In 1800, the Bartholomew Hotel, a long one-story house, became another nearby resting spot. Yet another patronized establishment was the Sherwood House. (SHS.)

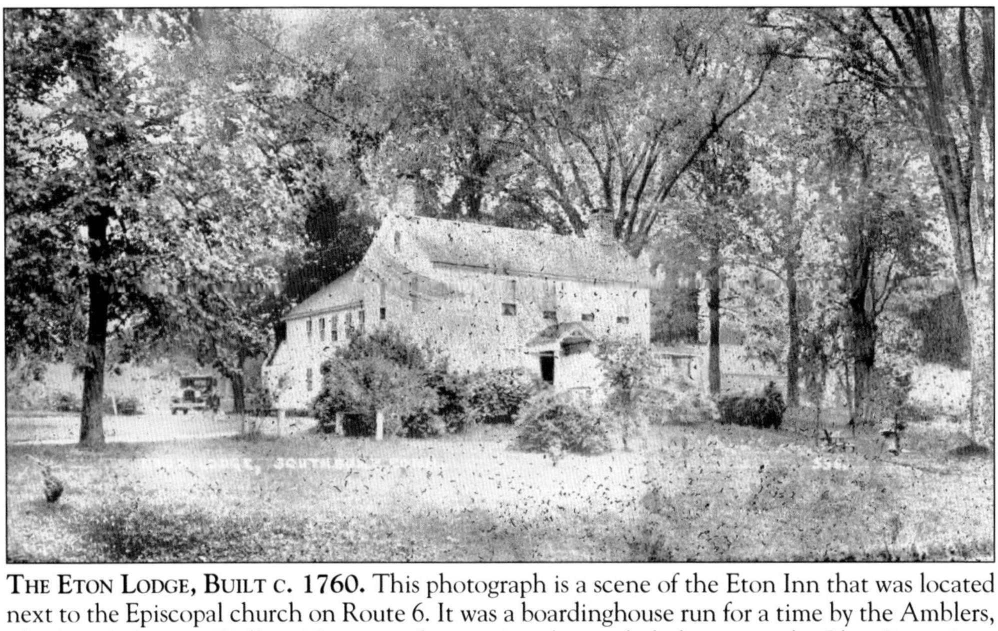

THE ETON LODGE, BUILT c. 1760. This photograph is a scene of the Eton Inn that was located next to the Episcopal church on Route 6. It was a boardinghouse run for a time by the Amblers, who boarded many Wallace Nutting colorists. Another early lodging was the Blue Goose Inn, which was built on Hull's Hill Road prior to 1800. It served as a restaurant for Southford mill workers and as a stagecoach stop. (TL.)

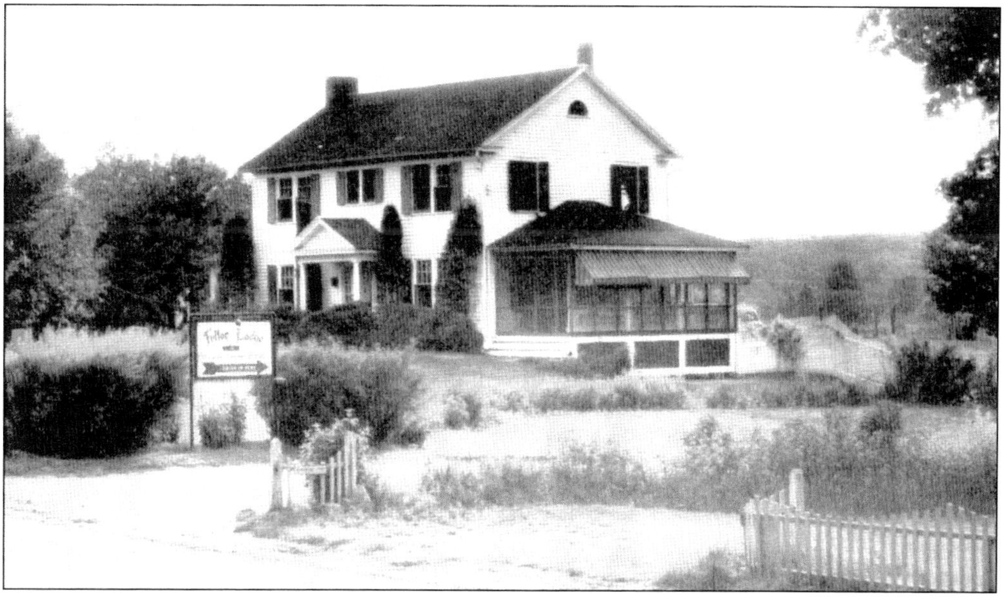

THE FULTON LODGE. This postcard shows the Fulton Inn that was located in front of the present site of Food Center. Fulton's advertisement read, "Situated in the town of Southbury, a typical New England Village, overlooking the beautiful Berkshire Hills on Route 6 & 202. 12 miles from Waterbury, 17 miles from Danbury, 38 miles from Hartford and 75 miles from New York City. Room rates $1 and $1.50. Free garage and afternoon tea." The lodge was previously known as the Oriole Inn. (TL.)

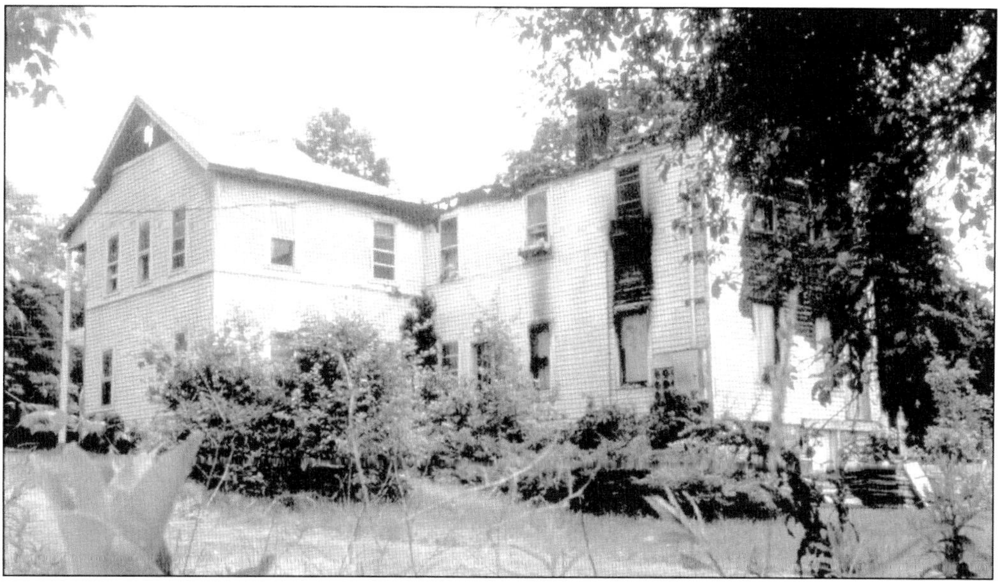

THE SOUTHFORD LODGE AFTER A FIRE IN THE LATE 1990S. This photograph shows the ruins of the old lodge after the fire. It was known as Boardman's Hotel and had been constructed in the early 1800s. It first functioned as a forge and was used by blacksmiths. The building became an inn after a second floor was added. It later became a tavern that served railroad passengers and was reputed to house a brothel. It has since been restored and houses a restaurant and several shops. (SHS.)

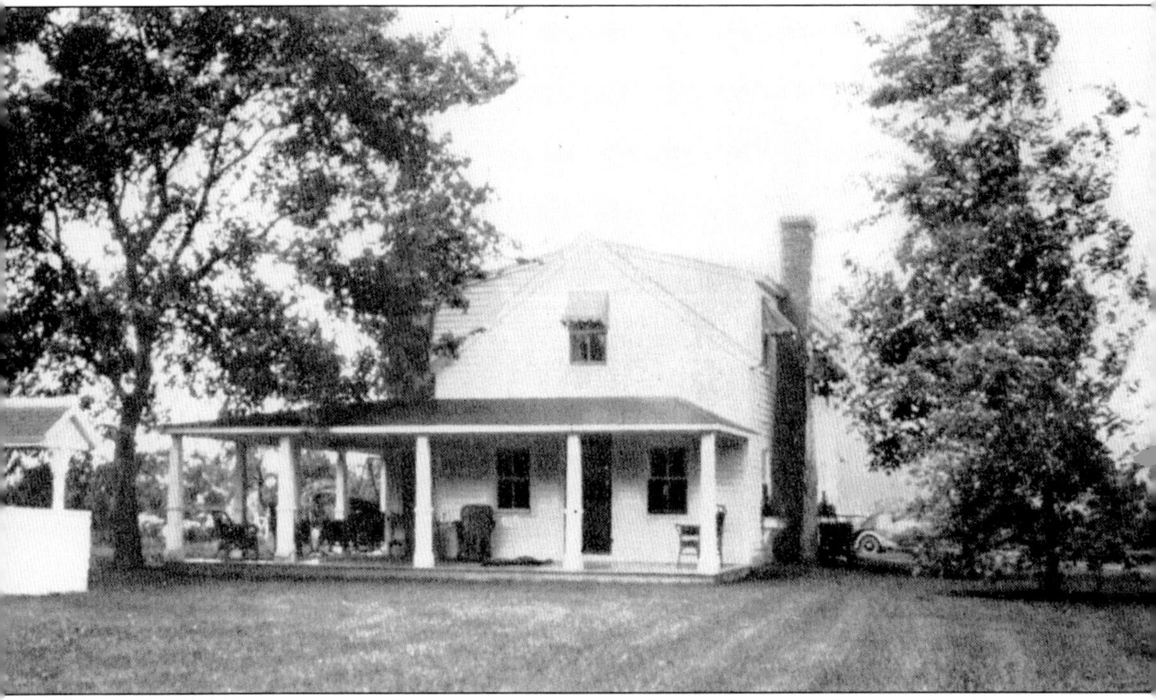

THE OLD HUNDRED INN. This picture shows the Old Hundred Inn. It opened *c.* 1933 as the summer home of the Browns. Over 80,000 meals were served from March 1939 to December 1939. In 1940, the Old Hundred Ice Cream Company started nearby. It was one of the first providers of packaged ice cream to food stores and other markets and restaurants in the tri-state area. Prior to this time, you could only buy ice cream at drug stores and confectionaries. (SHS.)

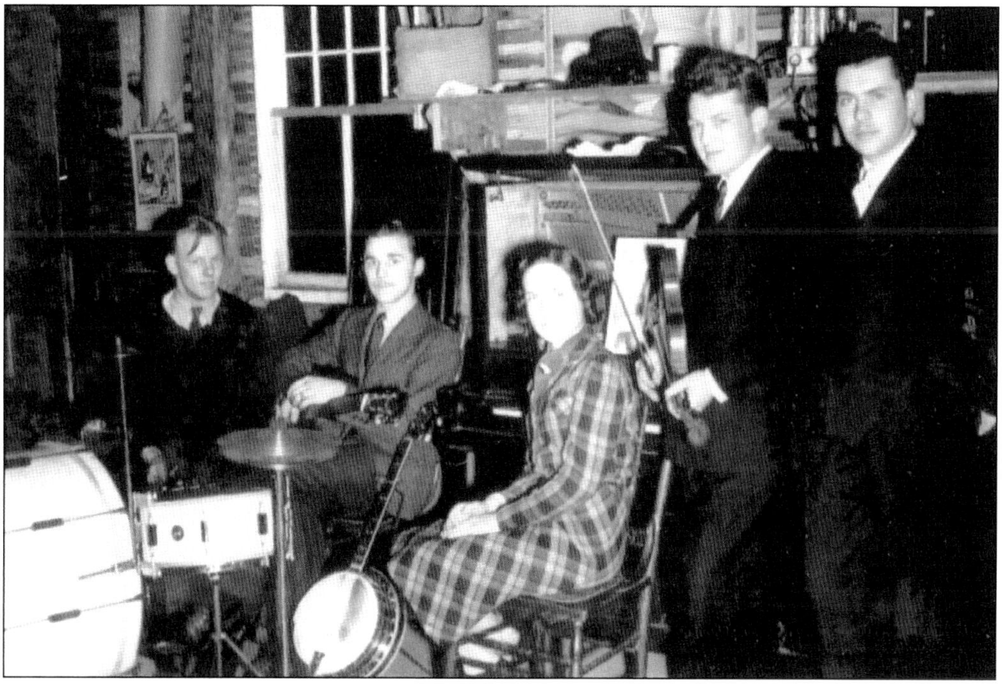

The Southbury Bills Square-Dance Band. This 1938 photograph shows one of the bands that was made up of locals. Included in the shot are Harold Doolittle, Ray Magas, Jim Norton, George Norton, and Bill Lautenschlager. Many people got together to play in bands as a form of entertainment. (TL.)

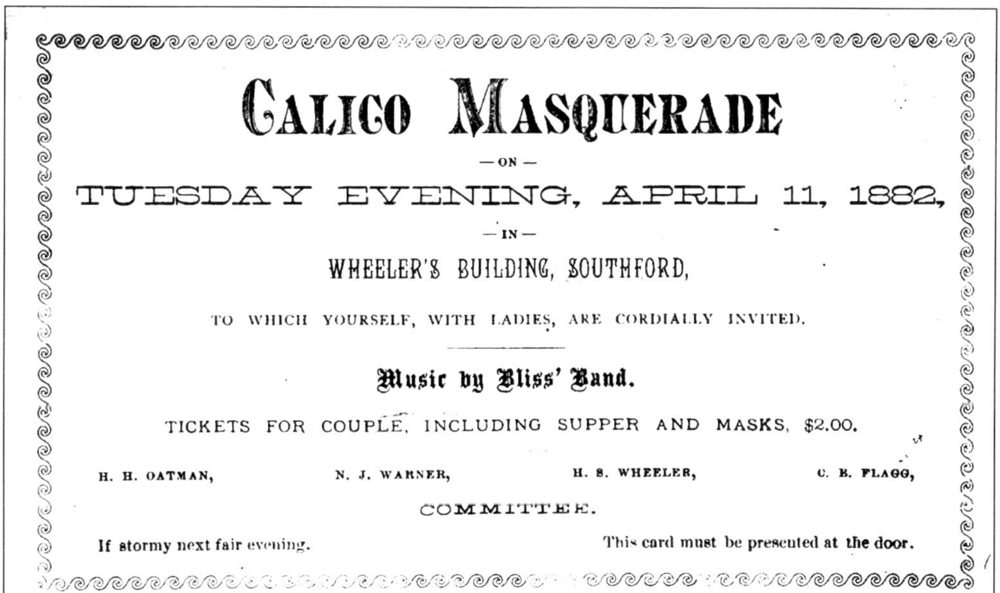

CALICO MASQUERADE

—ON—

TUESDAY EVENING, APRIL 11, 1882,

—IN—

WHEELER'S BUILDING, SOUTHFORD,

TO WHICH YOURSELF, WITH LADIES, ARE CORDIALLY INVITED.

Music by Bliss' Band.

TICKETS FOR COUPLE, INCLUDING SUPPER AND MASKS, $2.00.

H. H. OATMAN, N. J. WARNER, H. S. WHEELER, C. B. FLAGG,

COMMITTEE.

If stormy next fair evening. This card must be presented at the door.

A Calico Masquerade Invitation. Seen is a copy of an invitation for a masquerade party. It was to be held on Tuesday evening, April 11, 1882. Music was from the Bliss Band. The supper and dance cost just $2. (TL.)

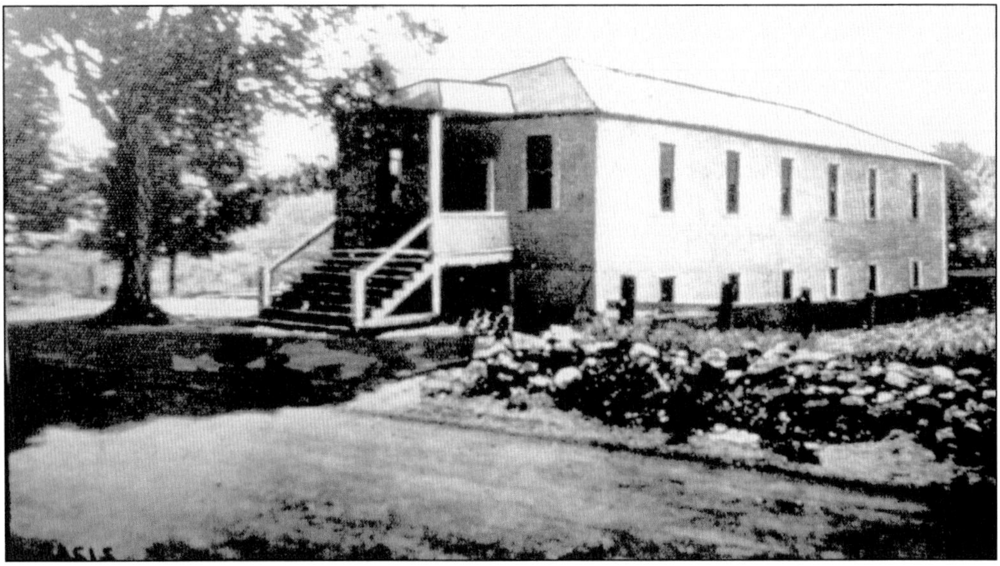

THE GRANGE HALL ON COMMUNITY HOUSE ROAD IN THE EARLY 1900S. The Grange was one of the most important organizations in a farming town. This hall was built from the lumber of houses that were torn down when the Stevenson Dam was built. Connecticut Light and Power allowed people to take the wood before houses were burned down. The building had a stage and held weekly square dancing, as well as plays, dances, and receptions. The Grange was also known as the Southbury Community Club. At one time, it served as the Southbury post office due to fire at the post office's previous location. Granges were developed as farmers' organizations in 1867 to bring together isolated farmers for education and social functions. The national organization was instrumental in the passage of the Granger laws of 1870s, securing public regulation of railroads and grain elevators. (SHS.)

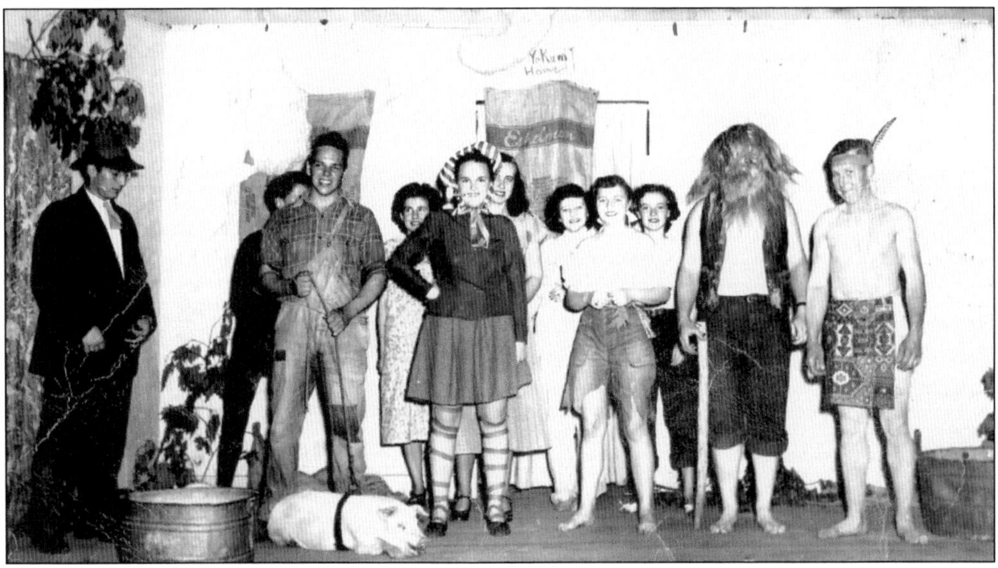

A GRANGE PLAY. This 1948 photograph shows locals hamming it up at the local Grange. Seen here are, from left to right, two unidentified people, Don Terrell, Lucille Grisgraber, June Moeller, Gladys Tschauder, Esther Coe, Katie Coe, Cynthia Weasa, Walt Harrison, and W.R. Cromwell. (RC.)

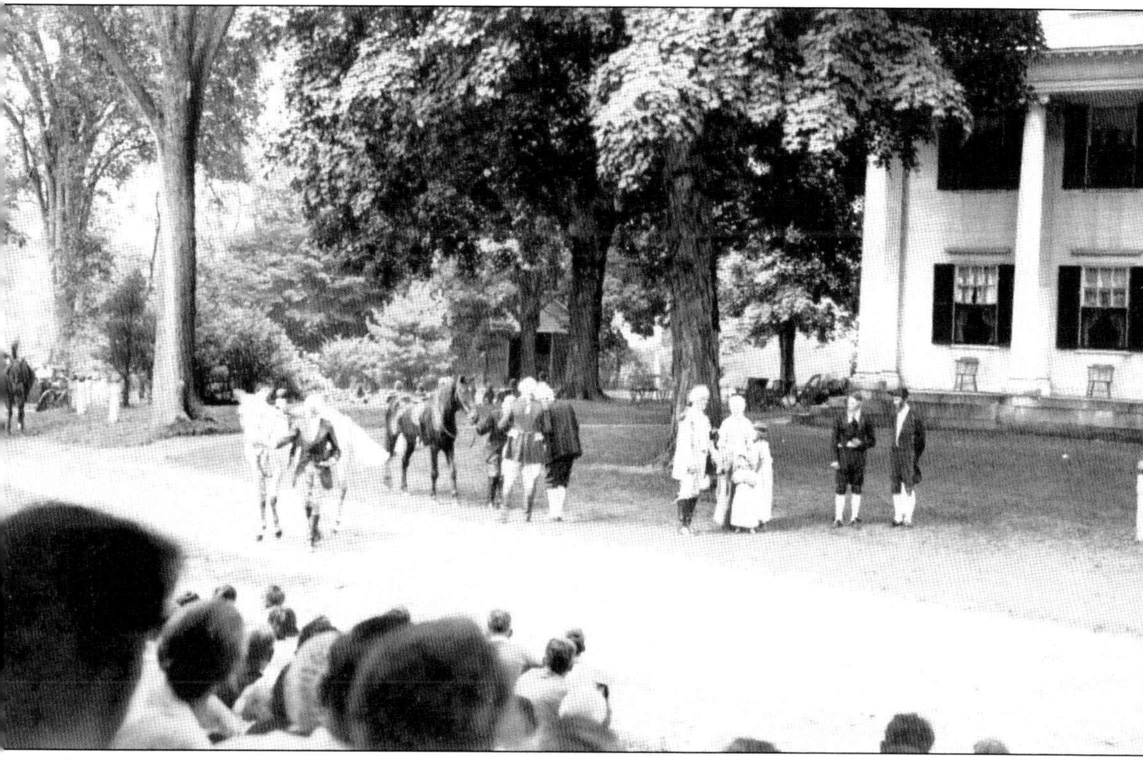

GEORGE WASHINGTON'S BICENTENNIAL CELEBRATION. This photograph shows the commemoration of Gen. George Washington and the bicentennial celebration in 1932. The festivity was complete with a parade and floats. A pageant was also held with descendants of old Southbury families. A white oak tree was planted for the occasion at the Episcopal church, and a military dance given by the Veterans of Foreign Wars took place afterward. George Washington rode through Southbury on September 19, 1780. (RC.)

THERE
IS
ONE STORE

THAT everybody likes, that everybody warms up to. Because everything that you buy is reliable. And the prices are always lowest for honest goods.

All through the month of August we shall be selling cheaper than ever; mark-down prices in every department—SAVING prices. It'll pay any one to do their buying NOW.

THE D. M. READ CO.,
BRIDGEPORT, CONN.

Social ∻ Hop,

Town Hall,

Southbury, = = Conn.

Committee of Arrangements:

A. F. STILES. E. G. AMBLER.

A SOCIAL HOP PROGRAM. Seen here is a dance card. The dance was sponsored by the D.M. Read Company in Bridgeport. Dances included many types, from the Sicilian circle to the two step, quadrille, lancers, waltz, polka, and Caledonian styles. Hawkins, who owned the Hawkins factory, which employed many local citizens, used to have dances and many other social activities for the employees and for the Wallace Nutting studio girls, who worked as colorists for his photographs. He had a bowling alley upstairs in his factory. (RC.)

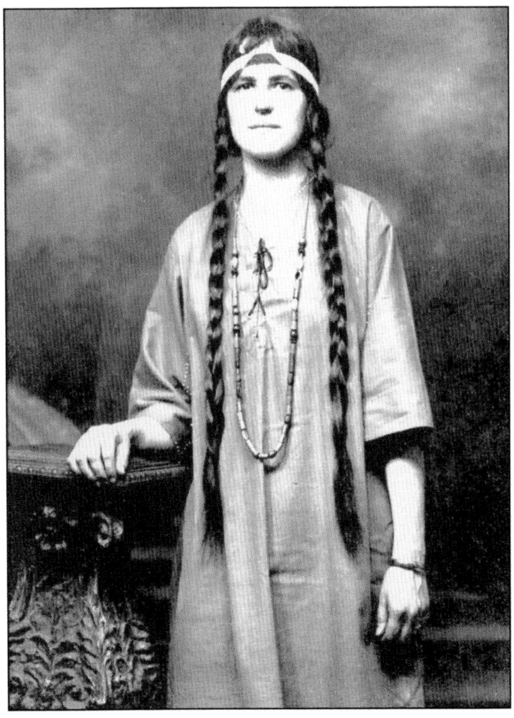

A CAMPFIRE GIRL. This photograph shows Matilda Hicock dressed as a Native American woman. Boy Scout Troop 60 was Southbury's first Boy Scout troop and organized in 1928. The first Girl Scout and Brownie troops were organized in 1933. (SHS.)

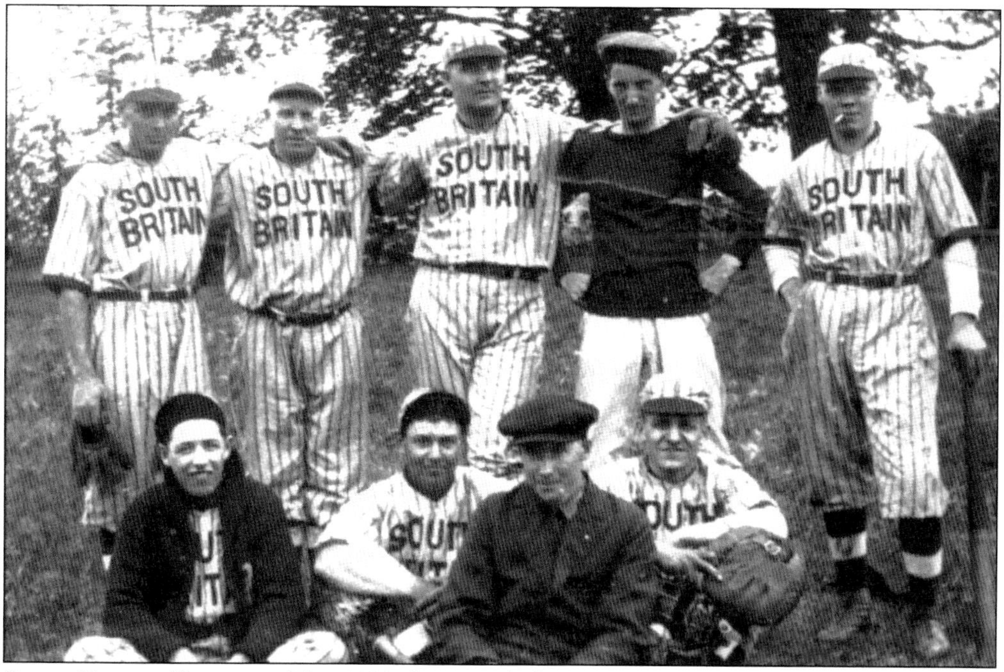

SOUTH BRITAIN BASEBALL. This 1920 photograph shows the Killer Team and includes, from left to right, the following: (front row) Arnold Cassidy, Charles Lautenschlager, George Grisgraber, and manager Greg Cassidy; (back row) George Manville, Jack Fleming, Roger Williams, George "Rip" Cahill, and Charles Manville. The shot was taken at Bill Schielke's field near the Fish Rock area of town. (DM.)

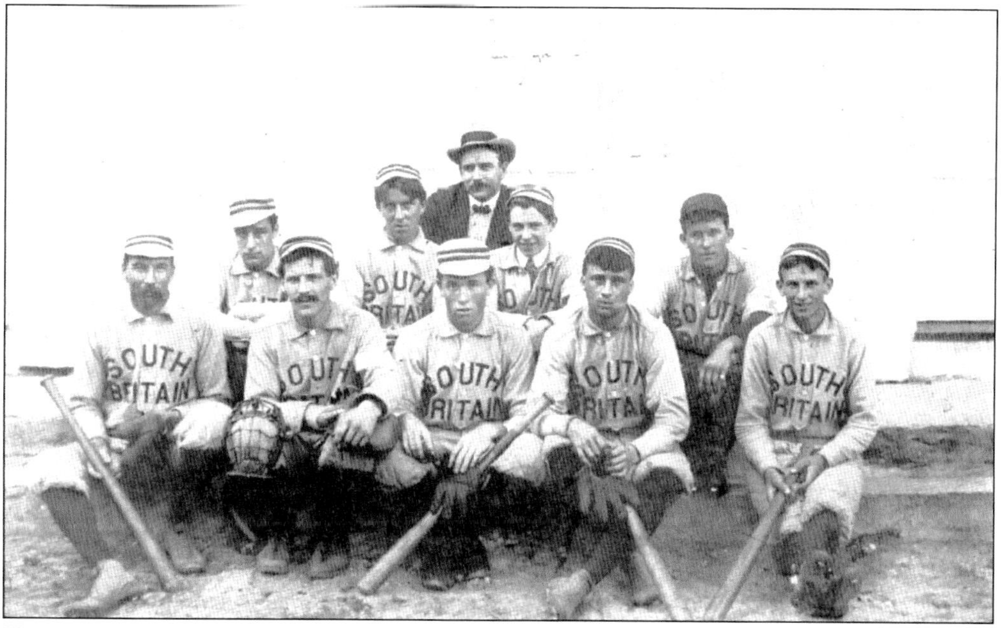

THE 1900 SOUTH BRITAIN BASEBALL TEAM. This photograph shows an early team sitting on the steps of the South Britain Church. George Manville Sr. is seated on the left in the first row. (DM.)

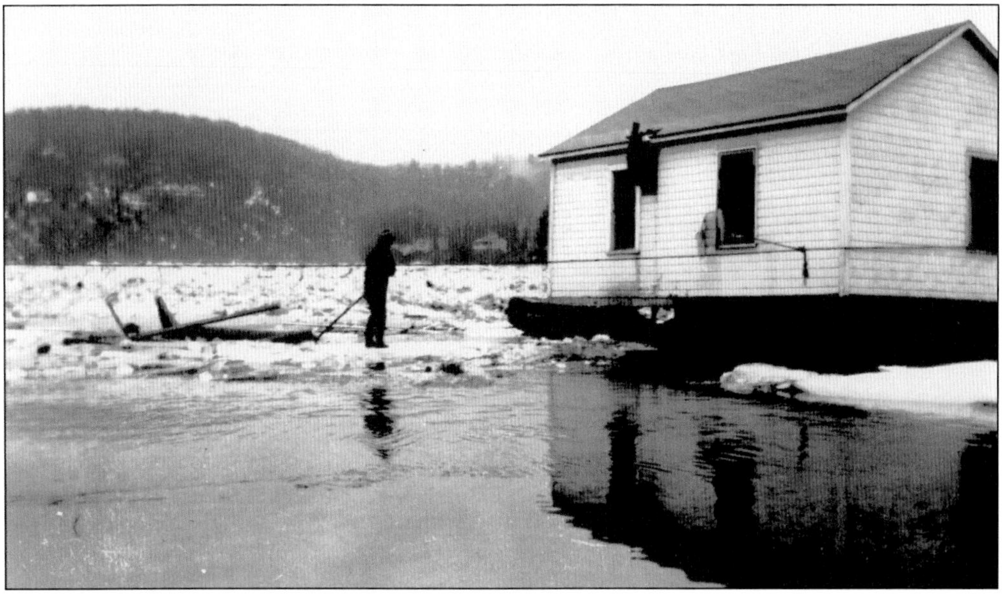

CHARLIE'S FISHERMAN HOUSE ON LAKE ZOAR. This *c.* 1936 photograph shows Charlie, who netted carp and suckers for trade in New York City. (SHS.)

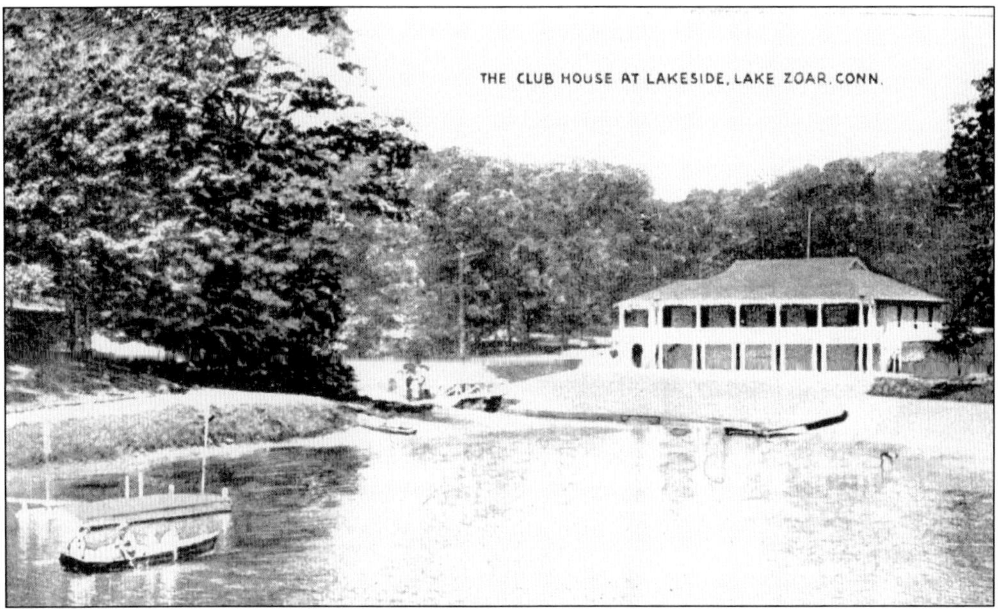

THE CLUBHOUSE AT LAKESIDE ON LAKE ZOAR. Seen here is a popular spot for Lakeside vacationers and residents. In 1948, there were 625 families in town. In the summer, the population almost doubled as visitors vacationed in the area. After real-estate entrepreneur Soule-Roberts moved out, the Lakeside Association took over and created a clubhouse. Lake Zoar was formed in 1919 by the creation of the Stevenson Dam. The name was taken from the old Zoar Bridge. (TL.)

A COUPLE AT PLAY. This shot shows the Lautenschlagers, Lottie and Wolcott, enjoying Labor Day in September 1914. (TL.)

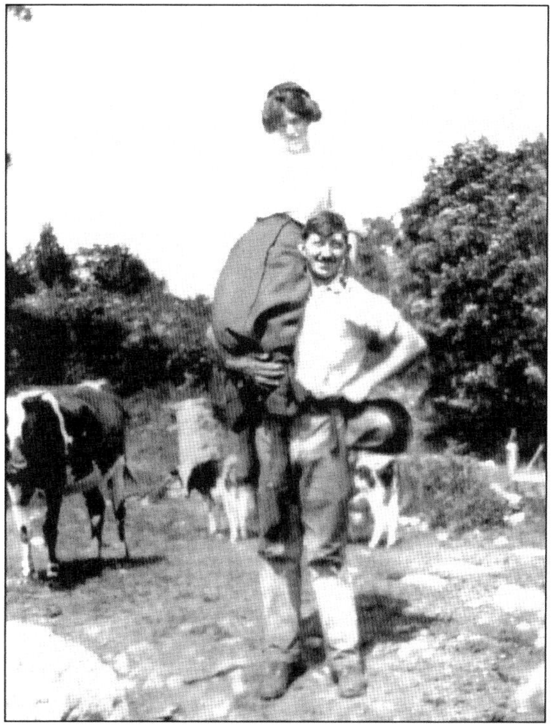

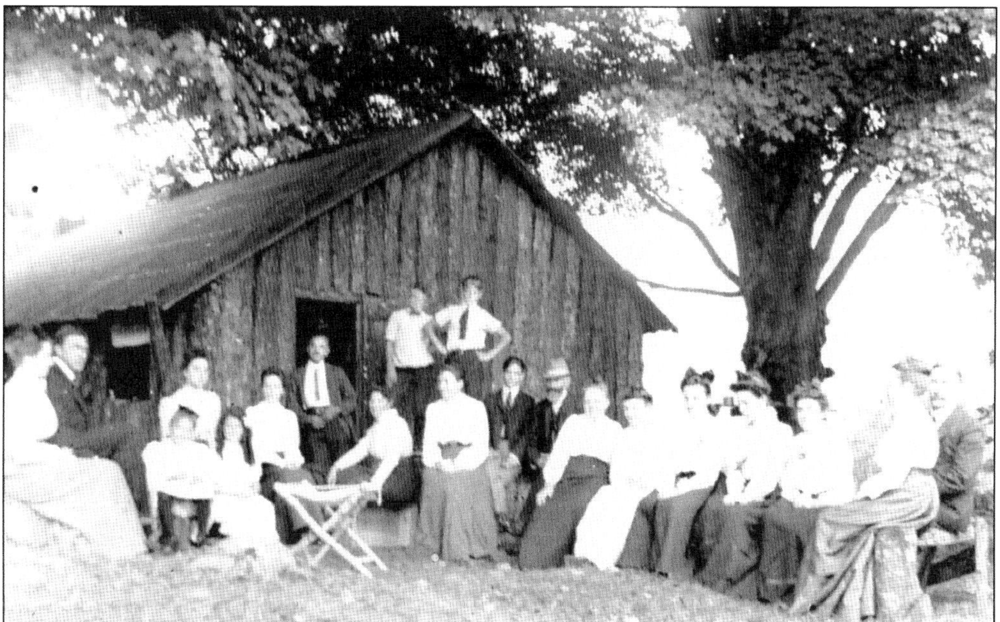

CAMP EASY. This photograph is of one of the many vacation camps in the area and shows women gathering to have some fun. Other popular areas were Oakdale Manor, Berkshire, Lakeside, and Cedarland. Some camps included Camp Rest Awhile, Camp Pomperaug, and the Cedars. In 1947, the town started a summer recreation program. At that time, there were 352 elementary and high school students. (DM.)

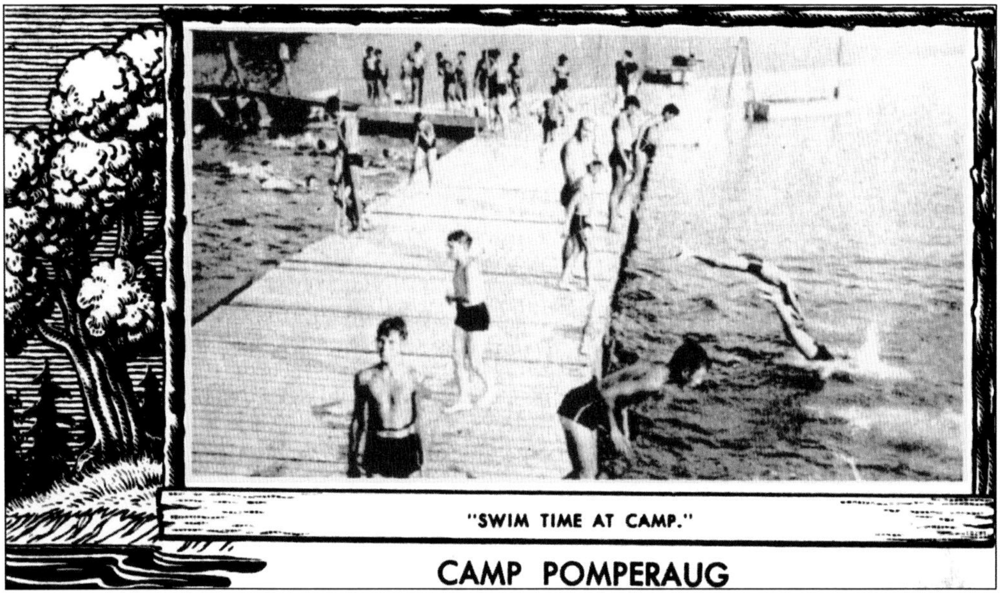

THE CAMP POMPERAUG BOY SCOUT CAMP. This postcard shows boys from Bridgeport enjoying water sports at the local Boy Scout camp. Many recreational areas were created by Connecticut Light and Power, when they built four hydroelectric plants to harness the Housatonic River's power. The meaning of the Native American word *Housatonic* is "place beyond the mountains." (TL.)

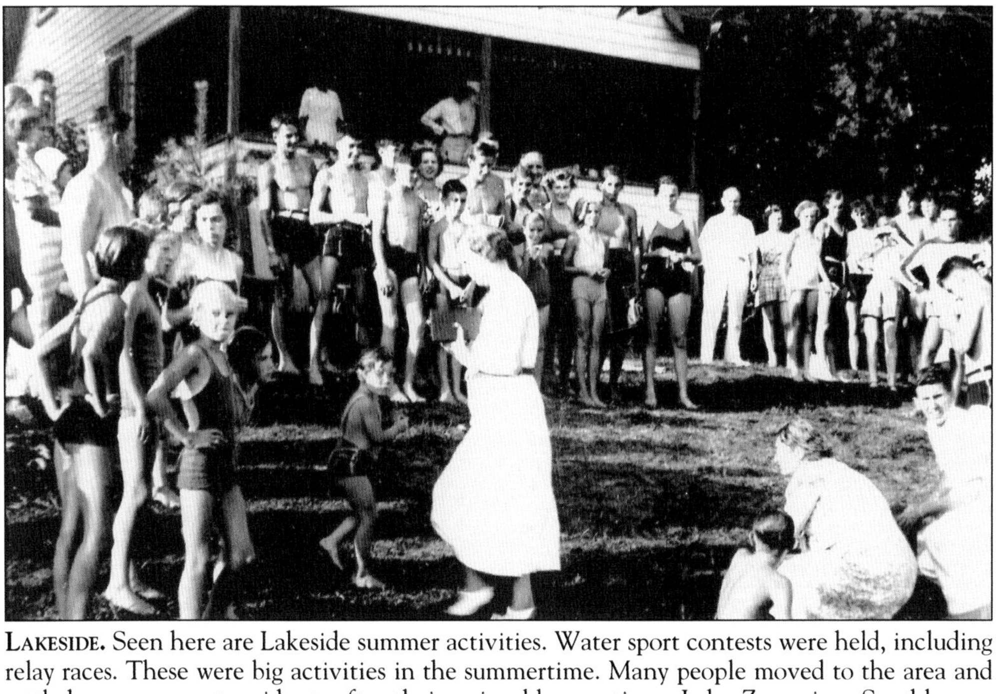

LAKESIDE. Seen here are Lakeside summer activities. Water sport contests were held, including relay races. These were big activities in the summertime. Many people moved to the area and settled as permanent residents after their enjoyable vacations. Lake Zoar gives Southbury a shoreline of about eight miles. (HH.)

Boys Fishing on the Village Bridge. This is an early shot of local boys Homer Bennett and Ely Hicock sitting on the bridge over Bullet Hill Brook. They are near the site of the former Green store on Route 67. (SHS.)

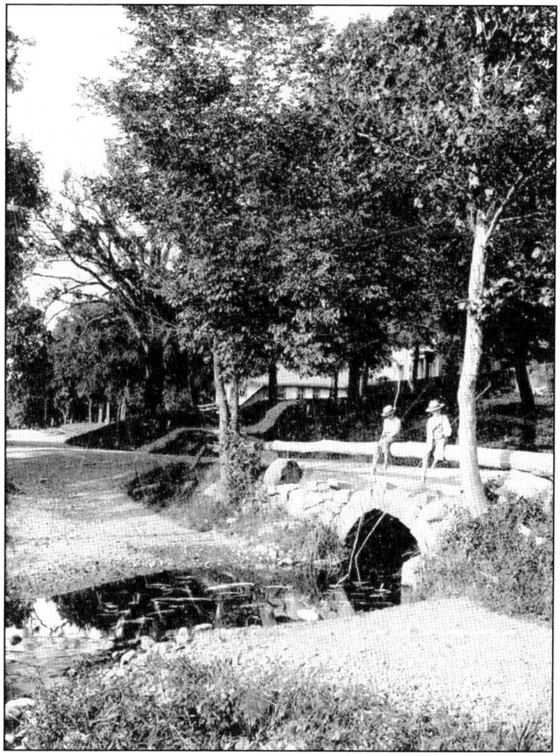

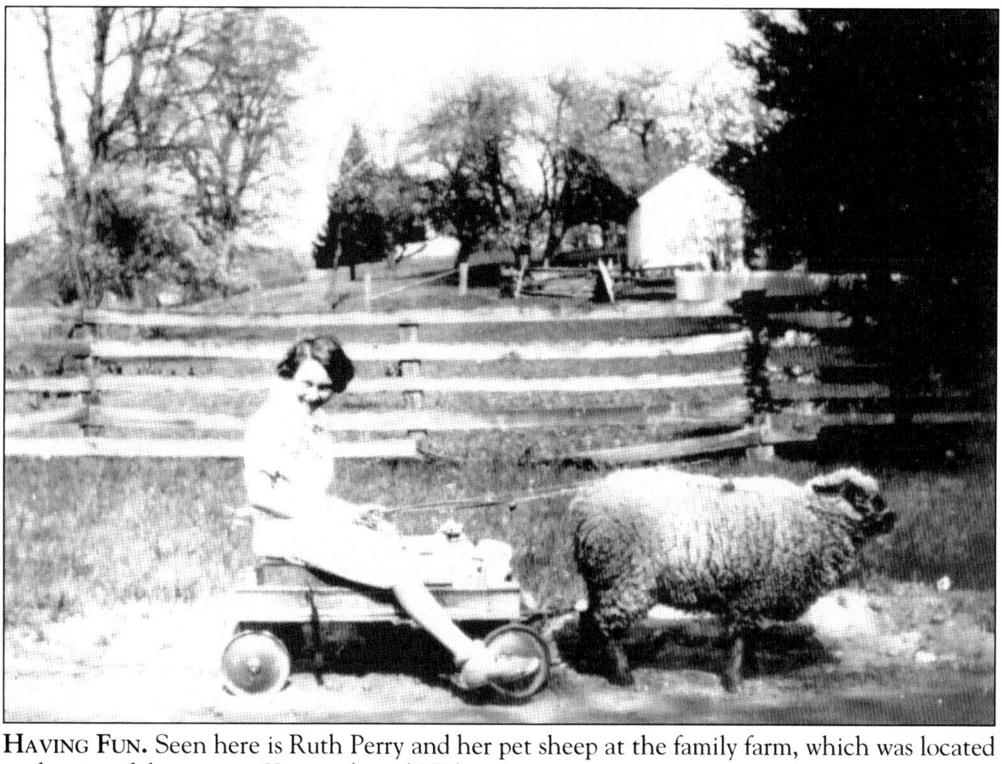

Having Fun. Seen here is Ruth Perry and her pet sheep at the family farm, which was located at the site of the current Kmart plaza. (AB.)

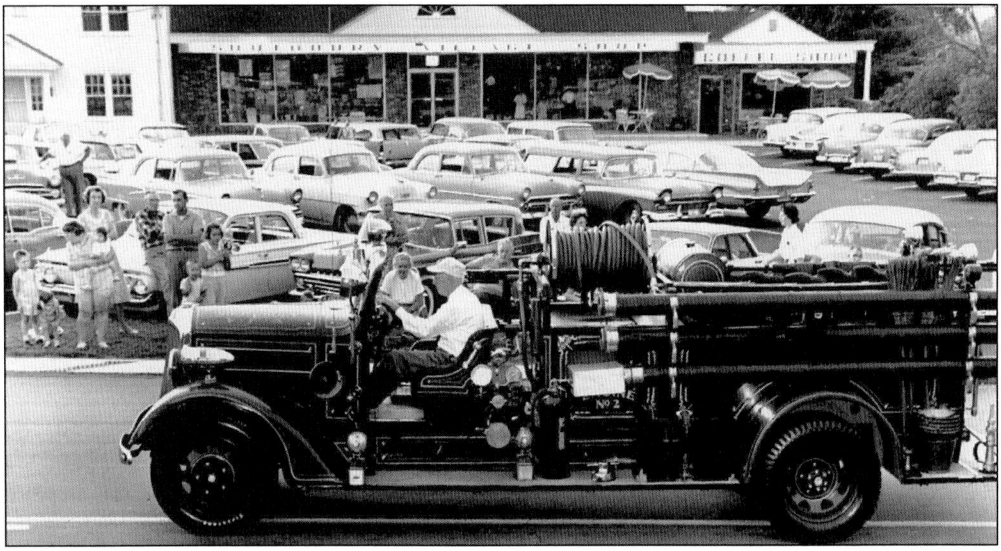

THE FIREMAN'S PARADE. This photograph illustrates the splendor of the town parade held in conjunction with a carnival. Fire trucks from the Southbury volunteer fire department are seen on Main Street in front of the Old Village Shop, which burned down. Also at the location were a post office, coffee shop, and the Southbury Food Center. The Southbury volunteer fireman's association was formed in the early 1930s. The first Fireman's Carnival was held a few years later, in 1936. (MCW.)

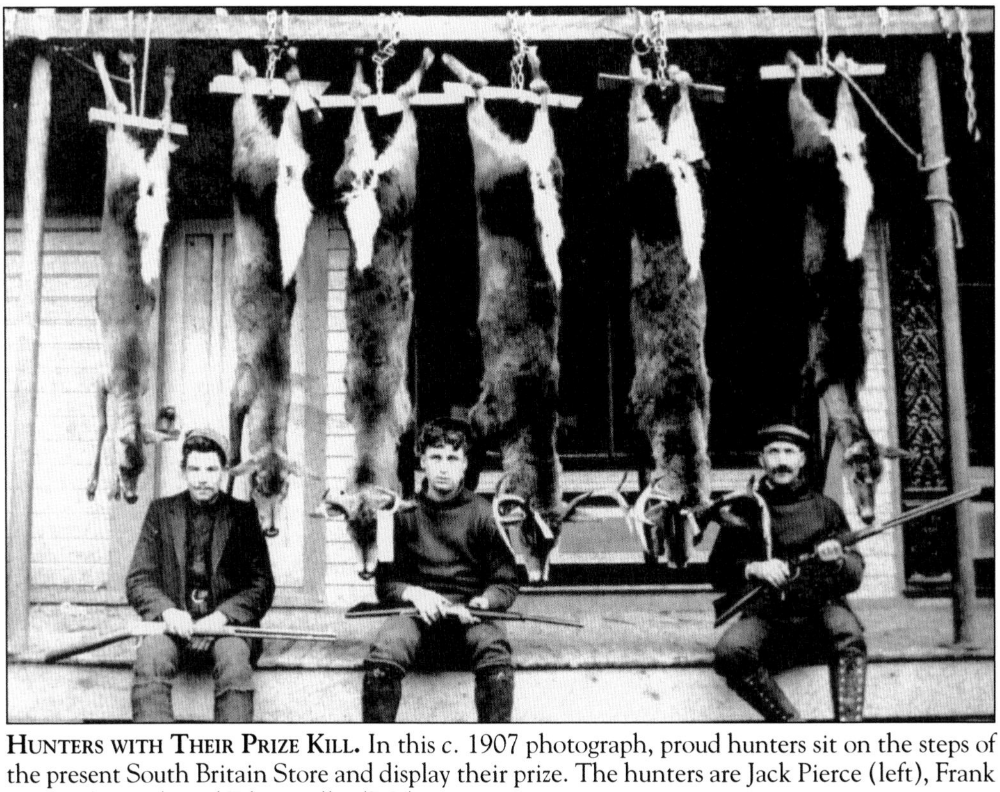

HUNTERS WITH THEIR PRIZE KILL. In this *c.* 1907 photograph, proud hunters sit on the steps of the present South Britain Store and display their prize. The hunters are Jack Pierce (left), Frank Bassett (center), and Ed Scoville. (RS.)

Six

THE THREE RS

18 Monday (December 1769) began school at Bullet Hill had 13 scholars
in the evening went to Singing meeting at Pam Wheelers
my wife finished weaving a piece of flannel for John Tiff of 24 yards
—the diary of David Hicock. (GHS.)

Until 1795, the ecclesiastical societies were in charge of all schooling. Each school district set its own taxes for the construction and maintenance of schools.

In May 1795, the General Assembly passed an act to distribute funds to towns to be used for schools. This money came from the sale of land in the Western Reserve. Southbury created a committee to receive the money. Records show that all school districts were to remain as they were on the records of the ecclesiastical society of Southbury.

The first town records mentioning schools, in 1741, gave permission for neighborhood schools in different parts of town. As indicated in the 1868 Beer's atlas, Southbury was divided into several school districts. These included Bullet Hill, White Oak, South Britain, Kettletown, Pootatuck, Wapping, Southford, Hulls Hill, Purchase, Pierce Hollow, Strongtown, and Translyvania. It was noted that the Pootatuck school building was only 16 feet by 18 feet in dimension.

Neighboring border schools included pupils from Woodbury, Oxford, and Sandy Hook. In 1741, payment per student was one-quarter cord of wood. Teachers lived with students' families for a length of time determined by the number of students each family had.

In 1870, a school for young ladies was held in the house just west of the South Britain Church. Between 1845 and 1860, Bucks Hill Seminary was run by Deacon R. Curtiss as a boarding school and accommodated about 30 young men. The academy was opened in 1829 in the Beardsley house in South Britain.

One-room schoolhouses were built in many areas of town until the Southbury Consolidated School was built. In 1888, a select school was run at the old town hall for several years. Parents had to pay expenses. As the population varied in each school district, children were transferred amongst the district schools. The White Oak and Bullet Hill Schools had second floors. These were used as the area populations increased.

In 1881, there were no schools for older students, and Southbury high school students took the train to Waterbury for their education.

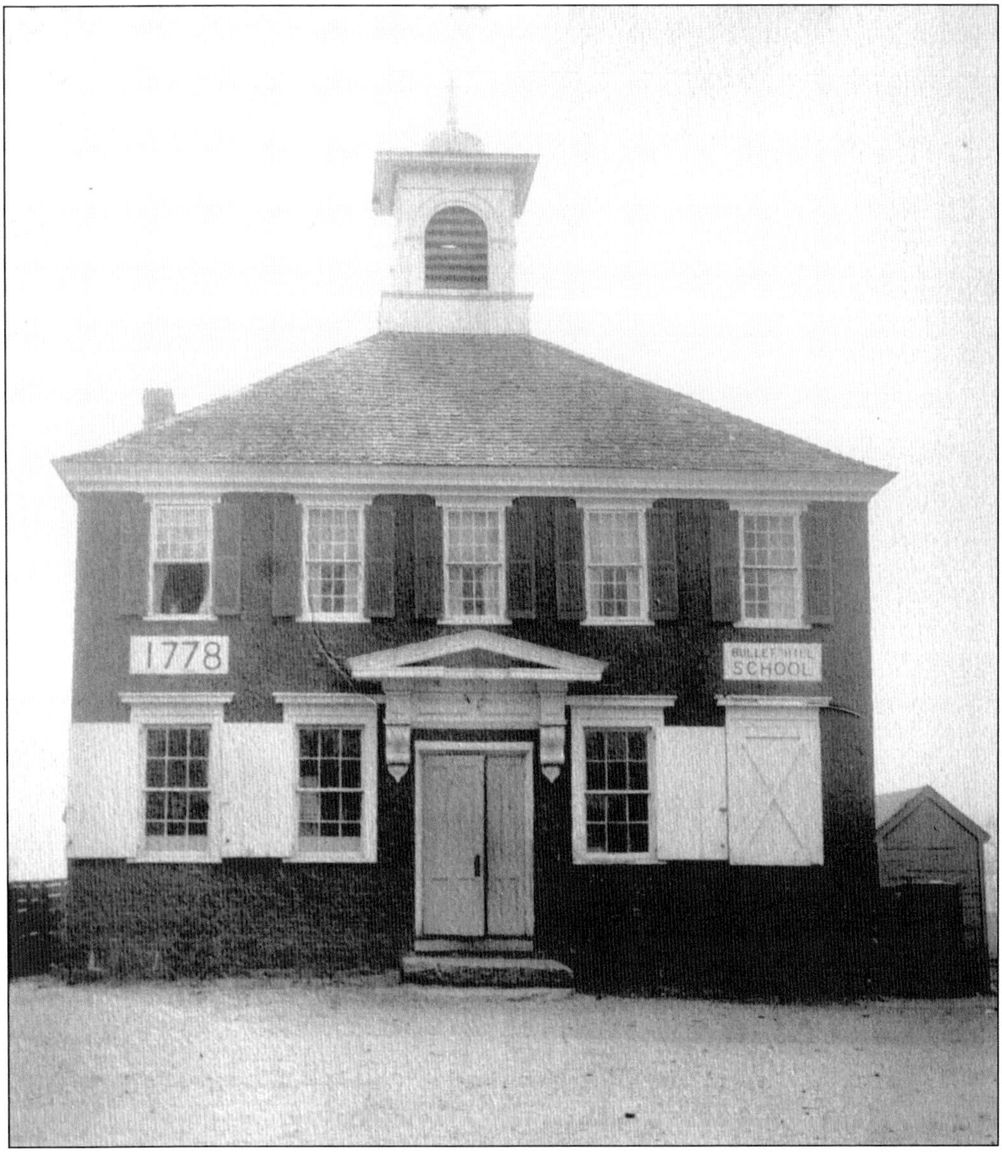

THE BULLET HILL SCHOOL. The Bullet Hill School is one of New England's oldest schoolhouses that is still in use. It is believed that its date of origin is 1778. However, research indicates an earlier date of 1762, according to Ancient Woodbury's town records. During the Revolutionary War, Bullet Hill was used as a site for the training band for firearm practice. On orders for the Woodbury training band, companies of young men who served as emergency militia were to practice twice a year at that location. Bullets used in the practice were dug out of Bullet Hill and melted down in the fireplace at the Bullet Hill School by women. The school is on the National Register of Historic Places and served as a district school from the 1700s until December 1941, when daily classes moved to other schools. The school is a unique two-story brick building designed in the Georgian architectural style. (GS.)

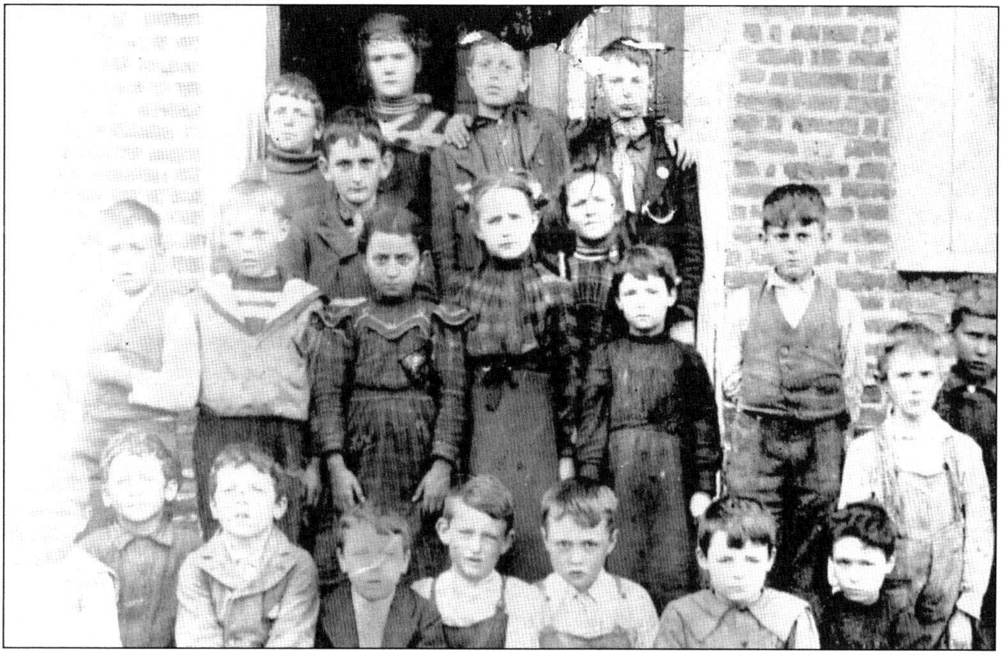

THE 1901 BULLET HILL SCHOOL STUDENTS. The only students seen here that can be identified are Harold Hicock (second row, second from the left) and Hulda Wilson Platt (second row, fifth from the left). (SHS.)

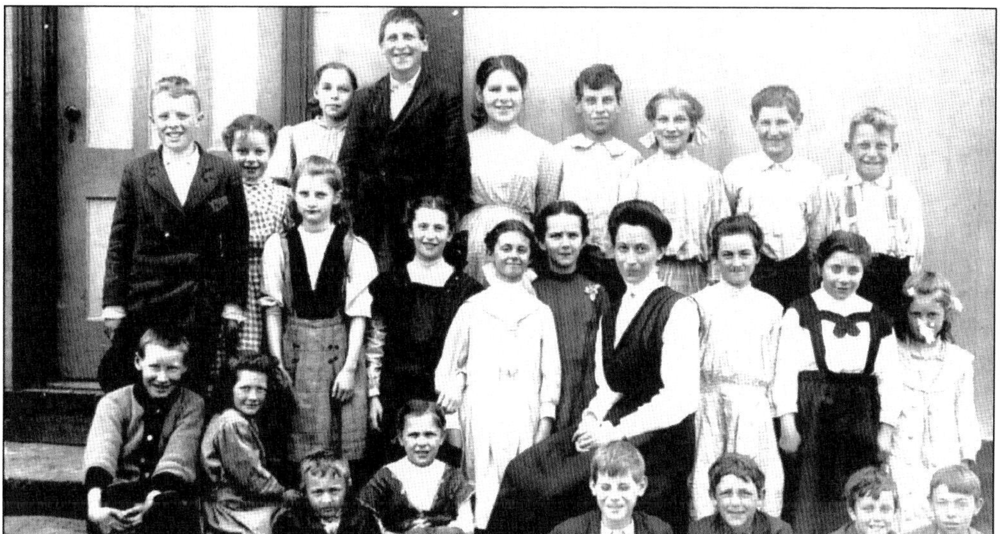

THE SOUTH BRITAIN SCHOOL. This 1910 photograph shows students attending the South Britain School. Seen here are, from left to right, the following: (first row) Greg Cassidy, Elizabeth Cassidy, Fred Fleming, Florence Spencer, Stanley Anderson, Bill Richmond, Wesley Hubbell, and Fred Spencer; (second row) William Fleming, Alice Erikson, Dorothy Richardson, Martha Scoville, Bernice Hubbell, Winifred Williams, Gertrude Beardsley (teacher), Helen Mitchell, Dorothy Taylor, and Annie Richardson; (third row) Bessie Spencer, Herbert Ingram, Esther Bezker, Helmar Anderson, Media Fields, Philip Lockwood, and Levi Stournson.

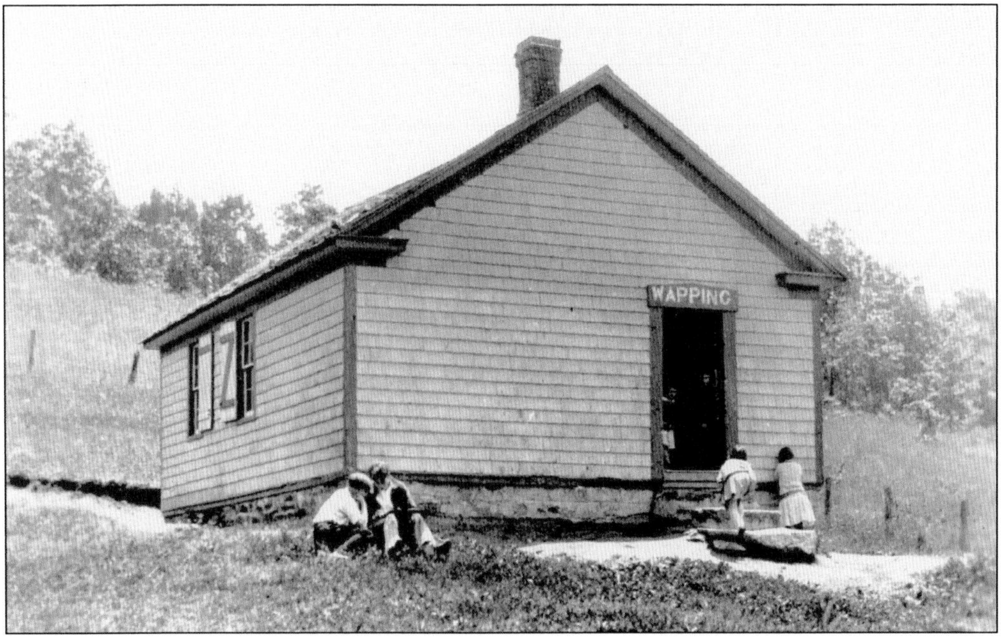

The Wapping School. This school was located north of the Rochambeau Bridge. It no longer stands. The 1927 Connecticut school register kept by teacher Doris Hotchkiss (Solosy) indicates an enrollment that year of 10 boys, ranging in age from 7 to 14, and four girls. Interestingly, fathers' occupations were listed in the record. Some fathers were farmers, electricians, masons, real-estate agents, factory hands, and railroad hands. One father was a railroad station agent. Hotchkiss held a permanent normal school certificate. (SHS.)

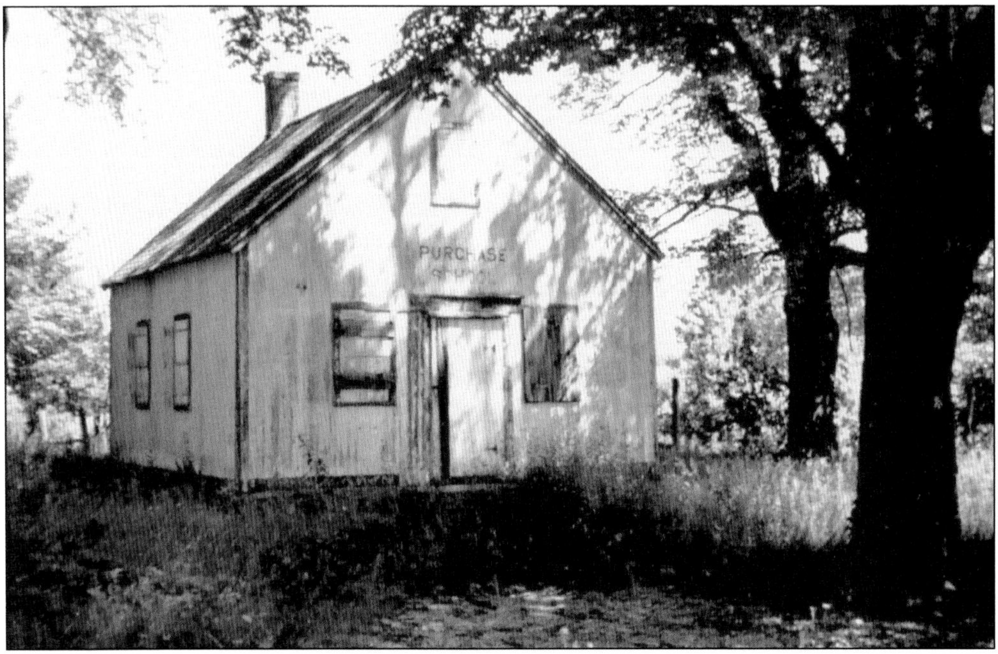

The Purchase School. The Purchase School, pictured here, was later abandoned. It was burned down to prevent continual vandalism. (SHS.)

THE TRANSYLVANIA SCHOOL. The Transylvania School was one of Southbury's early school districts. For a time, it disappeared from Southbury school records. Woodbury school records c. 1896 noted Transylvania in their town. Since the school was geographically located right at the border of both towns, and disputed sections of it were located in each town, bitter conflict arose as to its proper assignation. Finally, the state officials were asked to step in and help resolve the problem. (SHS.)

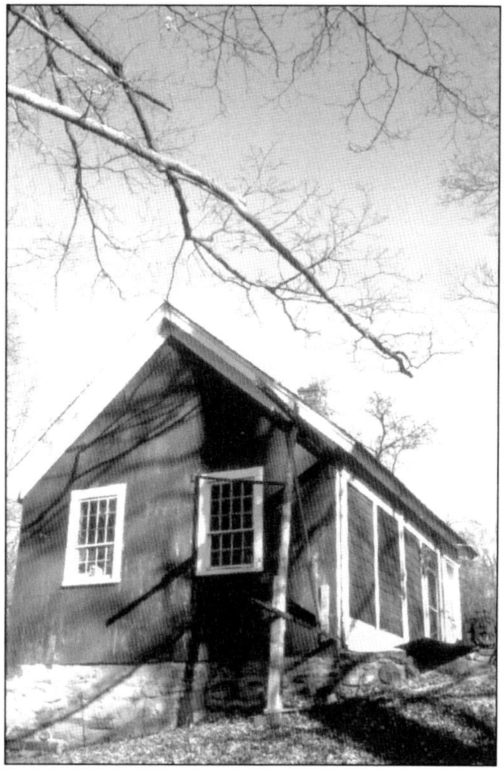

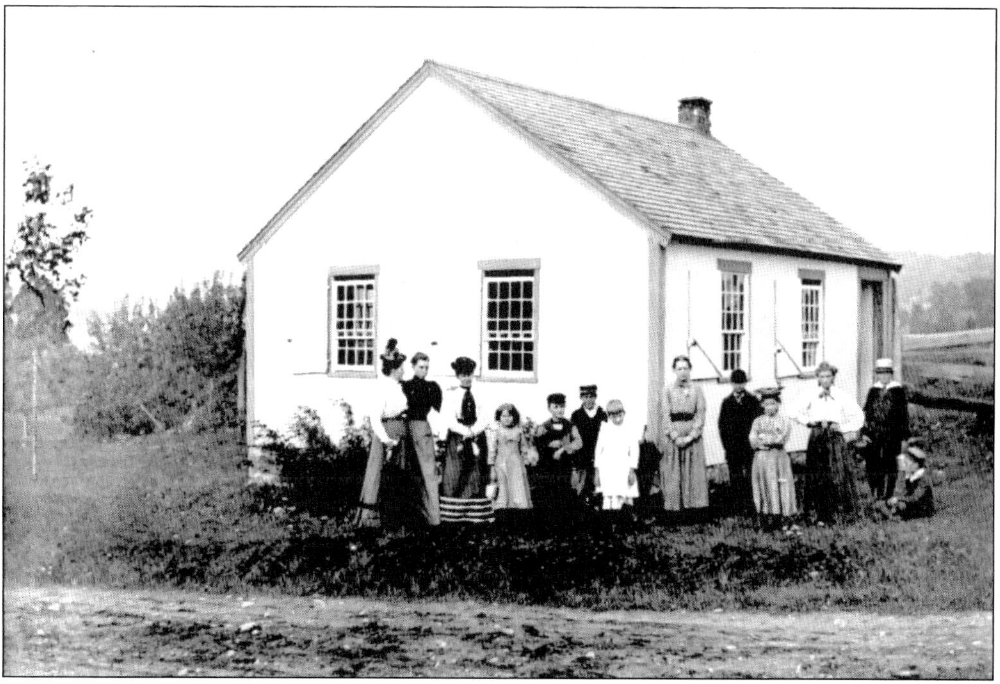

THE PIERCE HOLLOW SCHOOL. The Pierce Hollow School was located where the laundry of the Southbury Training School is currently located. When the training school was being built, coffee and goodies were sold to the workmen as a fund-raiser for class trips. (SHS.)

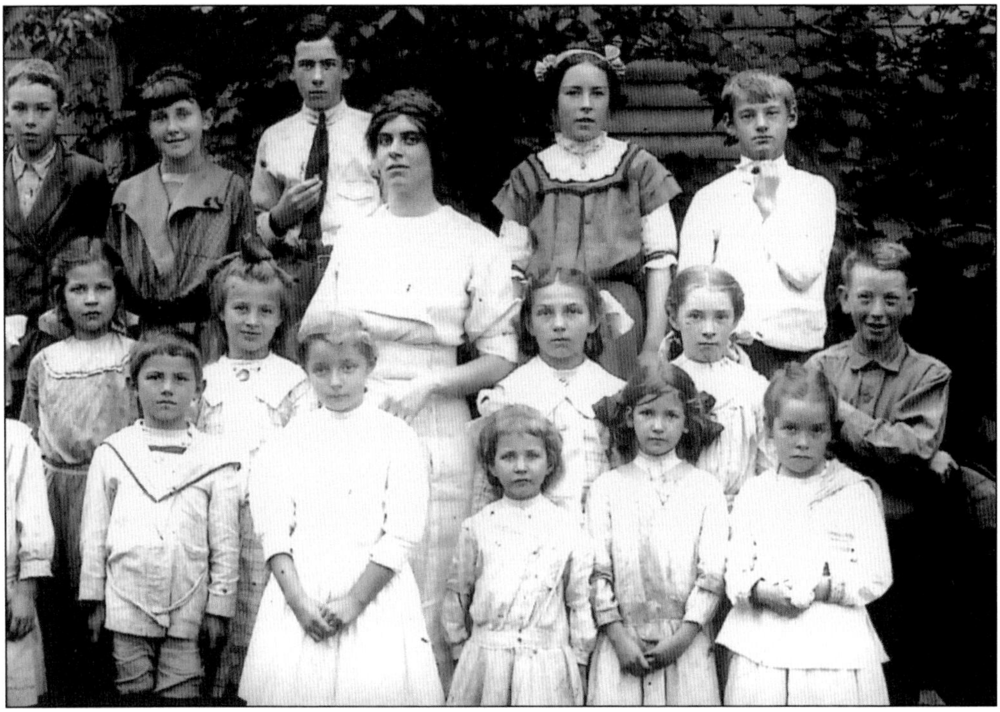

White Oak School. In this 1911 photograph, 11 students are pictured. They are, from left to right, as follows: (front row) Rita Hunnihan (not seen), Otto Englehardt, Isabel Smith, Elsie Wilson Mitchell, Helen Wilson Cahill, and Thalia Bennett Anderson; (middle row) Martha Wilson Hicock, Anna Ehrhardt, Gertrude McBath, Mildred McBath, and Arza Bennett; (back row) Hubert Leeke, unidentified, James Malane, Janie Pierce (teacher), Jeanne Leeke, and Howard McBath. (AB.)

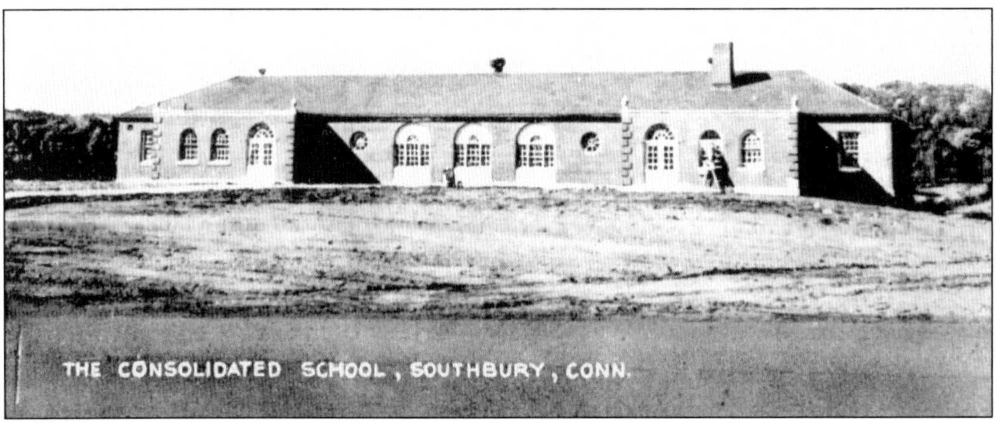

The Consolidated School. The Southbury Consolidated School opened on January 5, 1942, with 206 pupils from the remaining six district schools throughout the town. At the same time, over 64 local students attended Woodbury High School. As the school population grew, a new high school was built for Southbury students on Peter Road. As the population continued to grow, a new high school was built in its present location on Route 188, near the Middlebury border. At that time Rochambeau Middle School, grades six to eight, moved to the former high school on Peter Road, and its former site on the corner of Old Field and Poverty Roads became the Gainfield Elementary School. (SHS.)

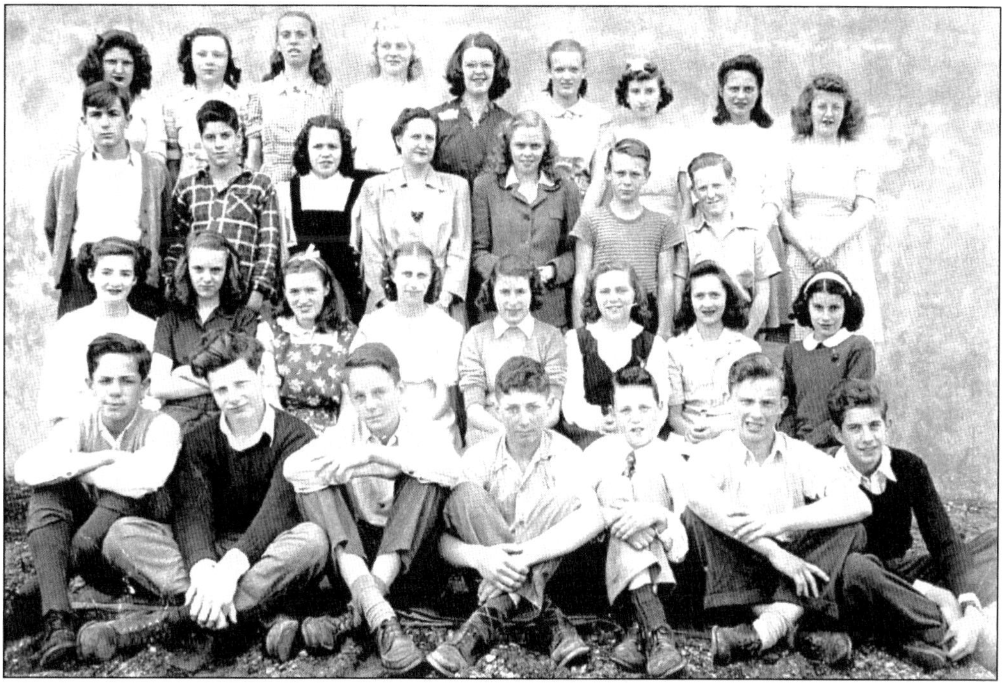

The Class of 1945. Seen here is the Southbury Consolidated School eighth-grade graduation on June 7, 1945. Students pictured are, from left to right, the following: (first row) Andy Williams, Ralph Pickard, John Petty, Garwood Platt, Richard Stephens, Jack Hoyt, and Joe Jameson; (second row) Florence Shea, Althea Hicock, Doris Lewis, Pat Hicock, Ellen McCarthy, Katy Coe, Dolores Klesitz, and Shirley Houle; (third row) Alfie Candido, William Houle, unidentified, Sarah Smart (teacher), Ellen Hicock, Ernest Ehrhardt, and Edwin Grisgraber; (fourth row) Shirley Makl, Betty Platt, Helen Hatfield, Alice Johnson, Lorraine Parsell, Betty Jane Lewis, Evelyn Barnes, Kathleen Ingram, and Arleen Grisgraber. (SHS.)

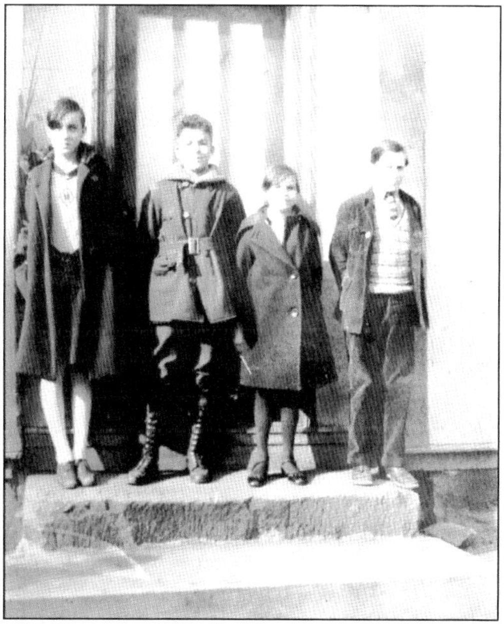

The South Britain Class of 1928. Seen here are students from an early 1900s class. (ML.)

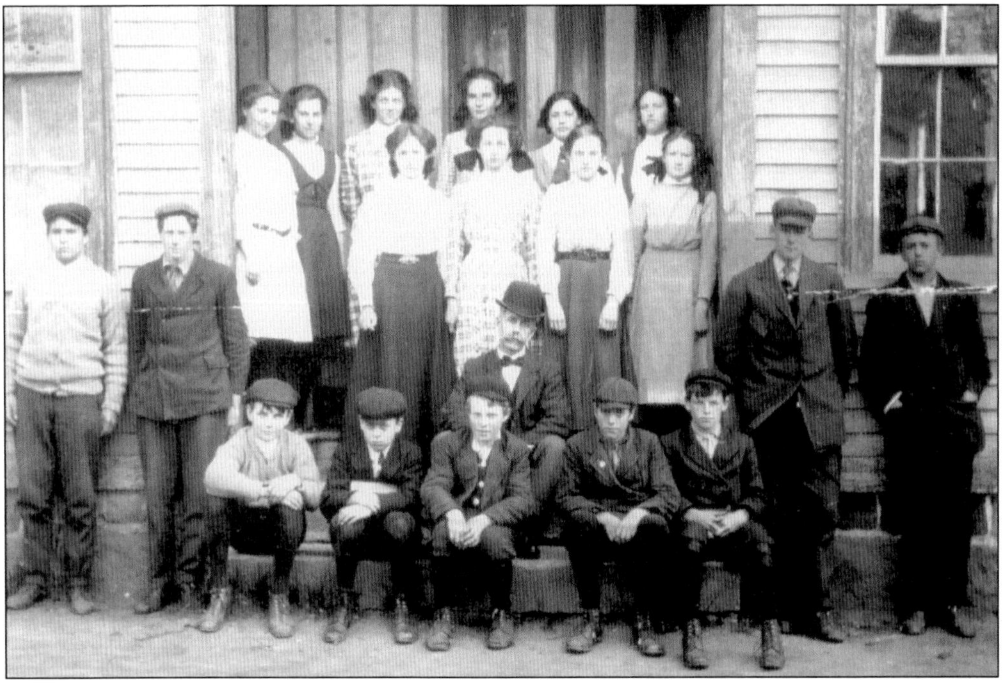

THE SOUTH BRITAIN SELECT SCHOOL. Above is the select school's graduating class of 1910.

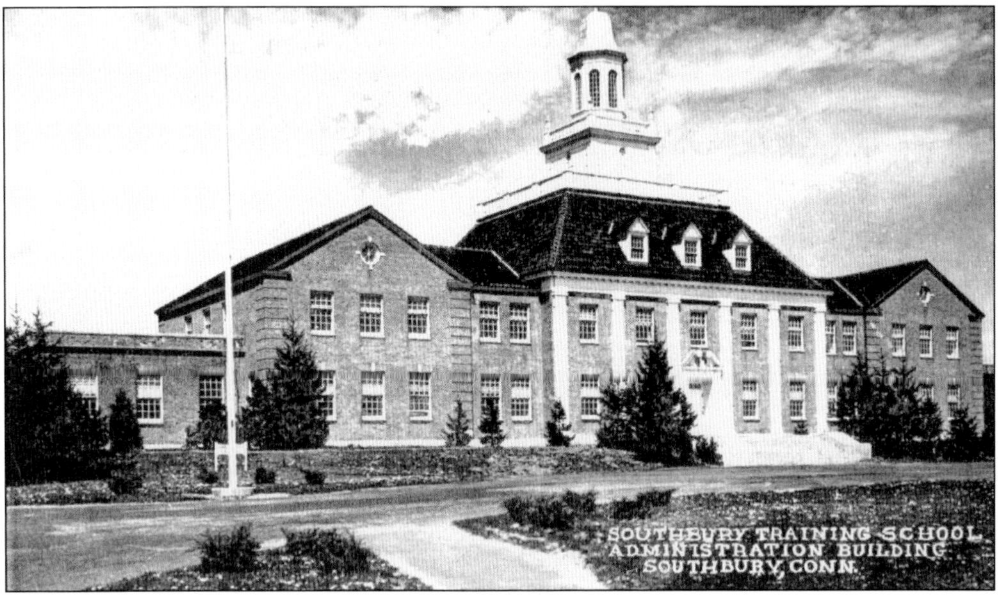

THE SOUTHBURY TRAINING SCHOOL. The school opened in 1940 and provided a new way to train people with developmental disabilities in a residential cottage setting. It was one of the largest employers of locals. In 1964, it had 764 full-time staff and about 2,000 residents. Many people moved to the area when this new source of employment started. Many community activities were held here, including bowling leagues, concerts, and other events. In place of a local auditorium, the training school offered movies on Friday nights and other recreational activities to town residents. (SHS.)

Seven

Shopping

There have been many changes over the years. The store has been enlarged, the horse stalls in back, which I used to rent, now hold refrigeration equipment. Times have changed, but it's still fun to run a general store. People still stop to talk.

—Carlton W. Tyler, former owner of the Southbury general store.

The country store served its citizens well. However, managing a store was not without risk. Since trade and credit were an important part of each day's business dealings, many store owners were unsuccessful. It was common for storekeepers to lose their business in bankruptcy in the early 19th century.

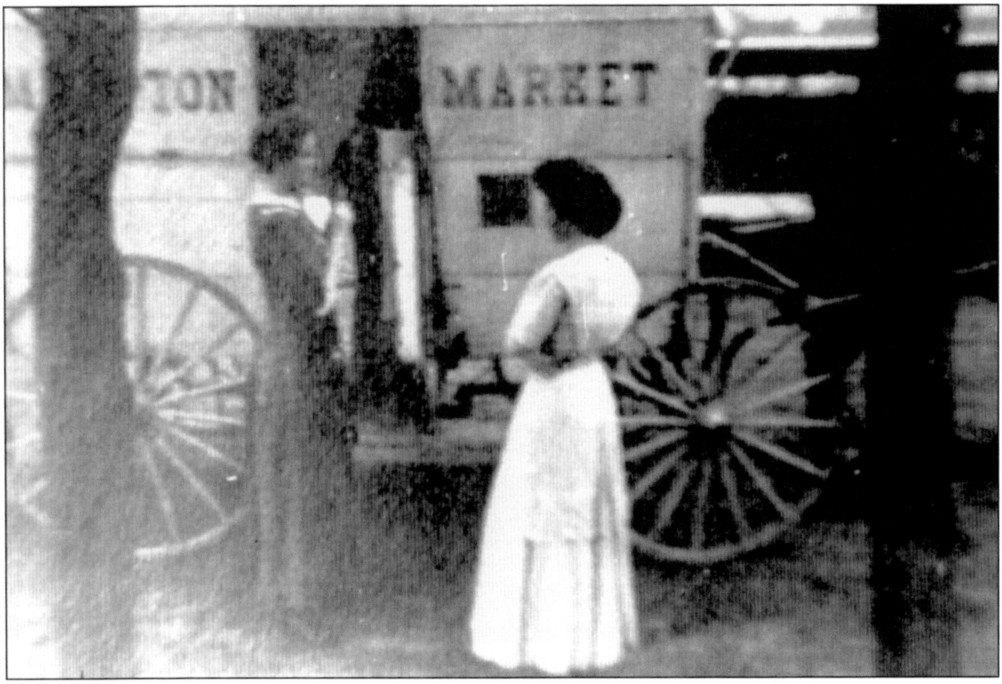

A Butcher's Cart. A butcher's wagon from a local market delivers meats as a woman shops for a family dinner. Later, in the 1940s and 1950s, Billy ? would go house to house selling fresh fruits and vegetables. Hughie Quinn sold ice, and ? Kamerzel sold fish. Initially, D.L. Condon peddled fresh meat with a horse and wagon, but ? Hatstat later drove a delivery truck for Condon. When gas was rationed during World War II, they also delivered groceries. (SHS.)

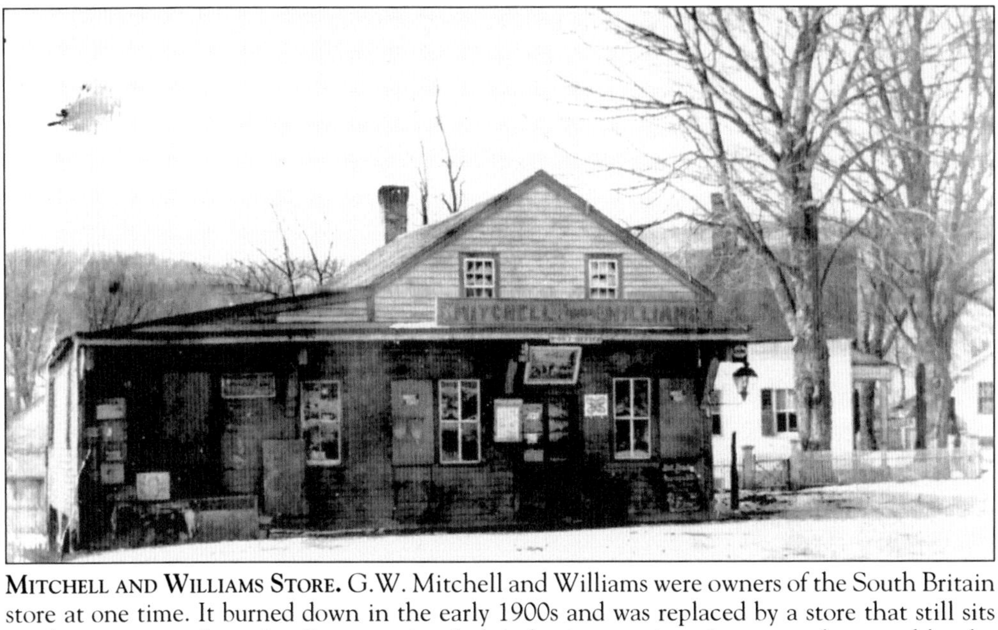

Mitchell and Williams Store. G.W. Mitchell and Williams were owners of the South Britain store at one time. It burned down in the early 1900s and was replaced by a store that still sits on the site across from the Congregational church. At one time, it was partly owned by the Scoville family. The second store was built by A.H. Wilson, who also built the South Britain Library. (SHS.)

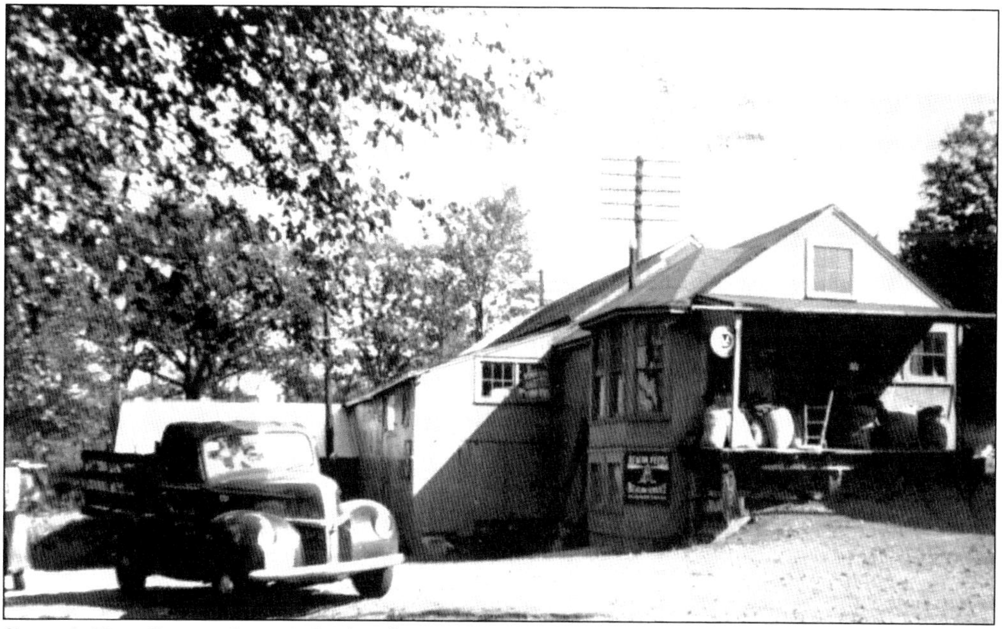

STONE'S FEED STORE. Stone's feed and grain store in Southbury was built across from the railroad station in the mid-19th century. It had a siding for trains to unload grain. (MCW.)

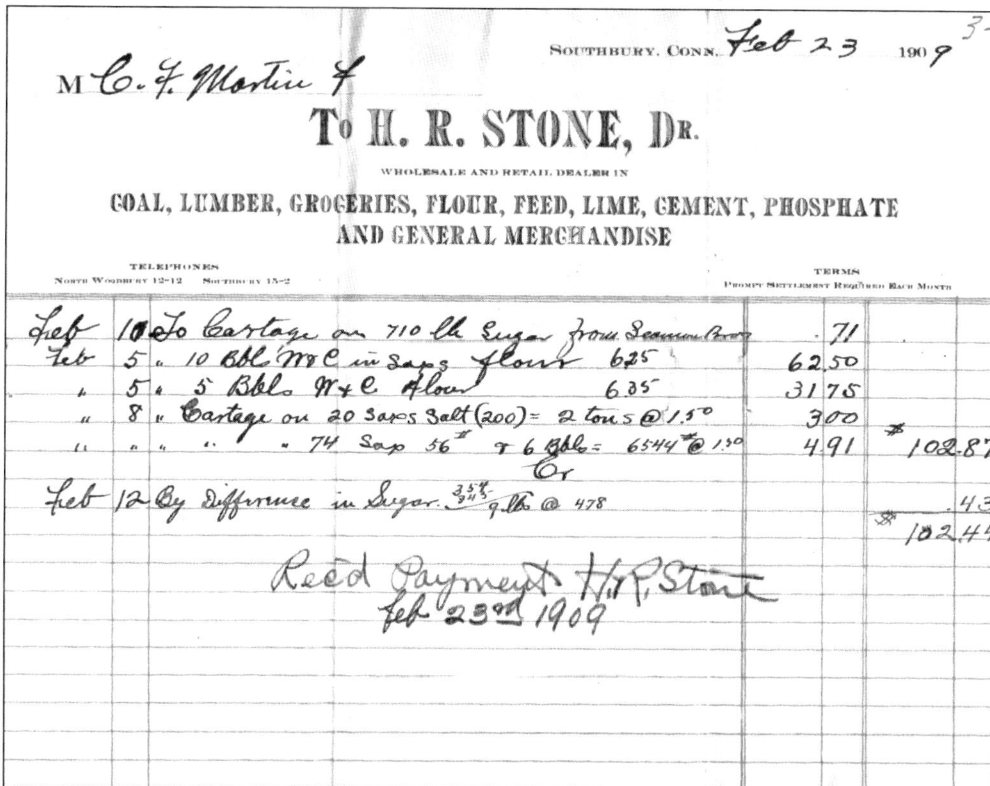

SOUTHBURY, CONN. Feb 23 1909

M C. F. Martin &

To H. R. STONE, Dr.

WHOLESALE AND RETAIL DEALER IN

COAL, LUMBER, GROCERIES, FLOUR, FEED, LIME, CEMENT, PHOSPHATE AND GENERAL MERCHANDISE

TELEPHONES North Woodbury 12-12 Southbury 15-2

TERMS Prompt Settlement Required Each Month

Feb	10	To Cartage on 710 lb Sugar from Seaman Bros	.71	
Feb	5	" 10 Bbl W&C in Sacks flour 625	62.50	
"	5	" 5 Bbls W&C Flour 635	31.75	
"	8	" Cartage on 20 Sacks Salt (200) = 2 tons @ 1.50	3.00	
"	"	" " " 74 Sacks 56# + 6 Bbls = 6544# @ 1.50	4.91	$102.87
		Cr		
Feb	12	By difference in Sugar 354/345 9 lbs @ 478		.43
				$102.44

Recd Payment H. R. Stone
Feb 23rd 1909

A HENRY STONE BILL OF SALE. This H.R. Stone bill listed some of the store's wares, "coal, lumber, groceries, flour, feed, lime, cement, phosphate and general merchandise." (TL.)

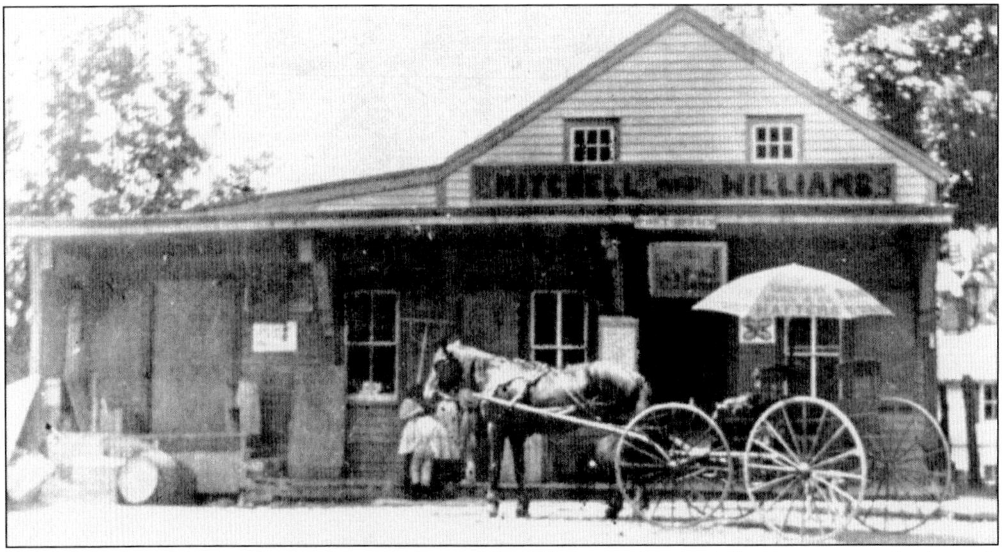

The Mitchell Store in South Britain. After this store burned down, it was rebuilt with great fanfare. A grand opening invitation flyer read, "Dance at Williams and Scoville's new store South Britain, Thursday Eve'g, Sept. 28th. Concert from 8-9 Tickets per couple including concert, dance, supper 50 Cts. All are invited." Written in pencil on the back is, "South Britain, Sept. 22- 05 My dear Hubert: Will you please post this in a conspicuous place. You may furnish a keg of beer and Florence a roast pig or turkey? Wish you might be here. Music by Bliss of East Village. Large time expected. Will enclose you a souvenir. Love to you both." The sender was Charles P. Williams. (SHS.)

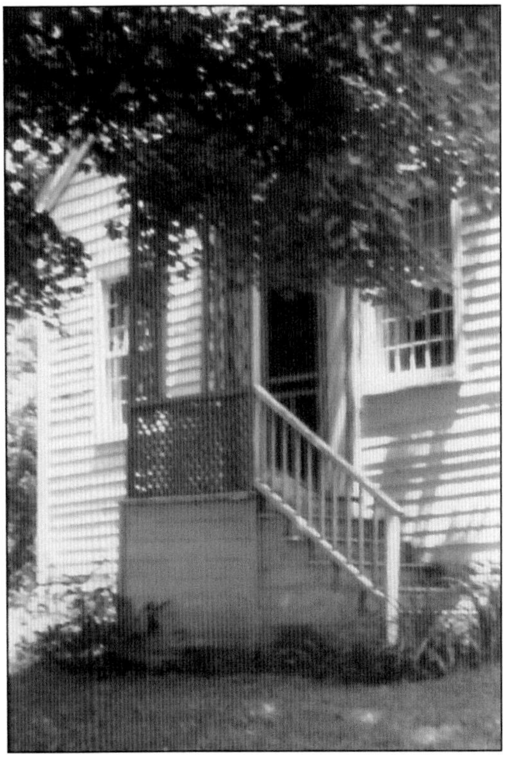

The Shadrach Osborne Store. The building that was Shadrach Osborne's store sits beside the Episcopal church. In the Revolutionary War, Osborne ran a commissary. He was appointed as a civilian to manage supplies for soldiers. He assigned a group of soldiers to protect a large pork supply after Danbury was captured. The supply was concealed southeast of the Southbury meetinghouse. The Hollow is still known as Pork Hollow today. Pork Hollow is East of the Congregational church. It is about a mile from where Shadrach Osborne lived. In 1811, he paid the highest town property tax. He was also the first postmaster of the town. Even before the Revolution, Col. Increase Mosley was also said to have a store. Some of Lafayette's troops are said to have camped there during their march. (SHS and LDM.)

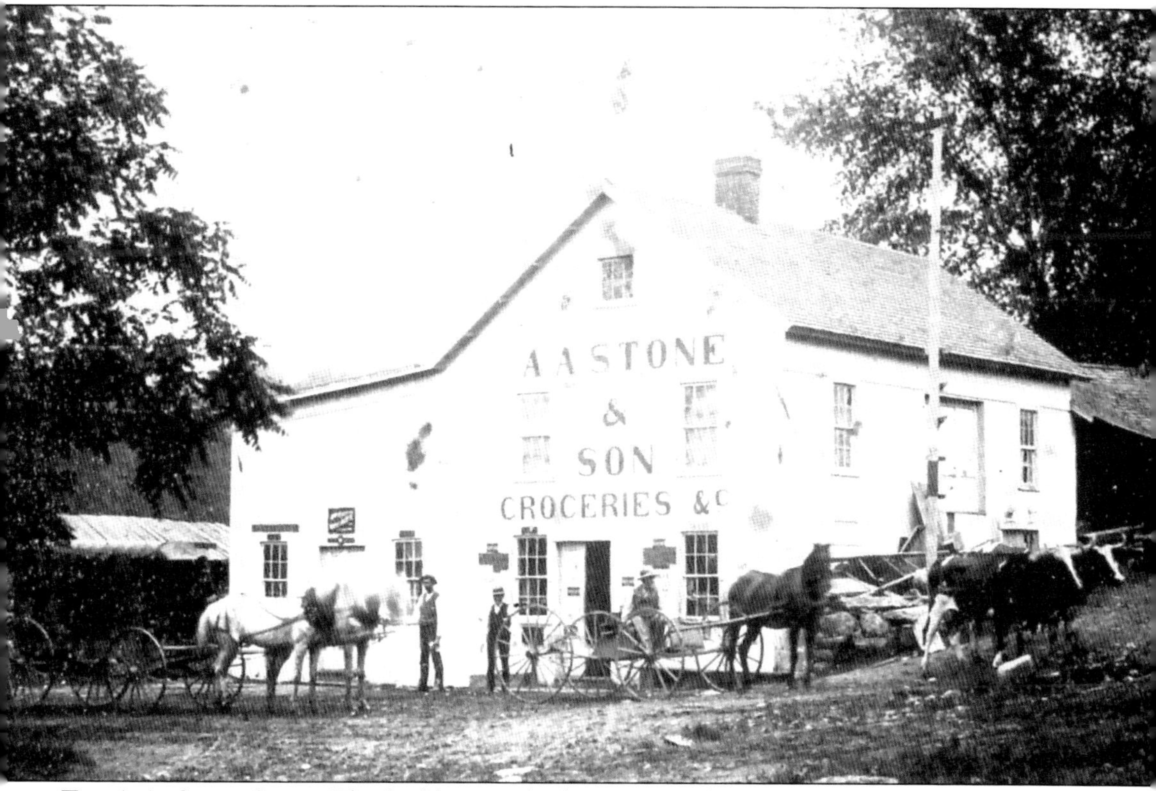

THE A.A. STONE STORE. This building was built in 1880 and initially housed the A.A. Stone and Sons store. It received supplies from the New York & New England Railroad, which was a line that operated between 1881 and 1948. Supplies were dropped off at depot station on the hill behind the building and were transferred by horse-drawn wagons to the store. The Stones sold groceries, feed, lumber, coal, and hardware. The store also had a grinding mill. Charles Stone attended the Centennial Exposition of 1876 in Philadelphia and was fascinated by Alexander Graham Bell's telephone. He bought two telephones that he wired from his grain and feed store (the site of the current Bullet Hill supply store) up the hill to the depot. Later on, he bought a ringing phone and strung wire to his brother's store in Woodbury, Harvey Stone's Feed Store (today's C.L. Adams). The next line was strung to South Britain. This was the beginning of the Woodbury Telephone Company. (SHS.)

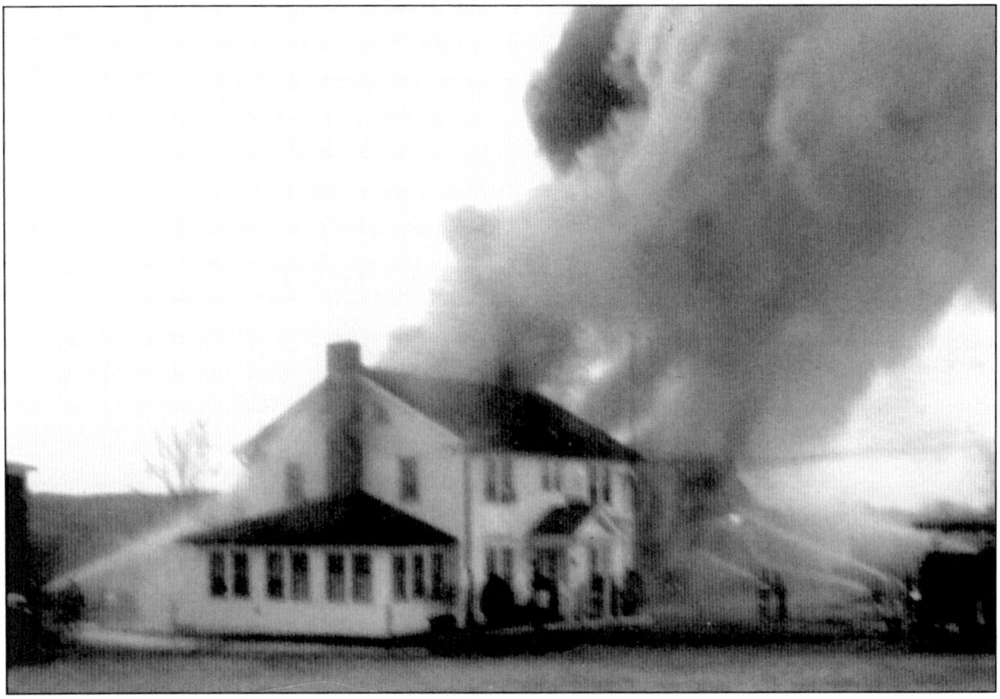

The Village Shop. On March 26, 1971, fire struck this shopping area and damaged or destroyed the Colonial Bank, post office, Village Shop, and coffee shop. Two firemen were sent to the hospital for smoke inhalation. The Nettleton house, which was at the back of the parking lot, was all that was left after the fire destroyed buildings to its right. The house was moved back through a field. (MCW.)

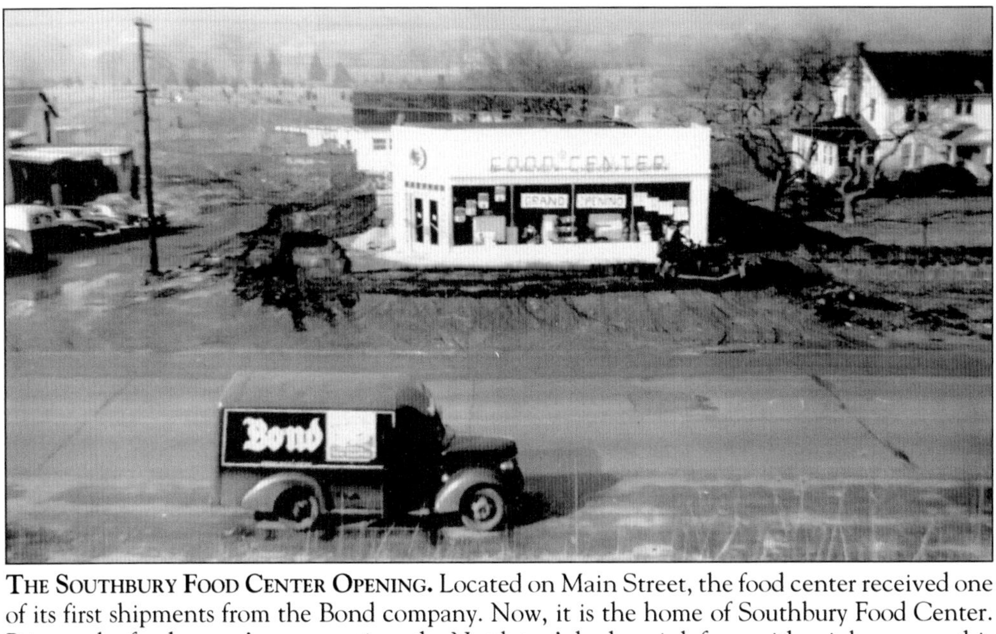

The Southbury Food Center Opening. Located on Main Street, the food center received one of its first shipments from the Bond company. Now, it is the home of Southbury Food Center. Prior to the food center's construction, the Nettleton's had a mink farm with mink pens on this site. (MCW.)

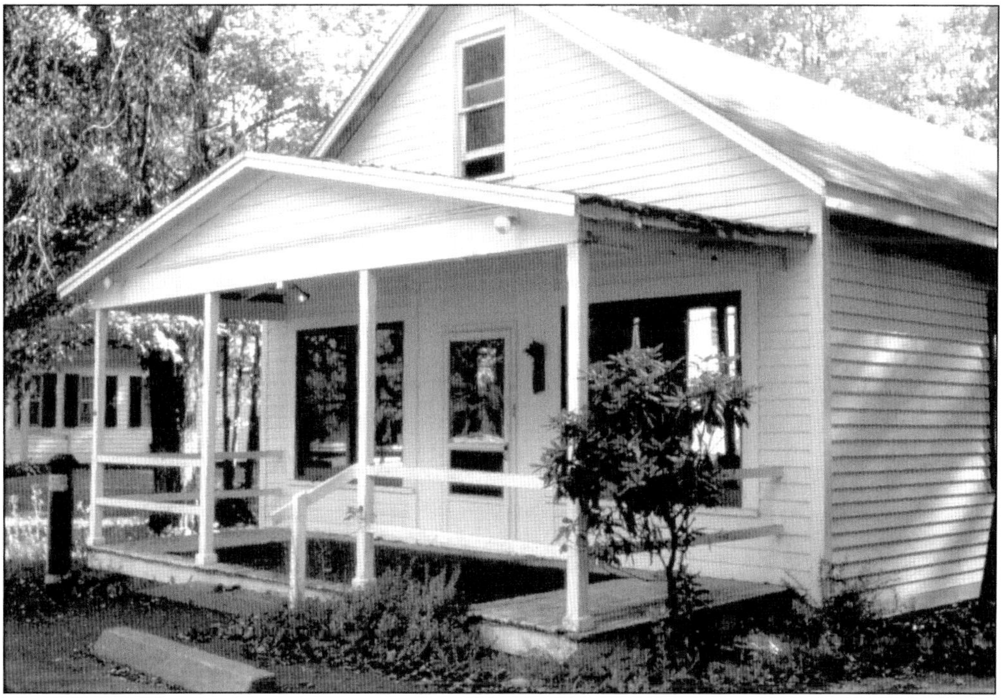

McCarthy's Store. This store was located across from the old town hall. It is now the site of Mitchell's Insurance. This is where the Bund inquired about supplies, thereby raising suspicion. (SHS.)

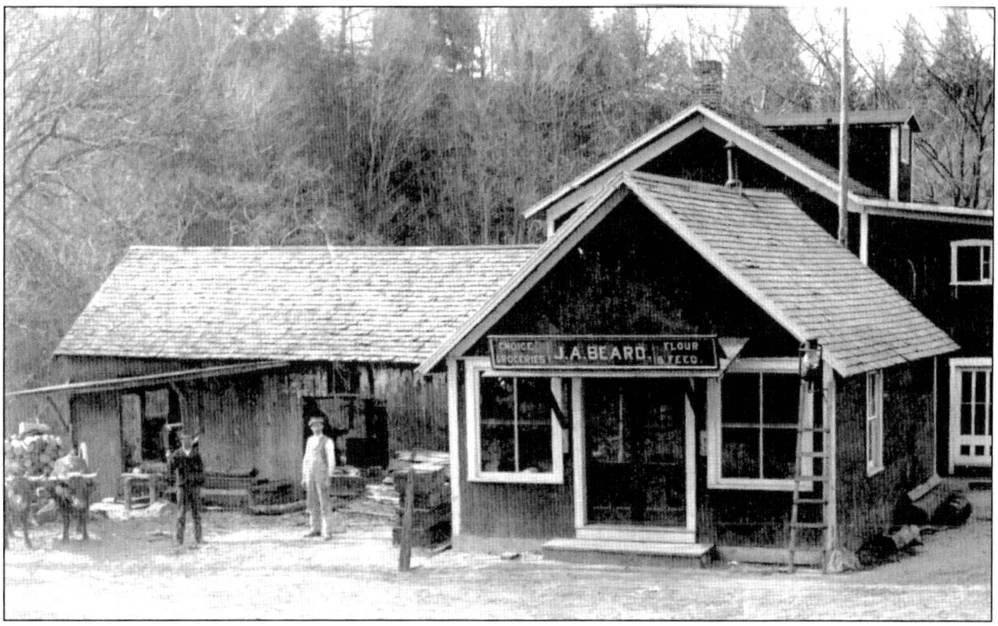

The J.A. Beard Store c. 1912. This store was located in South Britain and featured "choice groceries flour and feed." A lamp is seen on the right side of the building. Oscar Swanson, who was 12 years old, used to be the lamplighter for these carbon-type lamps. (SHS.)

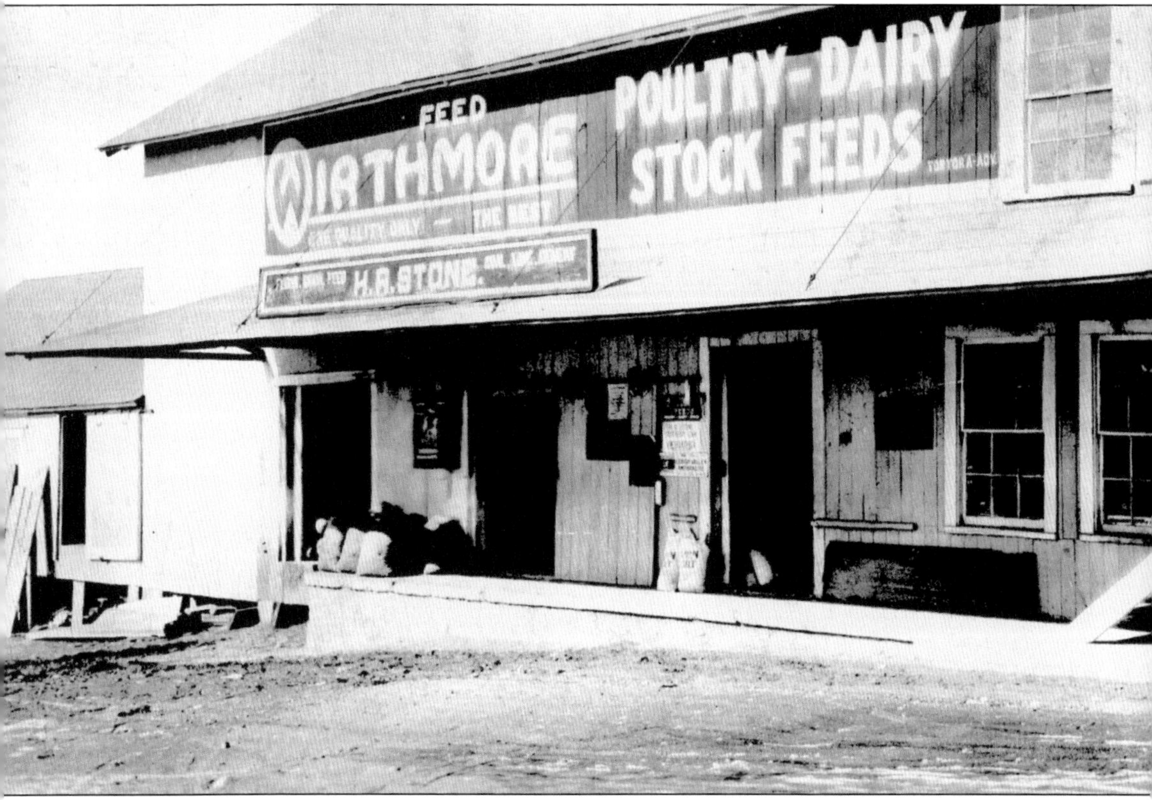

THE STONE STORE. This store was located in Southford. The Southford creamery was next to it. (MCW.)

Eight

Sacred Places

Layd out a burying place in Southbury and Woodbury, according to the act of the Proprietors in said town as will appear on record in 1741 at the northwest end of that hill that Deacon Hicock's dwelling house stands on.

—Woodbury Land Records, May 15, 1741.

All life revolved around the church in the 1600s. Originally, the church not only served as a house of worship but the seat of government. In the earliest days of the Pomperaug settlement, only members of the church were allowed to own property and vote.

The church has played a significant role in Southbury, starting with its earliest roots, as the Pomperaug Plantation's birth was directly related to religious dissension. The second ecclesiastical society was created due to the difficulty in commuting long distances to church. Many times a "ride-and-tie" means was employed, where a farmer with a good horse would ride part of the journey and leave his animal tied-up for another person to ride.

In 1686, one church and one ecclesiastical society existed for all of the areas of Ancient Woodbury, including Woodbury, Southbury, Roxbury, Bethlehem, most of Washington, Middlebury (the Quassapaug region), and part of Oxford. Travel difficulties for the ever-extending settlement created the necessity to form new ecclesiastical societies with churches. In 1731, Southbury formed the second ecclesiastical society. In 1766, South Britain established its own society. The building of church parishes continued. In 1770, the first South Britain Church was built. In 1790, the Southbury Methodist Church established services at the Bullet Hill School.

Many beautiful sacred religious sites exist in town, including old churches and associated historic cemeteries. Several of the more well-known burial sites include Pierce Hollow, Middleground, South Britain, Georges Hill, Pine Hill, White Oak, Sacred Heart, Warner, the French family vault, Crook Horn, and the Lone Grave farm.

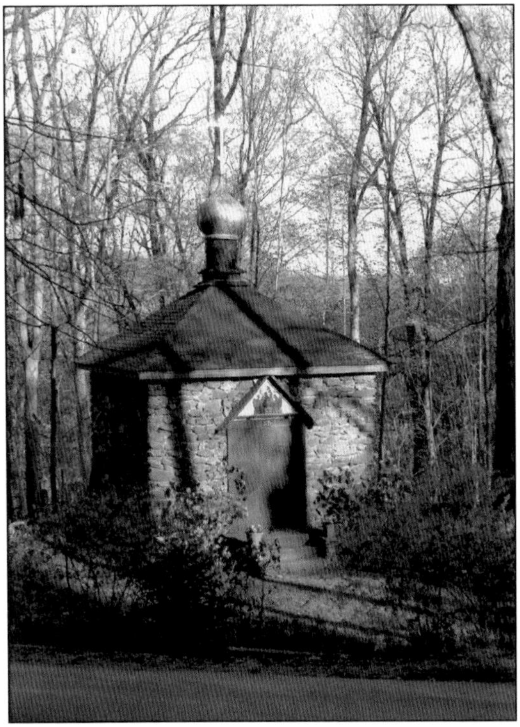

St. Sergius Russian Village Chapel. This chapel took six years to complete, with construction from 1926 to 1932. The Russian Orthodox chapel sits in Russian Village, which is also known as Churaevka Village. The chapel is named for St. Sergius of Radonega. Many Russians moved to Southbury following the Russian Revolution. Few of the first settlers' descendants remain today. Many of the original cottages are now gone. Only about 8 of the original 26 Russian families live in the area. The St. Sergius Chapel is listed on the National Register of Historic Places. It is a memorial to the Cathedral of Christ the Savior in Moscow, which has been destroyed. (AS.)

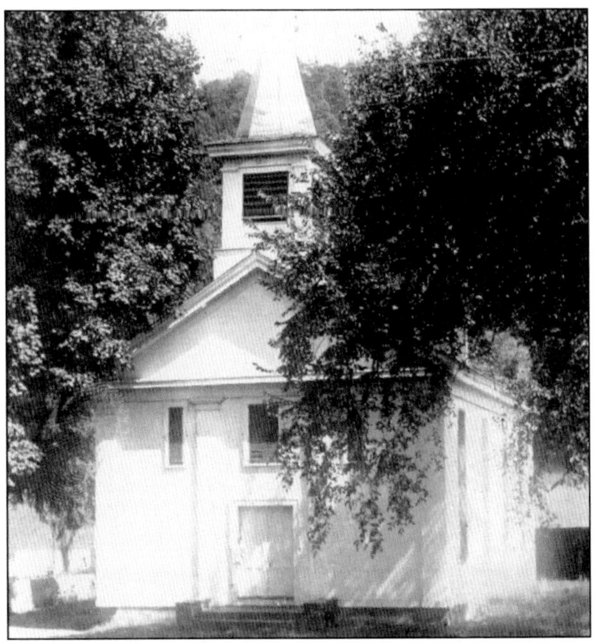

The Methodist Church. In 1803, a Methodist church was organized and met in the schoolhouse in the George's Hill area. The Southbury Methodist church was established in 1790. Services were held at the Bullet Hill School. The town population was 1,738. (SHS.)

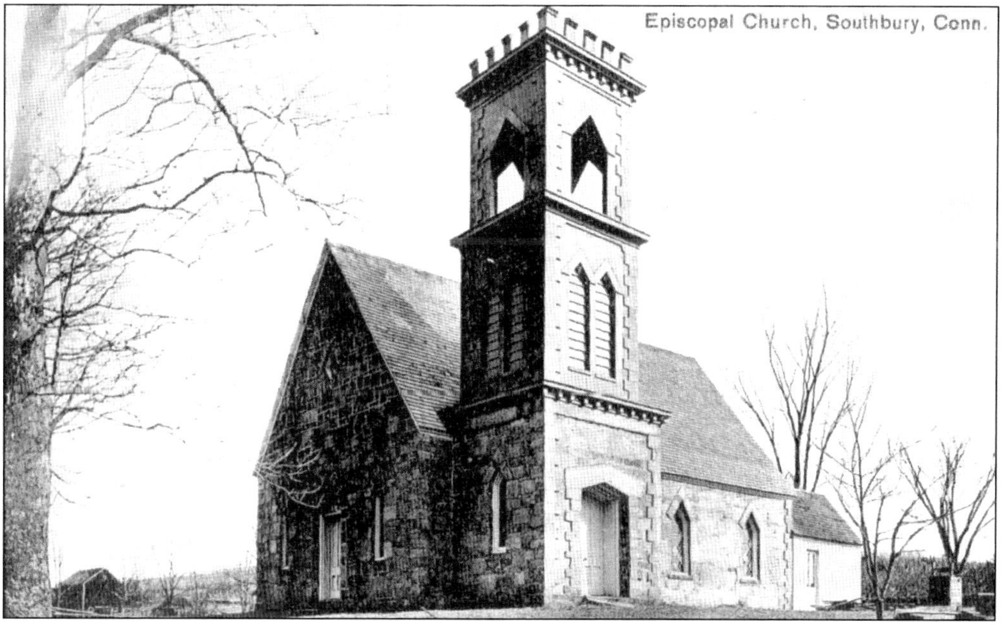

THE EPISCOPAL CHURCH. The parish of this church was organized in 1843. Like many early church parishes, the Church of Epiphany originally held services in the nearby Bullet Hill School. It was started as a mission church known as the Church of the Resurrection. Rev. Fred Harriman donated the present site in 1857. This property was part of the land owned previously by Shadrach Osborn, the owner of the purchasing and issuing commissary of the Revolution. In 1858, the name was changed to the Church of the Epiphany. It took an entire week to raise the cross supports from the floor to create the roof. A derrick was used. (SHS.)

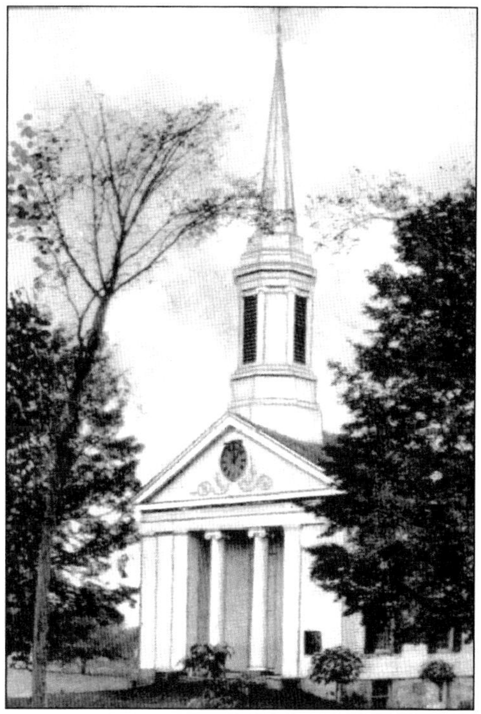

THE CONGREGATIONAL CHURCH ON MAIN STREET IN SOUTHBURY. The old church was replaced in 1768. The new church was constructed on Main Street, near Old Field Hill Road, where the old burial grounds were located. The United Church of Christ is the oldest congregation in Southbury. The Congregational church in South Britain is oldest church building in Southbury. The church was founded in 1766, in response to a 1761 petition. The sponsoring group was the second ecclesiastical society of Southbury. (SHS.)

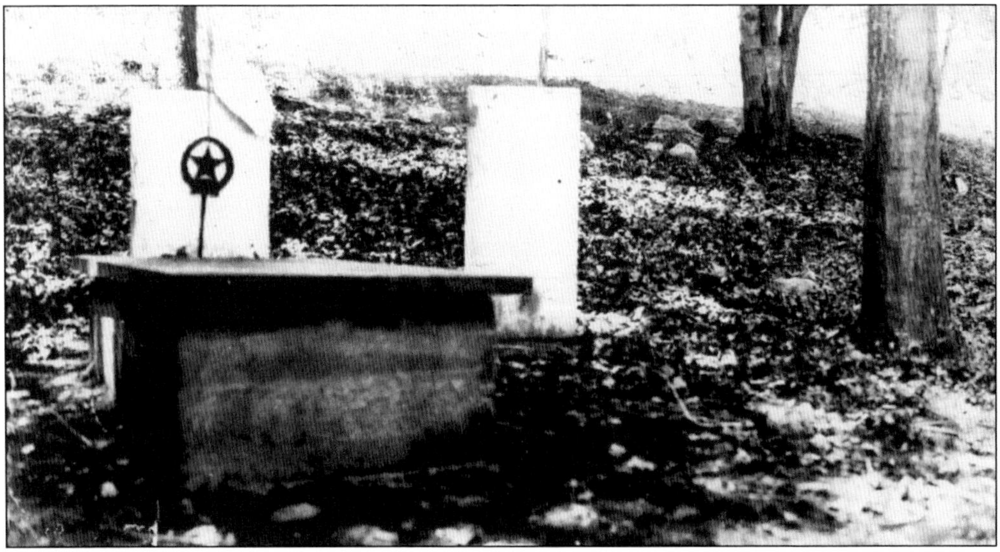

A Revolutionary War Soldier's Grave. Seen here is the site of a grave in the woods off North Georges Hill Road. Ancient Woodbury contributed many men and provisions to the war. Over 850 men served in 1775, when there were just 10,000 area inhabitants. Prior to this, in 1690, the governor of New England set forth a decree that all men between the ages of 18 and 65 had to go to military training two days of every year. In the area of Southbury, all of Litchfield County trained together. (SHS.)

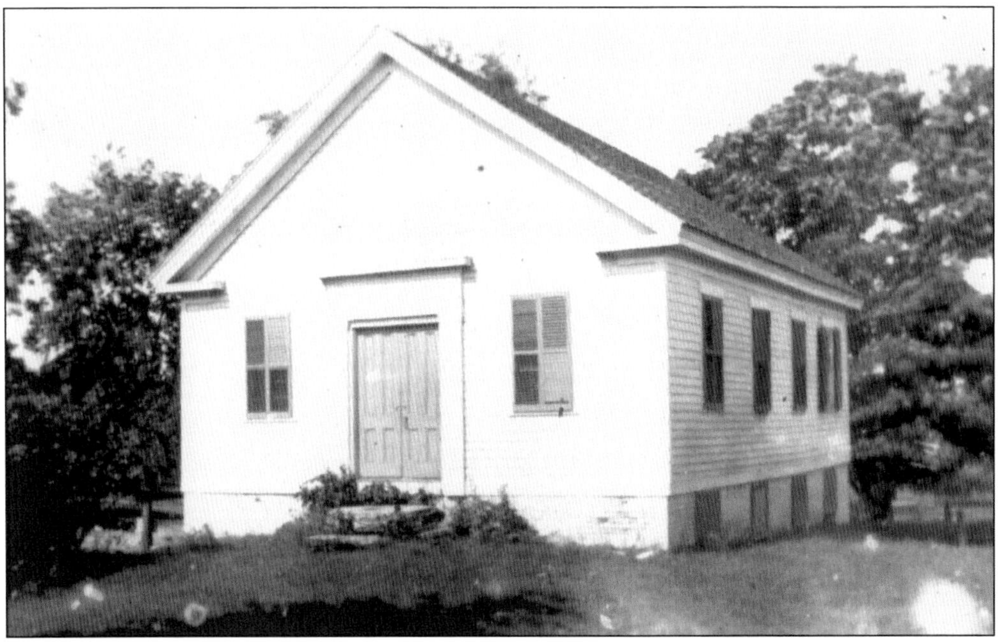

The Southford Chapel. Also known as the Union Church, this chapel was built in 1830. Many regular attendees included the workers at the nearby paper mill at Southford Falls. When the mill was suspended in 1888, attendance fell. The building is at the junction of Routes 188 and 67. Southford was named because of its location between Southbury and Oxford. The name is constructed of the first syllable of Southbury and the second syllable of Oxford. (SHS.)

THE SACRED HEART CHURCH. The first Catholic Masses were held in 1862 at the Francis Grant home. The first Sacred Heart Church was located in the White Oak section of town, and the first mass was held on Christmas 1884, with a parish of 40 families. The church was considered to be a mission church until 1940, when a resident priest was assigned. In 1958, a new church was built on the corner of Routes 6 and 172 at Sand Corner, when the parish numbered 250 families. The area was named due to the sandy nature of the land there. (SHS.)

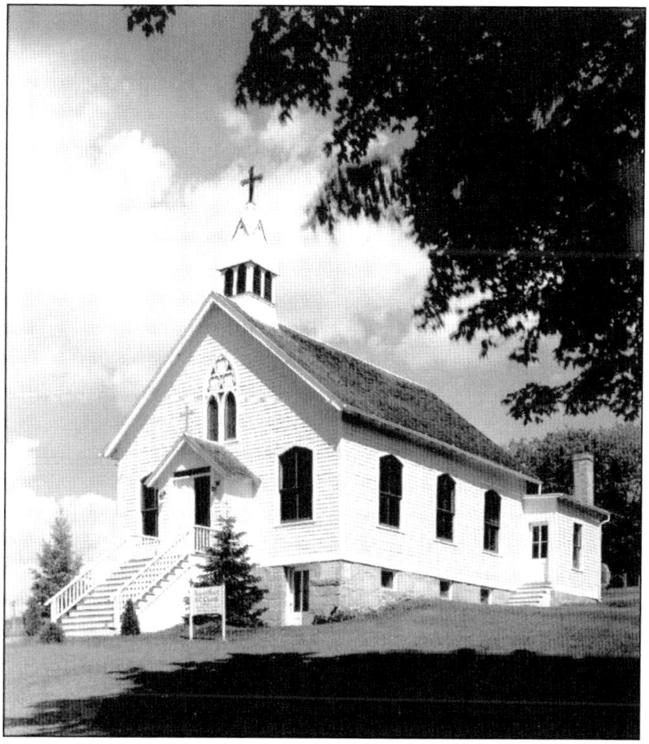

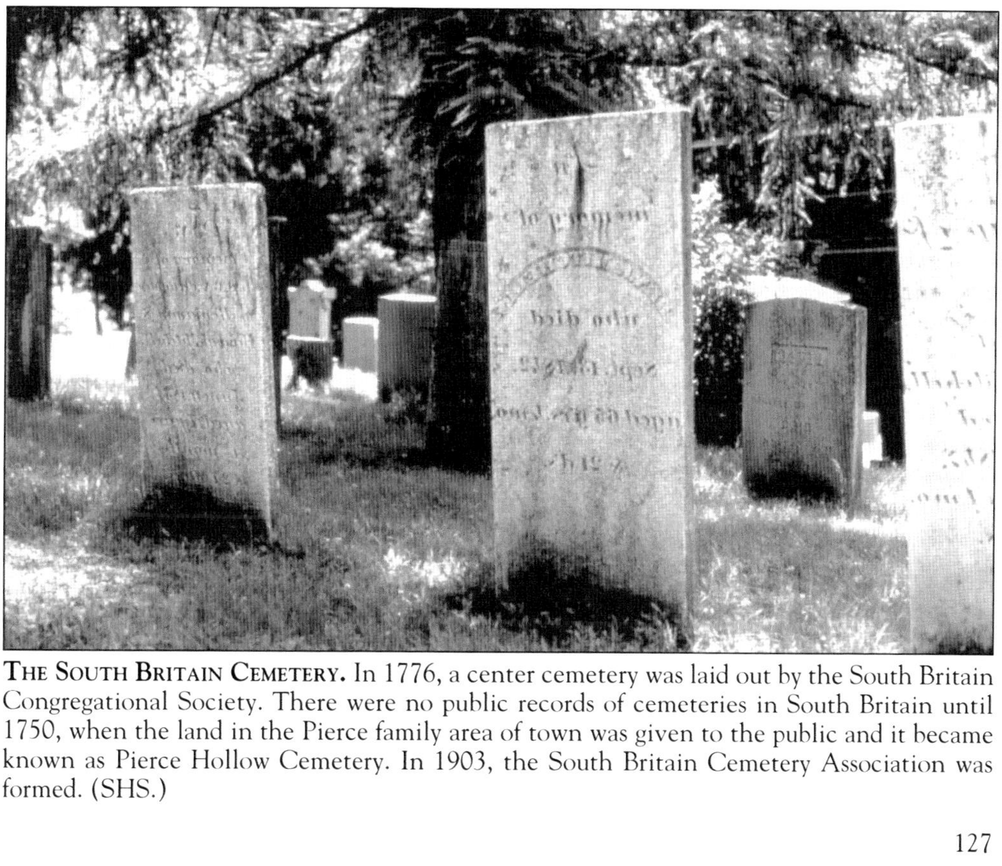

THE SOUTH BRITAIN CEMETERY. In 1776, a center cemetery was laid out by the South Britain Congregational Society. There were no public records of cemeteries in South Britain until 1750, when the land in the Pierce family area of town was given to the public and it became known as Pierce Hollow Cemetery. In 1903, the South Britain Cemetery Association was formed. (SHS.)

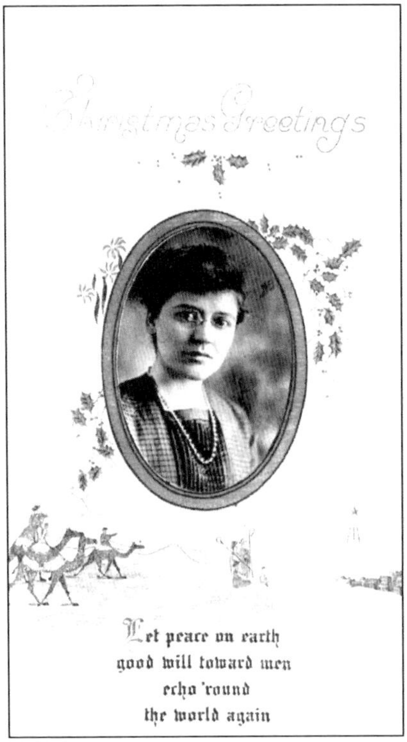

A Methodist Deaconess Christmas Card. Men were not the only ones in church leadership positions. Deaconess-pastor Elsie Stowe served Methodist churches in South Britain and Newtown in the early 1920s. (ML.)

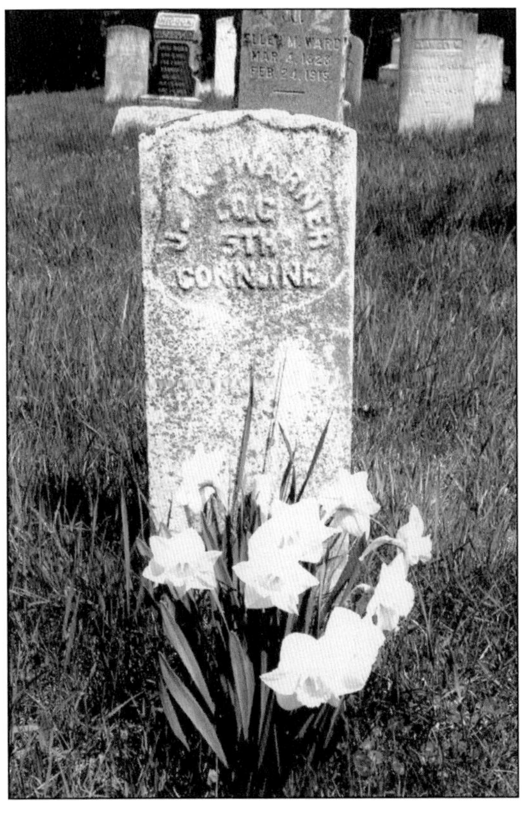

The White Oak Cemetery. The White Oak Cemetery is the second oldest burial ground. The Woodbury land records of 1741 read, "Layd out a burying place in Southbury in Woodbury, according to the act of the proprietors in said town as will appear on record in 1741 at the northwest end of that hill that Deacon Hicock's dwelling house stands on." The area contained 2.5 acres. The site was positioned at the northern end of the common (now incorrectly known as King's land), and the church was located at the southern end. Slaves are reputed to be buried in the entrance driveway of at least one of these graveyards in the ancient White Oak section. The oldest cemetery in Southbury is the Pootatuck Indian burial ground in the general area of River and South Flat Hill Roads. The sites of the original Native American village and burial grounds are in the area of River Road along the Housatonic. (AS.)